An Inconvenient Lie

SECRETS IN LANGUAGE

To a real friend
Elizabeth Lawry.

Louise Gouëffic

Louise Gouëffic

Library and Archives Canada Cataloguing in Publication

Gouëffic, Louise, 1933–
       An inconvenient lie : secrets in language / Louise Gouëffic.

Originally published as: Mind is not a plaything.
Includes bibliographical references and index.
ISBN 978-0-9690277-2-0

1. Language and languages—Philosophy. 2. Language and logic.
3. Truthfulness and falsehood. 4. Thought and thinking. 5. Meaning
(Philosophy). I. Gouëffic, Louise, 1933– . Mind is not a plaything.
II. Title.

BD241.G698 2010   121'.68   C2009-906995-4

Edited by Andrea Lemieux
Design and layout by Kim Monteforte, WeMakeBooks.ca
Cover art by Jim Albert, ideasondisplay.com
Index by Judith Brand

 Sapien Books
Box 906
Lakefield, ON
Canada
K0L 2H0

info@inconvenientlie.ca

Printed and bound in Canada

CONTENTS

ACKNOWLEDGMENTS

I am most grateful to the many people who have given me their moral and intellectual support for my ideas and my work. I thank Dr. Douglas Rae, posthumously, of the University of Western Ontario, London. He invited me to present a paper at the Comparative and International Education Society (CIES) World Congress in Montreal, Quebec, in 1989 on the research I was doing. This gave me an incredible boost in confidence in the work I was doing.

At this Congress, I met Dr. Richard Hirabayashi, now deceased, of the University of Calgary, Alberta, who from 1989 to 1996 gave me his unconditional support and friendship.

At the same Congress, I also met Dr. Susan Robertson, now at the University of Bristol, UK, who has been supporting me and my work since 1989 to the present day and has given me much-needed constructive criticism. Thank you, Susan.

In 1996, *Breaking the Patriarchal Code: The Linguistic Basis of Sexual Bias* was published by Sandra Brown of Knowledge, Ideas and Trends, Manchester, Connecticut. I thank you, Sandra, for giving me this opportunity. Soon after the publication of my first book, I presented a paper at the Organization for the Study of Communication, Language and Gender (OSCLG). There I met Dr. Anita Taylor from George Mason University, Fairfax County, Virginia, and Dr. M. J. Hardman of the University of Florida. Both have given me support and constructive criticism. They invited me to write a chapter on my work for their publication *Hearing Many Voices*. Thank you, Anita and M. J.

My biggest thank you goes to Dr. Vandra Masemann, professor at the Ontario Institute for Studies in Education (OISE) at the University of Toronto. She has not only been a staunch supporter of my work, but also a stalwart defender of my work throughout all the years since 1989. At a conference on education in Dijon, France, in 1992, as Chair of the final session, she related my work to many of the papers discussed at the conference. This is the kind of support needed by one who is doing research and analysis in a heretofore forbidden and taboo subject.

Because of her fearless defense and support, I was able to keep the courage to go on and not lose my focus or my sanity, and to go on to write *An Inconvenient Lie*. No mere thank you can ever be sufficient here, but anyway, Vandra, thank you so very much.

My thanks go out also to those who brought together the physical aspects of the book: my editor, Andrea Lemieux, who with her expertise made the book take wing; Jim Albert for his apt and colorful cover design; Kim Monteforte for her handsome book design; and last but not least, Heidy Lawrance, who oversaw the production and printing of the book.

LIST OF ABBREVIATIONS

a.k.a.	also known as
AS	Anglo-Saxon
BCE	before the common era
ca.	*circa*, about, approximately
CE	common era
cf.	*confer*, compare (see, by way of comparison)
Eng.	English
Fr.	French
gen.	genitive
Ger.	German
Gr.	Greek
Heb.	Hebrew
L.	Latin
m.	masculine
n.	noun
nom.	nominative
OE	Old English
OFr.	Old French
pl.	plural
SK	Sanskrit
v.	verb
vs.	versus
WMD	weapons of mass destruction

INTRODUCTION

As images of failed patriarchies, monarchies, theocracies, and humanities parade through the pages of the past, self-entitled lords tell us that
it is not the system that is flawed, *it is the species*. So I stepped outside
the system and into the language, against all unwritten laws and social
pressures not to do so. I wanted to see for myself where the flaw lay
and what was flawed.

Systems are communicated in language, symbol by symbol, name
by name. Patriarchy, rule by man-as-F/father, the system that set racism,
sexism, and class structures as "the way things are" in language, is
the basis for the most ideological menaces on earth. I found that the
language contains and uses divisiveness as a method to control the
masses, dividing people using gender, race, wealth, and class.

Everything in our species that has a name is a language issue.
Examining language developed under patriarchy, then, might reveal
what it is that is flawed.

Since patriarchy is the only system we have and know, philosophers
repeat the key assumption underwriting it: that our species is *man*kind
as *man* and wo*man* with moral imperatives set by God directing all
"human" action, the species so favored by God was *special* as mankind.
Few, if any, philosophers start with the premise that our species is an
animal species consisting of two speaking beings, both having minds
that can make language to communicate, and that this activity entails
using the tools of logic, observation, time, space, experience, evidence,
trial and error, interrelationships, and probabilities to name what exists
in reality.

Mind as we know it in ourselves today took millions of years to
evolve, starting with crude signs and sounds. It took hundreds of
thousands more years to develop the useable system of sound symbols
we call language. From the first symbol we made from myth, superstition,
fiction, fear, and necessity, *we* started the long, arduous process of
developing mind through language. We needed symbols to name reality
and accumulate facts in order to make sense of our existence and to

communicate this to others, first and foremost our young, to teach them to survive and live successfully in the reality that is planet earth.

The first act of creativity of our species was making *sounds-that-name*, and the second was using these *symbols*. Reflecting reality correctly in symbols as symbol *makers* goes to make our self-identity and creates our self-image as symbol *users*. Symbol making and symbol using involve the act of *thinking*, affecting all behavior. Language deeply affects our behavior. From an acorn comes an oak, not a giraffe. This is the bedrock of making symbols to use as tools to think for ourselves.

We made bridges, wrote music, and invented bowls by first making useable symbols to communicate "how to do" them. Symbols we make that are based on what exists in reality have implications for mind and morality because we use them. We *make* symbols that we *use* for ourselves. As a species, we are *thinking animal life* precisely because we make and use symbols in, with, and through the mind. We are not wool-making or silk-making animal life. We are symbol-making-and-using life.

The purpose of this book is to look at symbols. Symbols let us look at thinking life. I examine the symbols confected under patriarchal governances to see why we believe our species is flawed. If some symbols are not consonant with reality, then these symbols impose a flaw. Flawed symbols can make us believe an "innate flaw" exists in our species. Flawed symbols do not prove that we have an innate flaw. They expose that "the flaw" is imposed through language. It shows what the idea of being flawed does to our species.

Thinking life is not about money and patriarchy as *special*; money and patriarchy do not stop bias, hate, aggression, or war. If our language is riddled with flaws, errors, and bias that make our species believe in an innate flaw, then the laws governing symbol making were disobeyed to fit a certain plan. If symbols embedding and hiding error were made *to fit patriarchy* as a system, then it is the system that is flawed and false, *not the species*.

False symbol making makes false symbol users patent liars. False mind activity lowers the intelligence. The need to "dumb down" fixes the masses as being deficient in mind; "the masses" cultured in ignorance by purposeful error. Is this necessary? In my view, this is a crime.

The presence of only one deadly false symbol damages every mind one by one, as users damage the whole species. We cannot make moral collectives, respectful societies, and honest citizens by running on lies embedded in symbols. It is easy to make names that go against reality and good reasoning; disguise it as "the Truth" and claim that the species is *born with a flaw*. As you will see in this book, it is easy to impose belief on an undefined, vacuous innate flaw residing in the species.

Where symbols reflecting reality-as-it-is are made and used to communicate, the mind comes to know a life-sustaining habit to further sustain and enhance almost all other forms of life. Symbols that name and describe reality-as-it-is, that is, true-to-reality names, are both practical and moral.

As a young learner, lies in names damaged my mind with the belief that the species I was born into had an innate flaw, original sin. Yet I was told that I was *special*, chosen by God; God the Father had created me. Sinful at birth by birth! Yet special in God's eyes as a sinner! This extreme contradiction had a disastrous effect on me.

In patriarchy, the Truth of being both "sinner" and "special" was doing me too much harm. And society believed "this is the way it is." But I saw too much unhappiness, flakiness, despair, poverty, prostitution, obscene wealth, pollution, child abuse, power obsession, military solutions, money madness, use of opiates, wars between men, many prisons for men, and the masses going to church for divine comfort— I saw that it was harming others just as much.

I was thirty-five before I started to *see* the web of lies embedded in symbols being imposed on my mind—*to make it weak and deficient*. Like a fatal colorless, odorless poison poured into a river renders it useless, it was a case of *a small deadly dose of lies in everyday names* having consequences far beyond its size. It confused me and too many others. The language confected by patriarchs did not allow me to think for myself, I was to believe in what I was told to believe in—as revealed by God, the Father.

What does a symbol system, that is, language, do to the mind? What kind of symbol system ought we to make? What really is in a name?

Stepping outside of the patriarchal confection of humanity led me to see that mind was being used and abused like a plaything. So I washed hundreds of symbols in the machine of reality with the effective and efficient soaps of logic, observation, time, space, experience, evidence, trial and error, interrelationships, and probabilities. All the while, the small dose of deadly lies-in-names had been polished to perfection for September 11, 2001, the preemptive attack on Iraq in 2003, and the global economic meltdown in 2008.

The mind knows when it is correct; logic, the facts, and their interrelationships make one see the right interrelationships in reality. I knew I was on the right track. This gave me a measure of comfort as I wrote this book. I found that thinking for myself is exhilarating.

The motive for writing this book is the idea that the mind is not a plaything. We cannot feed the mind just any old thing and expect it to be believed. The mind evolved in nature, with nature, to be a life-sustaining organ for our species that would be more than sufficient to solve most of our daily and larger problems. It is a rational proposition to say that mind is a *sufficient* life-loving organ.

Patriarchy's scholars embedded falsehoods in symbols and names and called it Truth, separating (Holy) Truth from the many truths in reality-as-it-is. Why? What do lies-in-names, flaws-in-symbols, do to the mind?

What are these embedded flaws-in-symbols? Who are "the makers"? We must know. Lies embedded in symbols called Truth are fatal to the mind, just as the many real truths are an effective antidote. Thinking for ourselves is far too much fun to miss out on in life.

Chapter 1

ENDING THE CONFUSION
IN MY MIND

The premise upon which I am more likely to achieve a rational understanding rests on two truths: that our species consists of two gender-different members, and the members of our species have minds. Our minds are necessary for the development and achievement of rationality and knowledge concerning our species. Our minds exist necessarily to be *logic-affirming agents* as thinkers and, as such, are the *foundation of rationality*.

Before I can discuss this standpoint, however, it is necessary to understand that minds exist in two members of our species, but that one of the two members was rendered insignificant during the 4,000-year reign of patriarchal terror. The foundation of thinking today rides on patriarchy's naming our species *man*kind; this name underwrites the corresponding belief that *man* is the mind of the species.

The impact of false theory on the trajectory of one life, mine, resulted in a mind that likely few wanted to hear from. A change in standpoint was scary. But after years of mental anguish and suffering from a condition having no identifiable cause, I saw that I had no true sense of self. Belief from the old standpoint had wiped out my passion to know. In the end, I could no longer relate the *symbols* used to talk about ourselves and our species with the *reality* of our species. My conceptualizing capabilities had broken down. Why had this happened? As importantly, how had this happened?

What led to the identity of our species as *man*kind or hu*man*? Is this based on reality? It did not satisfy the criterion for my having a true sense of self. I was "in man" as a wo*man*, yet I was not a man. I didn't have the same rights as a man. Adding to my confusion was the contradiction of being born a sinner, yet being *special* to God, a supernatural, All-Creator Father, a male who *revealed* man.

How was I to create a real sense of myself with an authentic identity, and thus *be* authentic? I was searching for an identity that reflected what I really was, a fully participating and contributing speech-using member of my species.

Human socialization taught me, when I was still a girl, that *moral autonomy* for my gender had built-in altruism, or selflessness—an *id* attributed mostly to mothers. It also taught me that *personal autonomy* was about virtuous selfishness—an *ego* attributed mostly to fathers. This dichotomy of autonomy by gender—selfless and selfish—struck me as false. I had seen boys "sow their wild oats" and called "good studs." Girls who let boys "sow their wild oats" were called "bad," or "sluts," and their babies "bastards." I could not see society grow morally on immoral double standards for its individuals. This started my examination of human socialization. Was there a political bias or logical error somewhere? Was I really selfless? And speechless? Did I have to accept this as "the way things are" in human society? Were my speech-using capabilities as a girl being muted or silenced in the identity of being human? If so, why?

I came to see that the silent coercion of social pressure to *believe* we were humans threatened my life as a thinking animal. I started to suspect that internalized imperatives imposed by ancient forefathers defined moral autonomy for me, since I was of the gender that could have a "bastard" by letting boys "sow their wild oats" in me in my youth. Moreover, the pathologies of others under the gendered double standards made me invent a pathology of my own, a sophisticated, superficial artificiality, denying the necessary side of myself—the wisdom and achievements of ancient *foremothers*. I was drowning in confusion. Something was radically wrong. So I pulled in all my focus, research, and analytical skills, all my learning, reasoning capabilities, and emotional commitment to analyze the problem.

Thinking agents want and need genuinely good things for themselves and for everyone else. Wanting genuinely good things for all lets you live in harmony with yourself, and thereby with *other selves*. Since the self has to do with other members of our species, common sense told me that *the entity of self* is not achievable *in isolation of other selves*. Neither then is one's identity. This singular insight propels my whole critical analysis in this book. It makes me stay constant in empathy for other minded selves.

To look at the problem, I stepped outside the belief in "man-as-species above all (others) in nature," *special* as sinner in the eyes of God, from a standpoint not examined in 4,000 years. This gave me a criterion for trying beliefs and the father's dictates that the mother's duty was to stay the moral course—for *man*—by being selfless. This made me alone responsible for the basis of my convictions, no longer using, or wanting, the *special* forefathers' dictates.

I was now morally and intellectually on my own. I could use reason-based binding rules regarding reality and employ rationality as I saw it in order to better see the species that evolved to develop mind. I chose to use rational axioms necessary to moral principles, such as Q is Q and $2 = 2$ in all cases. Nowhere did I allow myself to use Q is and is not Q or $2 = 1$, or 3, whichever made things better or easier for me.

My convictions held that moral responsibility stood on rules based in reality that we ourselves can see and embrace as rational beings, and my greatest desire in life was to be a rational animal, a thinking being thinking for myself. It was the only kind of being I could be.

To my surprise, I found that "human" beliefs were useless. They *un*limited good reasoning by imposing belief in the *limitlessness* of humanity embedded in being *special*, that is, above all other life forms in God's eyes. I could choose any belief willy-nilly, as long as it was in line with the beliefs of being human. It was like belonging to a religion, and humanity was its name! Why?

I needed and wanted knowledge, and for the first time in my life my needs and wants were coherent. I wanted facts and true premises. I needed to know how the facts and premises related. Relating facts correctly makes knowledge; true-to-reality symbols carrying truths about what is related on planet earth enables thinking for oneself.

I discovered that knowledge of myself—the relationship between my body and my mind—as a thinking animal enhances my whole life. It limits my choices to facts obtained from probabilities, allowing me to do correct reasoning. Rational choice was now a real possibility. What a glorious day this was! I chose that day to be a committed, transparent, and mentally clear-thinking animal and enjoy myself as this kind of animal, which evolution had started in creating two members with mind. I no longer believed in *perfectible, limitless humanity*, where "human nature never changes." I knew now that I was a limited-by-my-own-reality thinking animal capable of solving my problems, because I had a mind sufficient to do so.

The concept of being a minded being capable of making speech, that is, being of the *sapient species*, was foreign to me at first. After decades of believing I was *special* as a human who was not a man, I had to practice the idea that the facts of having a mind and being a speech-using animal identified me as being among sapiens. But I found this true-to-reality identity only by stepping outside the human box. Eventually, I adjusted to my real identity, because true symbols communicate useful facts. Prebiased fantasies do not. This motivated my commitment toward acquiring and accumulating correct information, logical relationships, evidence in reality, and the physics in material nature wherever it led me. I wanted truths that were *see-able* in reality, including *the knowledge of myself as sapient agent*. It was the only kind of animal I could be. I could not be a bear, a sheep, a bee—or a man.

There was no loophole for me that could—or would—let me off the hook. There was no exception to any rules of logic that would let me go outside the limits of thinking. There was no divine being that would zap things to fit or bless a prebiased fantasy. But I did not *want* to get out of any limits set by reality, nature, and logic, because they held most of the paths to facts for correct thinking, truths, and sweet emotions. In my view, to violate any rule of logic or law of nature existing in reality creates the *common evil*, evil to be shared by everyone as if the species, *special in the eyes of God* and *born in original sin*, hid the "innate flaw." I saw that the flaw had poisoned my mind and blocked my self-identity as a contributing speech user.

The *common good* in reality's limits led me to see that limits are not what humanity wants. It loves "free will" and glorifies the limitless "perfection of man" without a conscience. Limitless humanity is in love with irrationality, loving contradiction, confrontation, and conflict as means and ends to perfectibility. Indeed, it embraces the "dialectics of dichotomy" articulated by Socrates more than two millennia ago. It loves ideas in opposition that divide the species into superior and inferior genders, higher and lower classes, and good and bad races to control the "unread" masses, thereby making it easy to impose the belief that the species is born in original sin and *special* in God's eyes. The liar and his lie are perfectible precisely because they are limitless.

I asked if there was anything in reality that did not have limits. Can giraffes fly? Can sky be "heaven"? The answer that kept showing up was only if some *special* forefather disconnected Himself from His physical brain to free Himself from the laws of reality to impose belief in a *limitless, bodiless*, All-Powerful Alpha Male in the Sky, an All-Creator Father in heaven as Truth. We were to believe that the F/father's mind can disconnect from His materiality: from limits. He can break out of his materiality and become a bodiless *male mind, Lord* God. Wow! What a neat trick! This is indeed being *special*. So how was this belief imposed so as to be believed by the masses?

A long time ago, some Father had to impose His "free-will" delusions on society. The slow passage of time had Him tell us that personal autonomy was above and beyond moral autonomy. Boys did not sin. Girls were seductive heaps of flesh making boys sin: Sex was at the center of it all, original sin, innate flaw, perfectible, limitless. So assuming personal autonomy as *Lord* in His own right, He became a psychological bully—with little regard for mind and reason in the species that evolved to use the brain that evolution had given it to learn how to think. That is, patriarchy entitles "special" men to be L/lords of creation through language, and these "L/lords" lord it over the rest of us by imposing belief in their Alpha-Male-Lordship-in-the-Sky fantasy. The circle closes in on itself.

So in the dichotomy of autonomy on two levels—the split-level method of dividing mind and body by gender, higher and lower classes, good and bad races—Fathers ignore the moral responsibility to stay within the limits set in reality. Personal autonomy without moral responsibility is like water without oxygen. Hydrogen is not drinkable. We cannot achieve rationality with half of mind, filled with *special* lies from *special men*, who received it from the F/father to boot. Mothers have minds and are as *necessary* to rationality, knowledge, self-identity, and society as oxygen is necessary to water. But in humanity—patriarchy—the belief was that mothers are breeders, not minded beings.

I saw then that humanity is real*ism*, not reality. Yes, there are two members. No, they may not be man and woman as humans. What does realism do to mind? It makes mind activity so complex and difficult that few do real thinking. It is too daunting *to do real thinking* using lies, so it is left to the intellectuals. The circle opens.

Who are these intellectuals? Since mothers were shut out of the higher halls of learning for 4,000 years, they are fathers assuming the personal autonomy to be *Lords* of thought. Men in seminaries from 300 BCE to 1850 CE were the few who knew how to read and write. They wrote what Fathers as L/lords of thought called Truth. The circle closes. And I saw my first *solipsism* at work. I wondered if the art of solipsism might not be the God-in-the-F/father Machine in having special limitless autonomy by virtue of his gender, that is, personal, and thus nobody's business.

We may be pleading ignorance here to the fact that when we go wrong in our thinking by shucking off limits, we go wrong in our behavior. But for the species that evolved itself capable of thinking and of naming reality—*making and using symbols*—it is every individual's responsibility to do so correctly. Maturity demands that one morally takes seriously the responsibility for limits that nature and reality impose, including those on the mind. Destroy one limit, and irrationality follows, like day follows night.

Solipsism in patriarchy is hard to explain. Usually it is a circular self-fulfilling aiming device that looks a lot like reasoning, but in patriarchy it is done by embezzling it through language. It is a set of terrorizing half-lies, cleverly wrapped in quarter-truths in names that come back as "proof" of what is assumed; for example, the father—(Holy) Father—making lies appear to be Truth, the most difficult lies to cull. I will do my best to peel off quarter-truths from falsehoods so that whole truths can be reset to use as a stable basis for the common good, restoring the right of both members of the species to think for themselves, to reestablish the foundation upon which rationality stands.

The goal is to want correct information, useful to the mind of our species. Knowledge becomes wisdom when correct information relates to other correct information consistently. This knowledge then becomes a tool that can enhance thinking life for the whole species, which then can create empathy for all other life forms. The facts based on and in reality build knowledge, creating intelligence, leading to wisdom.

Mind is not a plaything. Either we train the mind to reason well with correct information and commit ourselves to doing good critical thinking consistently, or we run amok on a rough frozen track of false information and biased fantasies called beliefs, living the whoring, grabbing, and warring life so evident in *special humanity* above all other life forms on planet earth.

So this book breaks many patriarchal taboos and throws out many patriarchal standards, the only standards we have had for 4,000 years. It also shows how patriarchal doctrines, laws, and commands have been used as tools that created the *common evil*. This intellectual disobedience of mine is necessary to return to the evolutionary aim of our species, being sapiens, thinking animals achieving rationality for the common good of all after a 4,000-year-long sabotage. My disloyalty and disobedience to patriarchy is to show the huge scaffold of beliefs that sabotaged our species, using gender to divide and conquer the masses. What is so hard for me to accept is that this was done with impunity.

Chapter 2

CHANGING 2 = 2

INTO 2 = 1

If we are to live with, in, and through the nature that is reality, instead of above it like L/lords and destroying it, we had better *know* that we are animals that make symbols, like sheep make wool, bees make honey, and silkworms make silk. Lies embedded in symbols used every day as names make us false individually and collectively, putting us all, yes—*all*—on a false track. If we are to live as naturally as possible as a symbol-using species, we had better make symbols that tell truths about ourselves. If we are to live as fully as possible as rational beings, we had better make symbols that clarify thinking life, not muddle it.

I sought for a "nice" way to explain how thinking life was, and still is, muddled. In reality, there are two members in the symbol-making species, and by this very fact these two minded beings make up *the foundation for thinking upon which rationality stands*. Two evolved with brains capable of making and using symbols, thinking, and reasoning. But examining the historical linguistic sources and social basis of 20,000 items of speech and symbols addressing our species across the Indo-European tradition since Manu named himself God 4,000 years ago showed me that one of the two minds is made insignificant in language. Therefore, it is 4,000 years too late to be nice, so I use a direct approach.

I use a three-pronged approach to separate lies wrapped in quarter-truths to show solipsism at work using the trajectory of slave law, symbols made to fit subjugation, slavery, patriarchy, and feudalism, and how belief in falsehoods is imposed. These cut across (1) making a name/symbol for bodiless Alpha Males in the Sky, (2) putting the name of the other thinker in the species out of usage, and (3) using *slave laws* to put all mothers and lesser fathers, the masses of "men," outside of rule-following identities and rational civilizing processes. Finally, I show how muddling makes us believe in deficient mind as if an innate flaw exists in the species. I show how belief in lies wrapped in small, gilded truths about our species muddle mind in the species.

"In the *name* of the Father and the Son and …" a bodiless being, a Holy Father—in the sky—having a mind that created earth simply by speaking it into reality. How did he get there? Why is "He" male? How do we know this? Or do we just believe? Why is H/he also Son and Spirit as well as Father? And standing above all! Is this fact, fiction, fantasy, or outright lie? What is His *name*?

What, really, is in a *name*? A name is first a symbol, a sound bite given a meaning. We make names. We make every symbol with a specific intent, including "in" and "on" as names of place.

Naming consists of the technology for making sound bites to refer to a thing; we make symbols to name what exists. It is more pliant than liquid or gas, which need containers to make them useable. Although we transfer the content of symbol making to dictionaries, and the content of symbol using to books, the "container" of the symbol, the speech item, is the mind. Symbols as names can be made to carry facts, create fiction, fit fantasy, or embed lies. Symbols used as names that are to become the content of knowledge ought to carry facts for truths. The problem is when symbols and names carry and impose falsehoods, fiction, and fantasies that become the stuff for belief. Every item of speech has a meaning that carries information.

Strangely, when one speaks of humanity, it is not about making symbols and developing mind. It is about (the centrality of) man as man and woman, human. It is *his battle between mind and body*, as if this were a battle. His in particular, since He can break out of his materiality and be bodiless, Holy Father, divine, living in the sky. Mind in H/him is not an organ for self-development in good thinking, reasoning, and rational self-identity. It is to imprint with His image as Holy Father,

Son, and Spirit in H/his battle with flesh—biblically, woman, body, sin. We are to believe creativity resides in the male mind: Woman, hysterical, *hustera*, Gr., uterus, is body. Thus Father, Son, and Spirit Inc. make *man* in *humanity* (whole species) omnipresent in name. God revealed man in His image. Life's purpose in humanity is to be man, the perfect creation of God.

A symbol like the name *man* in man and woman as human is omnipresent, because it is the one-and-only *name* for all members of a class, and the class, regardless of properties, distinctions, relationships, or logic, is meant for all time in all places for all purposes for all symbol users. Bigger than life, the name *man* takes on a life of its own, God-like in power due to a clever phenomenon: the absence of a name for the other thinker in the same class, made anonymous by naming her w-o-*man*. This makes us repeat *ad infinitum* the one-and-only *Name*, man, for all members and the class. *One name fits all*, the only Name in use, and therefore Holy. It posits omnipotence and omnipresence, giving *man* omniscience as mind and defines H/him as divine, God, bodiless, holy mind! Thus H/he is above all others, above all laws, outside of all limits, *special*.

To give a picture outside the gendered model as described above, let's say "fig" consists of "fig" and "apfig" (apple).

Fig names both items and the class to which all belong. The figness of the *apfig* is impossible to disprove, the name fig in *apfig* proves it is a fig. "Proof" stands on the *name* fig, the only symbol now in use. Abracadabra, *fig* added to *ap* makes the apple a fig, putting the names *apple* and *fruit* out of usage. Fig is now special in reality, made so by name. That the apfig is "a fig that is not a fig" is never said. Belief is that the apfig is an apfig. Q is Q!

To succeed with apfig, crucial information is missing, for example, fruit and apple. Fig, the real fig, takes the power to name the class (fruit) by its name and rename the apple the apfig. Fig names *all* as figs and is thus *special*, above all others (fruits.) Fig names all; there is no need for fruit and apple as names; they are banned, making apples anonymous as apfigs irrelevant to fruit, now figs. Fig and apfig become the stuff of belief. *The knowledge and truths of apples and fruits are lost*. Fig imposes belief in fig and apfig, calling it *higher* knowledge.

"Knowledge" in favor of fig = belief in fig. You don't see the cart pulling the horse to Q is and is not Q.

The fig fiction shows that belief and knowledge are not the same. One problem in *man* is that society behaves as if they were the same, the source of many problematic issues hard to describe and explain in solipsism precisely because belief = knowledge as *higher* "knowledge."

It's easy to rename the apple an apfig. But apfig misinforms and misleads. Apfig can be defended by saying "names are neither true nor false, they are just names." Names are made with intent, aim, purpose, and much deliberation stated in premises, and with specific linguistic techniques that must be obeyed, not out of thin air. There is no such thing as "just" a name. Every name that is made is made to serve a purpose. Apfig embeds and communicates a lie. To believe that the apfig is *higher* knowledge is to behave as if the apple is a *fig*, it becomes Truth.

As you believe, so you behave. Call a child stupid often enough and she or he will come to believe it and behave as if stupid. Belief takes over the mind when it is labeled knowledge, worse yet, when labeled as higher knowledge. Here is the real thing.

We speak of our species as mankind. We say man consists of man and woman. The name of *man* is used four times, regardless of any evident distinctions, categories, concrete differences, properties, relationships, or logic, as if the properties of being man are common to all members and the class. There is a big problem for logic, reality, nature, knowledge, and education in this.

In reality-as-it-is, being man entails only being male.

So when we say "mankind consists of man and woman," we are saying *man is and is not male*, as we would say an electron is and is not a negative charge. Q is and is not Q is spoken into reality abracadabra by "The Word" and made valid in "The Word" embedding the lie to be believed. "In the beginning was the word ..." Two men, man and w-o-man = man, or 2 = 1 man. This is not about two speech users = two minded beings. It is the start of the terrorizing nightmare of conning the fusion of belief with (*higher*) knowledge into one, Truth.

"Man is and is not male" set up the *original necessary inconsistency* in the mind; today "man" is Truth, belief—fact. What we have here is the birth of an *innate flaw*, the species believing that *man* consists of two men. Man is the only name used for the two members and the species, all three categories of classification. As the name for all *man* speaks and acts for all minds dictating "we are *all* men regardless of sex." The other thinker is anonymous and irrelevant as w-o-tacked-onto-man, the not-male man. So deeply is this believed that "all men are created equal" is writ in constitutions.

Faith in the belief that "this is the way things are" is set for eternity. Thus, like fig proves fig the *name*, man proves man; solipsism starts here. The basis of probabilities and proofs is set on its ear.

To perform this magic of transmuting the other thinker into a "man," he must disembody himself, be immaterial, bodiless, be a *mind* outside of mind with supernatural powers. He deems the other thinker to be *opposite*: body, not mind, H/his *battle* between mind and body justified. "The word" tells us of Adam: mind is strong and perfect; Eve: *not* male, weak, imperfect, *not* man, sinful, flesh. *Opposites*! We believe in the *necessary inconsistency*, man is and is not male, like sheep follow the shepherd leading them to green pastures. Sheep believe in male—and not-male men.

Necessary inconsistency, contradiction imposes belief in the lie. When man is both male and not male, the trick is to call him "generic man." This hides the lie to pass it as "fact." Claiming *generic* precedence and not disclosing that man assumes being both, male and not male, then, playing the grammatical game of *context* to hide false entailment, *man* is *de facto* special in that he names the whole species when he is only one-half. Abracadabra, male part = whole species, voilà, mankind. And *generic he* for both genders as grammatical law repeats the male and not-male opposites in *man*. Repetition becomes a tactic in the strategy. He inflicts anonymity on one-half of the species as *not* men named w-o-men, taught as "fact," then Man of opposing genders believes "mankind consists of man and woman" en masse. Belief and faith in these lies is moral and good; indeed, it is higher knowledge.

The violation of logic in the reality, nature, and existence of the thinking species is the crime of *necessary inconsistency*, smuggled in as an *innate flaw* by man's philosophers. Embedded in names, it would confuse the mind and make us fear and hate reason and facts. It would push aside reason-based wisdom and make the species embrace irrationality—faith-based fantasy—with open arms. Indeed, it would threaten the foundation of thinking. Name man God as disembodied mind and God exists! It is comforting to believe that God sees the least sparrow that falls, where large-scale deception and lies proliferate. This not only comes from the old belief in the magic of names, it also comes from a much more thoroughly sinister past, as we will see in Chapter 4.

The inconsistent proposition—man is and is not male—follows from "man consists of man and woman." No argument refutes that male and not-male poles—opposites—are embedded in man through the name man. This embedded *necessary inconsistency* is the worst crime against mind, an *original lie* transmuted into an *innate flaw* meant for all to believe in and share. None equals it to date. It would poison thinking about what the species is; it set up the machinery of *enemy* making: "Opposites" feud, either you are for me or you are against me. W-o-man, you are a man!

When *man* is *not male, he* is *w-o-man*. There is no time nor place nor situation when man can entail being not male. *W-o* is an ad hoc prefix with a dubious and devious etymology. In reality, w-o cannot change man entailing being male to entail also being not male, when in reality *being man entails only being male*. Man cannot be both male and not male. W-o-*man* in all contexts is a man (in name) who's not a man (male) in reality. Q is and is not Q operates as a tenet in man. Opposite, not male, repeats "Q is and is not Q" in man is and is not male. Politics, belief in *opposite* men and repetitiousness begin. Then man and woman are registered as lexical items in dictionaries, law imposed in language, *lex*, L., in lexical meaning is law. All the while, circular reason, the word *man* in w-o-man proves man, solipsism. His Special Name "proves" w-o-*man* is a man, and by this fact the whole species is human, mankind. Repetitiousness starts to make solipsism big, intimidating, unfalsifiable—and thus infallible!

Necessary inconsistency is dittoed in the man who's not a man. *W-o*-man embeds man in symbol like apfig embeds fig. The lie bamboozles mind. We then believe that there can also be a metaphysical, bodiless, supernatural male mind Lord God outside materiality to abracadabra wo*man* into existence. Thousands of years of believing in the fantasy that "H/he creates her," *innate flaw* and all, and we now fear looking at reality. It is a huge understatement to say that maturity is compromised in this process.

W-o-tacked-onto-man cannot be the correct name for *the other-gendered symbol maker and user, the other thinker*. Although it is true that a name is not the thing so named, cause and effects have to *relate in name* as they *relate in reality*. A *symbol* has to be *in consonance with reality* to name or state a fact. A not-male man cannot cause feminine effects; this is self-contradictory, false, another lie. The ecology of mind is not only compromised, it is also effectively changed for the worse. Lies believed as Truth start the process of making mind deficient.

Her true-to-reality name/symbol is missing, *absent*, she is anonymous. The *absent name* (like apple and fruit in fig) is the *modus operandi* for belief in bodiless, minded, Holy Alpha Males in the Sky. The missing mind of the *other* member, the absence of the *other* thinker, gives man the power of omnipresence, omniscience, and omnipotence, with H/himself as Creator Mind, God being the symbol intended to name this power to do and be all. W-o-tacked-onto-*man* makes belief in God-man plausible. He/God creates her, a man who's not a man, impossible in reality. Yet w-o-manly duty to stay moral, autonomy dictates that she sing from hymn-to-Him books. Like man, God did not know that consistent cause-and-effect entailments exist in reality to be reflected in speech! Methinks man and God to be the same guy.

The politics of repetition do not stop with woman. The covering symbol *hu*man further bamboozles us. We see *w-o* is mere sound gadgetry to distract and get away with violating logic. *Hu*-tacked-onto-man pretends to include both a man who's a man and a man who's not a man. Just repeat Q is and is not Q again and again, and again. Believe. It's higher knowledge! Cocky, self-righteous repetitiousness of the same violation of logic done by *special* fragile egos hides the lust to control the "opposite" not male, making names like wo + man and hu + man to inflate their egos to Alpha and supernatural. The name woman flatters the male ego. As does hu-man! Thus belief in lies is "our innate flaw" embraced as Gospel Truth: God revealed man in His image as man made the male-based, male-centered species in his image—as I "obey" the grammatical law of generic "he"!

The irony in this is that we are constantly bombarded by violence called "crimes against humanity." This shows that man does not address mind as a thinking organ for self-development, but as a sponge in both "men" to be imprinted with bold and cocky biases and lies about the species being man. Humanity, four times Q is and is not Q, created Hitler. Who/what else gave Hitler the permission to be G/god Himself? Where and when did anyone on planet earth ever hear of crimes against the mind? The reason why these are "crimes against humanity" is that man = mind. The *opposite*, not male = body is not a mind. Like w-o-, the gadget hu- does not change the meaning of man, male only.

Man, woman, human, and mankind stand on large-scale repetitiousness of male necessity and necessary inconsistence communicating a living "Q is and is not Q" in language.

Large-scale necessary inconsistency is law, embedded in the common everyday symbols man, woman, and human. This is serious irrationality of immeasurable magnitude. We have no symbols to distinguish the categories of two different-gendered beings in the speech-using class and the class of animals that evolved with a brain and body that holds the symbol-making mind. All are men named man. Ironclad politics in lousy logic, reasoning sung in hymn-to-Him praise for fragile egos needing their own ditto God-man to support his secret lies as "sacred." "The purpose of life" in humanity is to be man. He is born in sin in the eyes of God and he is His (own) "perfect" creation.

So around the globe, men could put their self-proving, self-infallible, indelible name stamp on all creativity in the cosmos, proving that the male attribute is indeed the creative faculty of reason: H/he is mind. She opposite is body, not male, not man, not mind. The ecology of the mind in both was as far away as the ecology of the planet. Both of the two "men" and the planet were thoroughly polluted! And the foundation of two thinkers upon which rationality stands was ground into rubble of muddle.

Reality is such that it seldom contradicts itself. Nature is not inconsistent. Logic relates thought rationally through the relationships seen in reality. The laws of logic for relationships between events are such that when A occurs, B occurs are found in reality. Acorn → oak. Bees → honey—not dams. In naming, describing, and explaining ourselves and our species, the bottom line is that the propositions are true and rational with respect to all probabilities. The propositions then should be analytic: *falsifiable*. To deny or doubt this criterion is to tacitly assume its validity. Logic is one of many steps to rationality, a very necessary one.

Infallible God-man, both male and not male, and a man who is and is not a man are self-inconsistent and not in reality, but unfalsifiable in view of absent necessary names to complete knowledge. Illogic damages both minds as symbol users, infecting the collective mind. The evil in the cumulative effect of believed lies, innate flaw, causes what I call *the common evil* for all to share. *The common evil* consists of the lies, biases, violations of logic, nature and reality made valid in lies-embedded-in-names that we must all share in and use every day, because *there is* (was) *no other choice, and no other voice*, the ground of infallibility.

If what is seen to exist in reality is not reflected in symbol, we mouth and repeat the given illogic until we believe in "the given," The *Word* of God-man, or Fig, a powerful fantasy that ordinary minds cannot grasp. Lies passed off as Truth are "gifted" to the masses, revealed by God-man, believed. Then belief (lies) is fused with knowledge as "higher" knowledge called Truth, when nothing could be further from the many truths in reality, adding to *the common evil*. The sum of crimes against mind for all to share is big, bold, and in your face. Faith-based fantasy, belief in God-man, replaces reason-based truths and earthly wisdom about the speech-using species, for there is no such thing as "the knowledge of God" without "studying man": To "know" God is to "know" man, and vice versa. Let us educate the masses in lies as Truth, and they shall obey. In the fear of God—all want to get to heaven.

Solipsism turns back on itself for validation: Man proves man. Like fig in apfig proves fig, and the fig god. "The *Word*" man as Name-All validates man's special status as naming agent, mind, zapped in on a simple, convenient, absolute, unfalsifiable One-Name-Fits-All. Repeated *ad infinitum* for three categories, when it does not apply to two of them, it takes on a life of its own and becomes too big to challenge.

Then Humanity is sold as a bill of goods when it is a pack of lies wrapped in quarter-truths.

Duplicitous simplicity, tedious repetitiousness, and constant appeal to base emotions (superior gender) are the major ingredients for the propaganda of an ideology. *Man* consists of man and woman as human, two men = man, a True 2 = 1 man formula is duplicitous simplicity, tediously repetitious, and appeals to male lust to control all, *special* in his own eyes as God-man. Mankind violates truths, logic, nature, reality, and mind, and is therefore an ideology, *manism* its apt name, "hu" being superfluous. "The *Word*" man, from Manu, 2400 BCE, self-named L/lord God, set up the Truth of supernatural, bodiless Alpha Males in the Sky. The differences between man and God, where two opposite-gendered men are Truth, are non-existent.

What does One-Absolute-Man do to mind? In the concept "man," there are many beliefs about *man* (ideology) and *man* (male), and when you put these together in one legion of beliefs, we see they make a few mortal fathers—Father *L/lord* immortal. And we are to believe in H/him as L/lord F/father to fulfill the duty of moral autonomy. Not only does this contradict autonomy and morals, it also imposes that facts are not essential, adding more evil to the crimes against mind, *the common evil*. It adds another miracle trick, the *transmutation* of earthly fathering, entailing the nurture of rationality, empathy for minds, support for life as life, and respect for other selves into heavenly God Fathering, rule by bodiless Alpha Male minds outside of mind. This is a giant leap into irrationality, with real fathering waylaid in the confusing process between father and Father.

So how do metaphysical Fathers in heaven make the leap from manhood in w-o-*manhood as cause* to *femininity as effect*, when being man in reality-as-it-is entails only being male? Why do we have only *manity* (as in *hu*manity) in a species having two different beings both necessary to the foundation of symbol making, developing rationality, and contributing to the process of civilizing?

There are two contributing minds in reality. Why then do we not also have *femity*? That *fem* might be the cause of femininity seems to support a more consonant and consistent cause-and-effect relationship, like man causes masculinity. Why hasn't this question been asked? This is the power of the unfalsifiable, infallible, one-and-only, fit-all, Absolute name—Man—imposed by absent names causing the anonymity of the other. Absent names (like apple and fruit) are missing items of information. The infallible One-Name-Fits-All stops missing information from being researched, because we do not know that information is missing in the first place, or what this information is.

Absent names are essentially *information withheld*. We have to conclude from this tactic that *knowledge* of crucial truths is *sin* in humanity, we must believe in man's "innate flaw." Belief in Lies is good for morality. Enter sky, stage right, *original sin*! What H/he tells you to believe is Truth. How evil!—And arrogant!

What do absent symbols/names look like? There is no name in Manism for the *being causing femininity that makes and uses symbols to communicate*. Yet she is the other necessary symbol maker in the species: She exists. In the next chapter, I show you items of language you did not know existed. You had no way of knowing they existed. Knowledge withheld is invisible. It took me years to find and gather these missing names. "Discovering missing data takes active concentration and thinking. Since data are invisible when missing, their absence has to be detected with the searchlight of questions and imagination" (Mayfield 1987).

The missing data in the next chapter show that absent symbols are indeed invisible data that once found and seen inform and enlighten. You see more clearly the convenient lie "gifted" by God-man in The Word. Man is and is not male, as man and woman is received information— the gift—from God we have at this time. A lie that is Truth, believed as higher knowledge. This confuses belief and knowledge in a big way. The knowledge of two necessary thinkers to achieve rationality is not in the picture.

F/fathers in seminaries were the few who knew how to read and write at the time speech was being advanced and standardized. These "holy" fathers claimed to have the voice "from God," when male centrality and superiority had been patriarchal belief for thousands of years. To fit this fantasy, they grabbed the privileges given "men" in subjugation, slavery, patriarchy, and feudalism and embedded male power in symbols, thousands of them. Fathers, with uppercase *F*, granting holiness, were/are higher than fathers and all mothers, so that what is *received* from the *Father* is Truth, solipsism at work, patriarchy embedding patriarchy in language to appear "natural." Circular reasoning turns the head 360 degrees at the speed of light, because the end is the beginning. "In the beginning was the word—*man*," this was the end of self-identity as thinkers. The unread masses can never read missing information to see what is done to mind, muddling it on a large scale.

Mankind is an inconvenient lie advocating male superiority into perpetuity for male dominance parading as Holy Truth, making it appear as if "this is the way things are." But *the bottom line in reality-as-it-is is that to achieve rationality at all if one logic-affirming mind is rendered null and void by clever anonymity as "a man who's not a man," then the two thinkers upon which the foundation of rationality stands is irrevocably muddled.* Irrationality stamped valid by God-man, loaded with fear, fantasy, fiction, and illogic invades on a massive scale with nothing to stop it from meshing with rationality, adversely affects both minds equally. The sophisticated octopus of FEAR keeps "mankind" Holy Truth, the bedrock of terrorism by terrorism for terrorism.

The price of one lie is the loss of many truths.™

Chapter 3

WITHHOLDING KNOWLEDGE AND MAKING MIND DEFICIENT

The following symbols are registered in the *English Dialect Dictionary*, 1900, and the *Century Dictionary and Cyclopedia*, 1911. Patriarchal bias appears in some definitions.

feme sole, a single female [sic]

feme covert, a married female, covered by a husband or male head

feme line, maternal blood line

femble, *Cannabis sativa*, strongest hemp plant, *feme* in nature, also as *fimble*

femicide, the killing of a woman [sic]

femmil, strong, firm, athletic, active, also as *fim*, quick and *fimr*, nimble

femlans, the remains of a feast

fimele, *Cannabis brevior*, also as *femele* (used in French, *feme*)

femmer, also as *fem*, slight, slender, made the symbol *femmersome*

femino, pertaining to a *fem*

femic, characteristic of a *fem*

femmel, to select the best, throwing out the inferior articles

femerell, a lantern on the roof of a kitchen

Other symbols containing *fem*, not of the Anglo-Saxon culture:

femme, French, a *fem*, from Latin *femina*

feminal, Latin, from *femina* → *feminine* → to *feminate*, to make strong

femto, unit of measure 10^{-15} (negative attitude toward the
symbol *fem*)

femulus, Latin from *famula*, feme slave of household, made "family."
In Latin, as in *femina* and *femulus*, *a* denotes feme and passive,
and *us* denotes male, active, a slave works, is active.

This list proves that *fem* had long ago named herself *fem*. It proves
that she used *fem* to name other phenomenon about herself, her sexuality as *feme*, and her life. It proves that she used *fem* as a generating
morpheme to make symbols involving her life and herself. It proves that
*she was fully aware that symbol making and naming were among
her creative abilities, rights, and responsibilities*. It proves that *fem*,
fim, and *fam* are variations. It proves that *fem* has the same innovative
name-making and name-thinking capabilities as man. She took the
task of naming herself seriously.

This information has been missing for hundreds of years. Few of
these names exist today. Few are in the common currency of the
language we use to speak about her in our species. In fact, she is not
defined as being "feme," *other* gender, but as *opposite* gender—not
male, astoundingly, fe + male.

sapience, from sapiens, the wisdom in good naming, wise speaker
sapient, wise, sage, *vise*, Fr., to focus (the) sight → wise (like
vine → wine)
sapiential, of or relating to wisdom
sapienter, being wiser (in making and using names true to reality)
sapiens, from L., *sapere*, to taste, sapid, having agreeable flavor
→ *savoir*, Fr., to know, *savourer*, Fr., to taste, *sagesse*, Fr.,
wisdom, whence sagacity, savvy. Taste and sight are the two
senses most involved in the definition of being sapiens. The
five senses give us the capabilities to find, see, and test
probabilities in reality to name facts. Being male is not one
of the senses.

Like the apple is banned as apfig in fig, fem is banned as w-o-man
in man. Like fruit as the name of the category is banned by making the
apfig fit in the fig category, so too the name for the category of speech

users, sapiens is banned as hu-man by making w-o-man fit in man. All become figs in fig. All become men in man.

The *fem*-based, *fem*-made symbols above show us that *fem* used *fem* as a base morpheme to make more symbols. They show (1) *fem* used with *e, u, b, t, m, l*, and *er, ic*, and *il*, and in vowel variation as *fim*; (2) that *fem* is an independent morpheme and is used as a generating one; and (3) that *fem is a symbol maker in her own right with man*. But with only "feminine" in use today, we cannot see all this missing information. Fem f.k.a. (falsely known as) w-o-man in man is the reason *one name fits all* succeeds in imposing belief in *man, whole species*. Missing or withheld information helps to deceive, to succeed with lies.

Before hu-man was coined in the thirteenth century, we called our species sapiens. Our species sought knowledge and wisdom by tasting what was good to eat, not poisonous to the body. Some of the first attempts at making sound-bites-having-meaning were based on "taste" of food. Survival depended on not ingesting poisons. When symbols not referring to food were minted, it is rational to say that our ancient forebears likely kept the rule of not poisonous.

But patriarchy saw what names could do for men and kicked speech back to "in the beginning," making symbols favor them to make fathers appear powerful. As dominators, they could wield power through language in the name mankind. The term *sapiens* is used very rarely today. The false cover word hu-man is the name of the species today. It is used to describe every characteristic from kind to violent behavior of every type, from gentle to criminal to war, invention, achievement on planet earth, one name fits all as fit-all adjective and noun. The absence of sapiens and fem impose that hu + man as man and woman is Truth, unassailable: infallible.

In most dictionaries, human is defined as "belonging to man." Coined ca. 1250 CE, etymology relates it to *homo* (gen. *hominis*), "man," and to *humus*, earth. This does not undo the premise *being man in reality entails only being male*, self-evident in its truth. Homosexual refers to males. Circa 1384 CE (100 years later!), hu + man grew into humanity, from OFr., *humanité*, from L., *humanitatem* (nom. *humanitas*) "human" nature, from *humanus*, *us* suffix, L., denoting male. But the *manus* is more complex and sinister than this, as we will see in Chapter

4. These dates show that man-favoring names were coined when feudal Lords, clergy, and religion ruled lands, seas, and skies, and religion used to rule the unread masses. Hu-man was coined later during feudalism!

One can see from this that hu + man came from the fantasy of the male as being the mind of the species. After 4,000 years of keeping fem out of the halls of learning, it was reality. So the species with male domination and his superior mind was revealed in Holy Books, and the Truth mushroomed with the invention of the printing press. The Bible contained the law!

In this book, however, I use "sapiens" to name the two thinkers, the two in our species who make and use symbols to communicate, fem and man. This is true to reality, precise, and just. Since "homo" means male being, *homme*, Fr., man, I do not use it with sapiens. There are two sapien*s*. I use "sapiens" to name the species because it is more precise by definition, and I use "sapien," without an *s*, for the individual. We are used to seeing *s* used to denote plural.

It is a truth seen in reality that no species of animals is male based. Sapiens are not male based in reality. There are two genders in the species: feme and male. Any symbol or concept having a male bias was coined under patriarchy for patriarchy by patriarchy, lasting so long that men believed they were the mind of the species, and thus the whole species. She was the body.

What happened to the reality-based *fem* symbols? Feminine, adjective, is the only symbol using *fem* in English, as such, then, it is a floater.

Effeminate refers to men, meaning *fem*-like—weak and powerless, implying that being fem is to be weak and powerless. Not only is this bad psychology, it is also another patent lie. *Femmil* means strong. Was her "powerlessness" first cultured by men, and then used against her? What made her weak? What precisely defines her as weak? The absence of symbols naming feme strength, for example, *femmil*, banned from language; fem were forbidden to use their minds.

Oddly, *feminate* is not in the dictionary, although *femmil* names feme strength. Fem have intellectual and body strengths different from men. But here is the conned fusion of meanings with the intent to deceive: If "effeminate" exists today as currency in language, then "feminate" made it possible (cf. immobile, mobile). But *feminate* is not registered in dictionaries. I cannot include it in my list above. Today, feminate, strong, is not registered in dictionaries as an independent symbol, but effeminate, weak, a lie, is. What strange goings on! How reliable are dictionaries?

Where are these symbols today? *Femble*, the strongest hemp plant, relating strength and feme matter in name was renamed "carl hemp," *carl* being the old Anglo-Saxon name for *male*. What is feme in reality and nature is now male in *name*: This is flat-out linguistic appropriation. *Feme*, a more logical name for fem's gender, was killed when a male poet in the thirteenth century wanted his couplet to rhyme with *maal* and changed feme to fe + maal (cf. apple → ap + fig), which later became male and female, more linguistic appropriation, and identity theft. *Femmil*, feme strength, did not stand a chance, banned outright. No one uses femmil today. No symbol denotes strength in femly attributes; femmil, femmility, and feminate are all banned, not registered in modern dictionaries.

I have never seen or heard the name *fem* used or defined in any positive way. But almost all weakness, flaws, and inadequacies are gendered *fem*inine. A ship can sink, taking 2,000 men down with *her*! She is a thing and more often evil!

In fact, the symbol *fem* is most often used to derogate. It is used to placate lesbians as a low class, to devalue femininity, and to crack jokes about "girly" w-o-*men*. The feme mind having been made deficient by lack of learning and experience, the name w-o/man as a man who's not a man stops fem from seeing *fem* as a good rational symbol she herself made long ago to use as her name. It even made the double-edged sword "feminist" used by both men of opposite genders to placate fem who want equality!

Mind is the target of the killing field here, as it is in all killing fields. War kills more minds than it kills bodies. Wo*man in man* kills fem as feme mind in sapiens aborts reason-based facts and diverts the mind away from consistent reasoning and rationality. The relationship between killing the mind of fem as fem and the consequence that it also kills the mind of man is not seen. Embedded illogic strikes both minds, making both deficient in staying consistent in reasoning. Necessary inconsistencies: (1) man = whole species, (2) a man who's not a man, w-o-man, and (3) human, covering both a man who's a man and one who's not a man. These inconsistencies work together and are a shotgun blast aimed at the head. The illogical pellets sink in and do their damage. This is war against the mind.

One by one, fem-made and fem-based names were put out of use and male-biased ones imposed. When Canada was a British Empire dream, a man named Buzovetski had to change his name to Cameron to get a high-status position, a much-loved tactic in patriarchy to shore up the superiority of certain men. Fem's identity as w-o-*man* shores up the pretense that man is superior and the whole species. *So the mind lost "fem" as a generating morpheme in symbol making to communicate correct/real information.* The species lost fem as a *symbol maker.* It lost her partnership with man to be *the foundation of rationality.* **It lost the goal in being sapiens.** All had to be men. All the absent symbols and illogic and falsehoods created mind *deficient* and readied it to accept an "innate flaw," original sin. Then mind was righteously deemed *insufficient* to go it without help—enter stage heaven bodiless/Holy Alpha Male minds called gods. The True God, Holy Father as ruler led the masses to green pastures, the masses now devout and obedient ruler followers in "man."

Fem-made ideas to this day are ridiculed and derogated. "Ms." is still ridiculed today. But reason, reality, and experience tell us that men would suffer equally from the same missing information. No fem, no checks and balances, no necessary other to develop rationality—the illogical and deceiving man as F/father, patriarchy, is all we have.

To lose her identity as fem is to lose her *original self* as a sapien. When fem lost her own *ratio*-based, mind-made symbol *fem* to name the cause of her femininity, she lost the power to be herself as a fem, *a logic-affirming, true-to-reality naming agent—with man.* She lost the wherewithal to be an authentic minded self. Her self-naming capabilities cancelled, her *deficiency* left her no choice but to yes the lie w-o-tacked-onto-man as her identity. Earth lost *the partnership of fem with man as sapiens, the foundation for creating rationality.* Instead, we got the hate-based, conflict-riddled human in his war of mind/man vs. body/woman with all the warring and whoring this would bring about.

W-o-man yes-ing the lie, this is where men lost out big time. W-o-man, created in favor of man, the load of nonsense tipped against men too. Trickery has a nasty habit of doing the boomerang, and solipsism boomerangs in a big way. Where man = whole species, the false rules.

Sum up the diversionary gadgets *wo*, *hu*, the capital letter doing something magical; the cumulative effect of inconsistencies plunge us deep into the belief that man is *special*/God-like/Holy Creator. Man, *man, and Man* are three different false sacred names that in the cumulative effect of their magic make belief and knowledge irrevocably "con" fused. In fact, two different beings, fem (in reality) and man, become One, *man as man and woman* and the idea "2 = 1 man" is made valid and imposed. Revelation, God's Word makes her rib-of-man *in* man; she is not to be *with* man to develop rational thought. The Taliban know this only too well! Even prepositions are conscripted for the Inconvenient Lie, the con of fusing two concrete matters feme and male to beget fe + *male* wo + *men*!

The systemic anonymity of *fem as fem* today is problematic. The name fem is not lexically registered. So in man's view of progress we do not see H/his eternal solution of *femic cleansing*, rendering the feme mind null by cleansing fem from the species as w-o-man. Her nature is manized as fe/*male* w-o/*man*, gifting her with value. Speech and logic are divorced. Fem is devalued as herself, her feme attributes as feme invalidated. This done, there are no moral qualms in putting her on the virgin-whore-slut plane below man, never defining her as a thinking agent in her own right on the same plane *with* man. Wo*man-in-man* is tacit belief. But it is not knowledge.

Prepositions, capital letters, wo, hu, lexical law, generic "he"—tricks conscripted for the ideology 2 = 1 man. Every trick of deception is used to make hu-manity succeed.

Man cannot use feme mind; her logic-affirming mind posits *fem*. *Hatred of mind* is in the *hatred of fem*. Wannabe L/lords did not see that it would disable male minds to the same extent as feme minds. Once in place, *hatred of mind* does not discriminate between male and feme: *It strikes all minds*. Hatred of mind necessitates control of minds. Hence stereotypes in gender-biased myths are "the highest knowledge"—faith in The *Wor*d of God, virgin body/sin as flesh and disembodied divine male minds exist. By a quick twist of speech, faith in male fantasy = "higher" knowledge.

Belief/faith in the existence of H/him G/god the center of 2 = 1 man is brazenly called "wisdom"! Believe in a childish package of gender-biased fantasy or else you'll go to hell. Be God-fearing or else He will punish you. FEAR.

Omnipresent man/generic man/Adam stands on being male. "Man is male" is descriptive. W-o-man not male is both evaluative and pre-scriptive. She is manned to have value: Fragile egos, Holy Fathers, set up "penis I win, no penis you lose." He gets the proving detail of penis. Details make "The Truth" look as though it is true, like the details of the male "trinity of God." But The Truth in false information has nothing to do with real truths. The Truth is blinded belief precisely because *fem* is absent, cleansed out of the species, not letting you see reality-as-it-is to weigh the evidence in the con/fusion of The Truth and truths, the trick of capital letters used in God-fearing 2 = 1 Man.

Such vicious games disconnect the relationship between symbols and reality, name and objects, and the relationship between objects in reality. As symbol users *we disconnect ourselves from our own natures as symbol makers*. When "holy" men made 2 = 1 man Doctrine, it harmed both fem and men to the same extent; it disconnected *the correct rela-tionship* between mind to body; it proved fatal to the development of self-identity; it arrested the acquisitions of skills to sustain consistence in rationality, self-integrity, self-esteem, and self-confidence. The self, deficient and small in the eyes of God, souls had to be invented, sepa-rate and distinct from the self. Enter salvation and the worship of God!

So what then is the personal *autonomy* of F/fathers? Is it being *L/lord* of the misinformed masses? Not to know fem is a co-creator *is* the way to create "unread" masses. When we say "the symbol-using species as sapiens consists of fem and man," the *transmutation* of man as father to Father as Lord is exposed. So many tricks impose con/fusion. When a father becomes the Father, look out! In the conned fusion of the two, a capital letter puts one above the lesser one.

Being *feme* is descriptive, reflecting what she is in reality. Being "not male" or fe/male is prescriptive and backhanded negativity. ***But above all, it is irrelevant.***

In $2 = 1$ M/man, then, we see that there are no checks and balances. Limitless rational*ism*, solipsism, imposes lies conned as Truth deemed "higher" than truths. The vast majority of fem are ignorant that they are fem in reality. But fem has such a large vested interest in w-o/*man-hood* that she does not see it as coercion to assent to H/his L/lordship's ego-lust to control her. Still less does she see the bribery in it. Falsely known as (f.k.a.) w-o/man gives H/him the personal autonomy to name the species man in general thought, science, and culture, making an "innate flaw" become reality in all places for all time in all situations meant for all sentient beings to share.

The most terrorizing consequence: The Doctrine of *man* became the "secular" "theory" of M/man. The species ruled by religious superstition and magic for thousands of years made the mind ripe for upholding the crime Q is and is not Q against mind into perpetuity.

Cheating at knowledge does not come into fem's suspicions. Indeed, she trusts history to the hilt of H/his Mighty Sword. Jane, Anne, and Tracy get the Sacred Names mankind, man, woman, and human in infancy, unaware it nulls feme mind. So later they sincerely, and even reflectively, assent to the premise that man consists of man and woman, at the same time, they sincerely, and even reflectively, dissent to the premise that woman is a man. Con/fused in misinformation, the game of context between *seminal man* and *generic man* keeps them loyal to the Truth M/man from the age of reason on. His solipsism revolving on "Q is and is not Q" made legitimate in lexical items *is law* in *The Word*. The lexical law *w-o/man* subjugates her *in man to man* and unknown to her makes $2 = 1$ man plausible for belief, repeated in all disciplines from birth to death. Infallibility needs support!

The false symbol w-o/*man* has a political purpose, to control fem's mind and body, make her deficient, flawed: no penis. But w-o- is mere decorative distinction between the man who's a man, has a penis, and the man who's not a man, has no penis. Hu (the secret in hu/man) speaks the magic candy-coated Truth w-o- higher than the real truth of fem, to control the seductive flesh-without-mind in H/his Word, the best mind-controlling strategy that could have been invented.

Clever sound gadgetry, capital letters, wrong prepositions, gender bias, false facts, and magic camouflage the fear of his own sexuality, the sex drive he named *vir*ility. His fear is transmuted into power over fem by imposing ignorance and superstition on her and the masses. Fem's sex drive is not even named, so it does not exist. Dare we ask how pro-creation takes place, non-consensual sex? Rape? Holy insemination?

How much more obvious could L/lord G/god M/man/u expose the fear of being responsible for his sexuality? *SEX* in man is bigger than life itself today. For if men believe femes have little or no sex drive, then it is easy for males to say they are *not* responsible for their hard-drive virility, because she could not possibly understand it. This seminal solipsism legitimates boys sowing their wild oats and girls penetrated to be sluts. Sex is good for boys—good studs, dirty for girls—sluts. *The gender split in autonomy is exposed: personal for boys due their hard-drive virility, moral for girls due to the—falsely proclaimed—absence of sex drive.* Since girls don't have a sex drive, how can they possibly understand what virile boys and men "suffer"?

So male is sex and males call SEX. How twisted can things get? This is basis for morality?

So big money is good for boys, dirty business for girls. Power and control is nice for boys, dirty business for girls. Power, money, and sex, the trinity in Lord Man is the same as the trinity in Lord God by sheer coincidence! The arrogance of H/his *special* claims zapped in on rep-etitious magic leaves you breathless. Does this really help men be more rational, compassionate, and moral agents?

Symbols addressing our species de-specify fem, merge her in *man* the One as w-o-tacked-onto-man. At the same time they overspecify male as both natural and supernatural—until she fears H/him who fears his self-claimed, hard-drive sexuality. We are not to distinguish (a) fem as a distinctly different being and what this does to mind and symbol making, and (b) the symbol-making skills requiring commitment to logic in both minds, the similarity necessary to distinguish the differ-ences. The connotative symbol *fem* being absent, fem is absent in history, science, civilization, thought, and mind. *Hu*manity is a terror-izing story of splits, an enemy-making machine of *opposites*: a "divide, conquer, and control" strategy solved only by wars soothed by whores. Divide the masses by withholding knowledge, conquer them with holy lies and they are easily controlled. And the project went global. So why did it fail?

Femic cleansing differs from ethnic cleansing. Fem are scattered throughout the species as wives, sisters, and mothers, necessitating a one-on-one targeting in the belief that husband, "the man of the house," is the head—mind. He holds the power. In ethnic cleansing, the group is identifiable by characteristics such as color, dress, and facial features. The killing too differs. Femic cleansing is psychological death, the death of the feme self as feme by knowledge withheld, killing the feme mind to wipe out any undesirable resistance to male control. The Nazis killed millions of Jews to wipe out the undesirable race—identified by a yellow Star of David. Lack of penis is a detail as visible as any yellow Star of David.

Sex difference defined as *not* male—*opposite*—is to have a deficiency in mind, man's battle of mind male vs. body fe + *male*. But in "penis I win, no penis you lose," the me-superior, you-inferior axiom can source hatred to "white penis I win, black penis you lose." In Canada, Professor Philip Rushton proved that black males had less intelligence: He measured the length of penises. The *bell curve* clinched this. No one before this knew that penises had neurons. In solipsism the comforting ritual of repeating Q is and is not Q, conned by knowledge withheld, causes the love of irrationality. The evil is that the unread masses have no chance in hell of ever reading this missing information. *That is, missing vital information makes the mind "deficient"—gifts it with an "innate flaw."* Fem as w-o + man did not know she was *fem*. How convenient for man! How deeply evil!

Absent symbols make a code of concealment in the code of R/revelation. The code of concealment is the sum of missing data imposed in false symbols called Truth; fem concealed as w-o/man in *revealed* man. Then the false name w-o + man deemed Truth—which is not the truth—is believed.

When *fem, feme, sapiens, and sufficient mind* are not named as existing, you cannot speak of them; these facts that add to truths and knowledge are lost. False symbols explain our species; they are all we have, giving plausibility to an *innate flaw*, a.k.a. a *deficiency*, a.k.a.

original sin, a living Q is and is not Q begun by imprinting *necessary inconsistency* in our reasoning processes without our knowledge, since patriarchal language as higher knowledge is all we have. This is morally and intellectually reprehensible.

Cultured ignorance imposed by withheld information is blinded belief, *Lorded* Truth. It gives no thought to the fact that controlling the mind with falsehoods harms men as much as fem—if not more. Lords engender violent splits, opposites opposing one another, feuding in "Words"—not knowing that symbols cannot discriminate once these falsehoods are let loose in society. They are used and believed by everyone. Aye! And there's the rub.

Civilizing ideas such as *femhood*, *statesfemship*, *femly*, and *hundreds of feme-made*, *mind-affirming ideas* about the rational state of nature and reality cannot be common knowledge to contribute to the *common good* of the species and morality. But this is the very reason why *moral* autonomy fell on the heads of fem/potential mothers as w-o-tacked-onto-man beings. She is to believe in the personal *autonomy* of the Father having the right to pull H/his free-willed, monolithic God-man out of his man-hat to make her submissive to the Father God, imposing the responsibility of morality upon her head. I call this ingenious gilded solipsism, the Holy Integral Solipsism, or HIS—ironically engraved on the holy wafer that can be transubstantiated into the body of Christ by "The Word."

Almost all legions of "men of both sexes" identify as *Lord*-based groups, every legion, patriarchal group, having a Lord of its own. That is, for each man-special legion of men (race), there is a One True God, a Father Ruler of men, *Manu*, Zeus, Ptah, E*manu*el, God, *Hu*, Allah, Manitou, Yahweh, Buddha. Any feme named as supernatural is devalued as god*dess*, lesser god, not even deserving a capital letter.

What happened to our species? First came the idea that fem was not to be her own naming agent as fem. Second, half the species became not-male men, to name the whole species mankind, which I now call the Grand Identity Theft of fem. Third, this put a deficiency in the mind; it imprinted Q is and is not Q in four false names for our species. Fourth, the Greatest Social Engineering Project on planet earth was put in gear to change two, fem and man, as two sapiens into two men of opposite genders into one man or 2 = 1 man as man and woman. Fifth, Fathers gave birth to many Holy Alpha Males residing in the Sky, supporting the culturally different patriarchies/races around the globe. Sixth, the Doctrine of man, religion, became the Theory of man "secular," pretending to separate secular from religious belief, state from church. Seventh, the *secret* in 2 = 1 man became *sacred*. Eighth, capital *T* Truth was not to be challenged, criticized, or analyzed as sacred. Ninth, voilà, infallibility!

The next question, then, is how did we come to believe in 2 = 1 man-favored-by-God? How did we come to accept Q is and is not Q as valid? It could not arise merely from *making* symbols. What led to such a devious and yet obvious falsification of our species? We can say for sure that it did not come out of a vacuum. Nothing comes from what is not a thing. There has to be an *origin*—an *in-the-beginning* aspect of the falsifying program—somewhere. What was the situation before the Christian God revealed man to be two men of opposite genders as doctrine, an act of highly arrogant fantasy about 2,000 years old? What events led to this fantasy? This takes us back 4,000 years.

■   ■   ■

From here on I use names that more truly reflect reality-as-it-is to expose the difference between realism and reality. Fem with man as sapiens is reality; woman in man as humans or two men of opposite genders as man, is realism. But the limitlessness in solipsism makes it hard to explain that Q is and is not Q in 2 = 1 man causes so many nasty curves in its secrets. Limitlessness zigzags erratically in its many secrets. (1) W-o-man included *in* man excludes fem as a thinker in the species. (2) *Being man in reality entails only being male* is not articulated in any books on man. (3) W-o/man is a man who's not a man is not articulated in any books on man. (4) Free will is *special* to man since God gave it to him born in sin. (5) There are sanctions against analyzing what is *sacred*! (Secret → sacred.) Just believe. (6) Belief has primacy over knowledge because it is "higher" knowledge! All these tactics are used to succeed. Knowledge withheld with infallibility is a potent force.

If one is not allowed *to name herself by her own insights in her right* to be a logic-affirming being, then her mind is deemed null. Deemed null she is not necessary to the speech-using species, except for her uterine services. That the two minds are necessary to be the foundation upon which rationality stands is destroyed.

Where did the idea come from that fem was not to be herself as a self-naming agent, not to be her own self-identifying agent? How, where, and why was this idea invented at all? What is the "In the beginning was the word …" of it all?

Chapter 4

SLAVE LAWS, WANNABE L/LORDS, AND THE FIRST OF FIRST LORD GODS

Symbol making comes *to us from* us through culture. Culture, the name we give to our social activities, including making symbols to communicate, holds our hopes and goals, individually and collectively, as well as the details of our daily lives. Sapiens make symbols like sheep make wool, bees make honey, and silkworms make silk. Each animal evolves capable of doing what it evolves itself to do with nature. The prepositions are with, in, and through nature, because we are a part of nature. We are not separate and above nature as a *special* species created by "The Word" of Alpha Males in the Sky, necessitating that we worship them.

We make new symbols every day to name reality. We expand our intelligence and creativity with every symbol we make that reflects reality-as-it-is. Then we use these reality-based symbols to create plans and programs that enhance all of life on the planet.

Symbols made to fit non-rational notions, nonsense, and lies expand ignorance, make you stupid. "Dumbing down" is necessary. Dittoing like a parrot the gifted false from those who believe themselves higher than others, ritualized in song and prayer, is rote, mechanical belief. Dangerous neuroses, hatred of mind, false evidence, and non-facts broadcast "the One-and-Only Truth" belief to preach "The Word," where you are either for me or against me. Born in the hatred of mind, racism and class structure take root first in seminal sexism, fem as w-o-man. From this nonsense come destructive plans and programs, such as grabbing, warring, and whoring.

The sapient animal as sapient evolved its capability to make symbols with nature's evolution. The brain that makes symbols determines that we live as thinking animals. Everything we do, think, and say starts with having to make sound-bites-with-meaning to use that develop mind and enhance thinking life to add comfort and happiness to our lives, such that it enhances all of life.

Symbol making and using determine life lived as thinking animals. Our "purpose" is to live *thinking* life as fully as possible to enhance minded life and all life forms. We are the stewards of mind and body on planet earth, and by this very fact the stewards of planet earth with, in, and through all other life forms. Being *special* and *above the law* is terrorizing fantasy.

Thinking life is different from all other life forms in one aspect, mind. There is no model for us. Thought is not in us as an instinctual or built-in device like wool making in sheep. It is not in us like making honey is programmed in bees. We must work hard to do it and do it right. We cannot imitate sheep, ducks, or apes. We have to cut our own path to make the neurons and synapses in the brain arrive at the right information in the mind to make useable knowledge. The whole exercise is about getting and having correct information and facts that are useable to use and work with.

The self-reflective factor in us must above all aim at truths about us. Sapiens as sapiens as naturally sentient animals possess common aptitudes and skills to live *rationally* side by side with one another and with all other life forms; they can make a rational framework for all life because they are self-reflective. They can empathize. Symbols ought to enhance life as thinkers to help sustain thinking life and all other life. *Life* lived rationally is central to thinking life, and thinking life is central to living with all other life forms.

It took millions of years to make useful language, but as fem and man, *we* made and still make symbols we call language today, an ongoing project. New symbols are created every day by both fem and man, for example, quasar. Many unnamed entities are being found and named as we speak.

We are symbol-making animals. Like sheep are wool makers. The brain is organic; it is not hardwired to overvalue male and undervalue feme. Feme mind and body acting *with* male mind and body must be named correctly to acquire truths about fem and man. Both symbol making and reproducing are necessary in sapient life, both necessarily also in species identity. To acquire these *truths* in reality, it is necessary to be constant in using consistence for rational thought. The many truths stop false power from defining life as death—to be in the arms of God, Allah, Jahweh, *Hu*, Brahma, Your Favorite Holy Male. Thinking life is thinking life. Q is Q.

No Alpha Male gave language to *man*. *Adam*/Man as whole species is false both in doctrine and theory. Language developed to fit male fantasy, he believed "him"-self higher than all others, above laws and limits.

Fem have contributed to language for as long as men have. But he banned and banished her symbols naming, denoting, and describing her half of the species. Why?

H/his fantasy makes the "purpose" of life as death for "eternal life" in H/his arms in heaven—or fear of hell causing psychoses that ignore rational deliberations in language. It imposes death = life-in-the-arms-of-Holy-Alpha-Males-in-the-Sky as goal. Inventing the soul, he also banned the self by splitting mind from body by gender. The self entails the body, a problem in "rising-to-heaven" language that poisoned both the goal in and the purpose of living thinking life.

The Holy Truth in mankind as whole species is institutionalized bias, an inconvenient lie stopping the many truths from being discovered and seen. Capital *T* Truth sucks on its sacred bull's tail as proof of its Truth; the word "man" proves man, which God-man gave to man.

We could not know the long-term effect of Manu's Law passing through 4,000 years. It brought about the false and terrorizing Doctrine-Theory of Man, the ideology of man, the gender that would give itself the entitlement to control fem, sex, nature, reality, rationality, and knowledge.

Rationality is not just logic. In this narrow view, rational*ism* is used to discredit reason. Rationalism sanitizes H/his solipsism. In revealed *man*—*mind* the 2 = 1 man Truth is proven by The Word (of God), which is man, rationalism. It destroys the truths of fem and man as two gender-different beings, duality, the truth of 2 = 2 and why rationality is often derogated.

So what imposed the fantasy that man was the mind and soul of the species? How did dual*ism* 2 = 1, the one-size-fits-all *man* become the Doctrine-Theory of Man con/fusing doctrine and theory into one belief?

In 2400 BCE, Manu of the Hindus put into law that mothers, wives, daughters, and sisters "should never be free of subjugation" (*Code of Manu*, Sloka V). The need to set up such a law blatantly shows Manu's fragile ego, his lust to control the other gender. Fearing his own sexuality, Sloka V gave him the right to control and take any girl of his desire at his convenience. No other reason but that of lust for control can explain the need to legalize the subjugation of half the species to the other half of the species.

The law gave all males power over all femes on a global scale. Men's sexual lust and hard-drive virility protected by law put supreme power and privilege in male sexuality. The law changed the direction of knowledge and mind in the species. Sex being the pivot on which the first legalization of feme slavery was writ, language had to make this law appear as if "this is the way it is." That is, *mind had to be redirected*, whence the goal of patriarchal codes in all major languages on planet earth. Patriarchal codes, language, had to communicate male superiority.

Sex became the great dividing axe of mind male and body not male. The collective mind in men turned to grabbing wives-as-capital (commerce) and for whoring. Conflicts between men arose; violence and serial tribal warring between rival patriarchs appeared natural. The collective mind in fem would plunge into total annihilation of self as an active agent in her species as she was transmuted into a submissive, weak, powerless, and penniless thing. How could not-male things understand hard-drive virility? It was beyond their empty heads. Feme slavery, now legal on planet earth, mothers became the wares for trade (*mer* + *x*, L., mothers as wares → commerce). Wives, warring, and whoring for commercial ventures were the first tastes of capitalism and wealth making.

The law went on its merry way from 2400 BCE for several centuries. Along the way, like Manu, other higher men, patriarchs with inflated male egos, created metaphysical clones, supernatural doubles, *God, Allah, Jehovah, Manitou, Buddha, Hu, Jahweh, Ptah—Emanuel—*fully supporting his right to control fem and feme sexuality writ in H/his Holy Books by men inspired by their own Alpha Males. Male; sexuality has never been analyzed outside this privilege nor reported forthrightly since Manu's Law made feme sexuality submissive and accessible to men by divine decree. God's word is final. It is Absolute. Virility is the sacred talent of the Creator.

Law is never just law; in every law there is a social goal. In Manu's Law, the goal is for fathers to stand together in solidarity against mothers. She is the enemy! The manu/facture of hatred for her mind and her sexual role was necessary for the law to succeed. Not superficial hatred for freedom from sexual responsibility, but a profound hatred of fem's mind to quell all resistance to his sexual demands, but unknown to him, the hatred of all mind. You cannot subjugate and mute half of all minds in the species without cutting all minds down to a dittoing pea. Man law made sex a wife's duty, rape an accepted act, and wife beating normal. Life was sex.

Institutionalized in marriage as husband-head, the myth male is and is not divine mind keeps the species believing. Few see that Q is and is not Q, for 2 = 1 man disables the individual mind by gifting it with a deficiency, making collective mind insufficient. The eternal slavery of fem in Manu's slave law would give men the idea of positing an "innate flaw" in fem that would come to be called "original sin" by another legion of men about 2,000 years later. Legions of men were always reassembling into new legions to face challenges from foreign men who wanted to be top dog. The big legions pulled the fantasy together in incoherent cut-and-paste, mix-and-match organizations called *religions*, showing that God, Allah, Hu, Ptah, Emanuel "revealed" feme subjugation in His Holy Book. Secular law was law in religion, cosmic support for 2 = 1 man.

A law nurturing hatred of half the species necessitates solutions entailing violence. Zig: Hatred of the not-one-of-us comes straight out of the idea that *gender divides mind from body*, an idea that brought on violence to impose the division. Fem were kept out of the halls of learning for millennia. *Gender-as-division* of mind and body, the cause of much *common evil* was born out of the rights of virility. False secular systems must use violent means to succeed and invent other false systems, religions, to shore up the first one. An inconvenient lie is shored up by other lies.

Zag: So male act, thought, and deed had to "progress" to the belief that a bodiless male mind existed to justify and make infallible male *part = whole* as mind. It follows that the mother was flesh without mind. Thus the battle *man vs. flesh* (about which many books have been written) started in the battle *mind vs. body* in man's gender-as-division of mind/male and body-flesh/feme. Historical philosophy rests on the fantasy that the father is *subject* of act, and the mother is *object* recipient of H/his act, from the model of copulation, preordained by the Father/supernatural double of the father in H/his law. Male control of feme sexuality received holy permission from *Lord Manu God* in 2400 BCE and has received it ever since. The rights of virility are law in $2 = 1$ man.

The road to $2 = 1$ man is paved with Manu's Law. Fem-made, feme-identifying symbols are banned or put out of use, gifting all mind with a deficiency, a Q is and is not Q as valid. Belief in *man* and warfare-with-whoring between patriarchs became endemic to our species, a species that as sapiens evolved its self to see, reason, think, and do mathematics on the knowledge that $2 = 2$ in reality. That is, Manu's Law redirected mind in time to the *2 = 1 synthesis of man* by *systemic femic cleansing*, holy/special man's eternal solution to linguistic, social, and physical domination. He banned her name, symbol, and identity from the knowledge of the species. This is like banning the oxygen necessary in the composition of water.

I doubt that rational men would support such evil. The crime done to mind in banning the knowledge of fem as fem, Q is Q, denatures and brutalizes males dictating w-o-men to be silent, submissive, and powerless, proving the false claim that men are superior and more aggressive by nature. Subservient ignorant wives lorded by virile stud-men central to faith-based fantasy of husband-head is taught in seminaries, where men fully using their neuron-loaded penises are free to claim that "semen is the first principle of everything" (*Christian Encyclopedia*). How did semen become the original stuff of all that exists in the cosmos? Whose semen is the prime mover's stuff?

Four thousand years of 2 = 1 man propaganda in seminal books redirected mind from reason-based wisdom to faith-based fantasy, belief in Lord Gods, Holy Alpha Males in the Sky, imposing irrationality as valid. Sex, the hinge of value, is in the edifice of the 10,000-term *Patriarchal Code* asserting man L/lord and special. The code reveals how self-important, self-titled F/fathers systematically imposed the idea that only males possessed the rational faculty. It followed that woman was flesh-without-mind "put on earth by God to please men," Lordship claiming semen to be the first creative substance. Seminal sexism seeds the profound hatred of bodies to be "activated" by semen, creator, virility, and penis. The ovum has to be "activated" so she has to be rendered weak, submissive, powerless, and penniless by law. Sex divides mind male and body not male. Thus the "whole" man in 2 = 1 man is a man-owning wife-as-slave. He heads the marriage as Mr. (and Mrs.) His Name. As Mrs. His Name, she is his possessed body/object. Possession by law for control!

Mind is skewed on *man* "in the Name of *Man*/u God." Manu claimed to be H/holy Father having divine credentials; he stamped the idea of *Lordship* on the masses. To be *in manu* is to believe and live life in Lord Manu's right to legalize feme slavery. To be *in manu* became the ruling idea for the next 4,000 years. The seminal Truth is 2 man (and wife) = 1 man. Fem would be wife-of-man, w-o-man, not fem; femic cleansing put into action. Lordship won. Four millennia later 2 = 1 *man* still overrides the knowledge that 2 minds = 2 beings. Mr. and Mrs. His Name for 2 = 1 impose the false math in marriage "in the name of God the Father." Ditto, ditto, ditto.

Belief in man lording/husbanding inferiors is law in *hu/manity*, *hu* doing god magic. The Medieval witch hunts leading to the burning of thousands of fem using their own minds expose seminal hatred. The Aboriginal Holocaust by Christian European settlers decimated 100,000,000 Aborigines in the Americas down to 18,000,000; the Jewish

Holocaust in Christian Europe took down 6,000,000 Jews. We have to praise ourselves for fast technological progress often because progress in rational attitudes toward *life is life* does not advance one iota.

The story of man as man and w-o/man is even more complicated than this. The idea of legal feme subjugation by Manu went through many ancient cultures like a burning bush of unexamined phallic passion among wannabe Lords, self-important fathers. Many kinds of non-legal slavery existed around the globe. The Greeks had a good one. But how does a patriarch emulate Lord Manu and stamp H/his own image to leave his own eternal seminal mark and legacy on planet earth?

About a millennium after Manu, the patriarchal Jews named Yahweh Emanuel, the Manu in us. Also as *Immanuel*, historical linguistics tell us that the Hebrew term is one in which *immanu* means "with" and (repeat of) *anu*, the first person plural suffix *us*(?) (leaving *imm* hanging). The *us* suffix in Latin denotes male. The *im* usually means "in."

This looks like confessional etymology. *Semenologists*, seminal etymologists, in seminaries would not refrain from lying. The issue is how much can we trust historical linguistics after imposing that we are all men regardless of gender, Q is and is not Q, and 2 = 1 man is Truth in doctrine, religion, and theory, secular.

Manu was a male life giver: a G/god who "gave birth" to seven sons! All Manus! We assume *s* denotes plural here. Then Germanus, Romanus, Parmanus, and so on appeared. Parmanus is a man from Parma. Is Germanus more than one germanu? Is manus an independent symbol? Or is it the political game of ambiguity? Or of needing more than one M/manu/Lord to subjugate femes? Historical linguistics does not enlighten us here; it is silent. Yet silence is not claimed to be a male characteristic: Silence, the Bible says, is w-o-man's duty! Why such a high usage of *manu/s*?

What does *manus* in the Old Latin term *hu/manus* mean? Surprise! It means "hand"—*neutral*! Manual makes this sound plausible. So we now have manus hand, more than one manu, male being, Manu, law giver, Lord, birth giver. How *manu* became *manus* as "neutral" hand is not explained. Historical linguistics is silent here too. Is this eclecticism or selective silence? Confusing!

But why did he add *hu* (ca. 1250) to manus, neutral hand? What did this do? It did not change the meaning as hand, nor clarify it. Therefore adding "hu" is suspect. Would it have a male connection after all? How does the *us* ending, meaning "male" in Latin, change *manus* to mean "neutral"? None of these ambiguities are answered in etymological research.

As "neutral" hand this puts a huge jinx in w-o-man! What is the wife of a hand? Is the neutral hand male? Why is the hand suddenly more important than the sex axe? Did the Romans see our species as hands? Not if you read about the Etruscans! Moreover *hu-man* is defined as "of or belonging to man." The snow job of ambiguity! How much more confusing can this get?

On top of this, generic H/he as grammatical law fits generic M/man. We are starting to see that man is a victim of his own seminal sexism. The doer of act is male because he is mind as neutral hand! W-o-man is passive, to be activated, remember? Solipsism boomerangs! Believe willy-nilly in sex-axe fantasy's confusing pseudo-facts—not good for everyone after all, is it?

How did hu-manus come about? If "hu" comes from humus, then more silliness is exposed. Man as God's special creature is above all animals. Since animals are as much from humus as "special" man, then why do we not have the hulion, hutiger, or humouse? If it is a vowel variation of *homo*, L., to assert male *homo*geneity of the species, then hu-manus clearly means manman. The Arab language contains *man-man*! What is a manman? Is he more man than man? Time goes by so slowly, but time can make man spout so much—nonsense.

About 2,000 years after Lord Manu's Sloka V, after the Hebrews named their god Emanuel, Roman patriarchs wrote their slave law. They called it the Manus, with a capital *M* and *s*. The Manus is the law: *the authoritative control of the husband over his wife*. The Manus parrots *in manu's* Sloka V law perfectly for wannabe Manorial and Ecclesiastical Lords alike. "Wives, submit yourselves unto your own husbands … For the husband is the head of the wife, even as Christ is the head of the church" (Ephesians 5:22–23). Sloka V and the Manus of the patriarchal Romans are identical. Ditto, ditto, ditto. Legal slavery boosted *special*, self-important patriarchs and priests: from Manu

2400 BCE to Manus about 200 BCE until about 1850 CE. The species endured some 4,000 years of nonsensical, senseless, cruel, and unjust times through patriarchy's slavery and feudalism.

So we now have manus, hand, Manus, law of control, suffix *us* denoting male, manu + *s*(?), man or men, Manu, Lord, God, Manu's Law, seven sons, many guys named Manu, and manus as neutral hand of men. The roster thickens. Dittoing is prolific.

The Roman Manus extended slave law to include the Lord's male slaves, after the model of Greek slavery. This was an improvement of Lord Manu's slave law and Greek slavery—*progress!* How we love progress. We now have full legal enslavement of males along with the subjugation and enslavement of femes. Yes, it's time for the question: Who were the enslavers?

By association, *manus* hand and *Manu's* Law come together as *neutral* hand-of-control in wannabe Lords. Lords had the M/manu/s— (neutral) hand of control—over all fem and most men as slaves, a neat sleight of "hand" through *The W/word manus* to Manu's Law. Left to do was add *Hu*, the tongue of Ptah-speaking man and creation into being, wow, foolproof magic! *Hu*, the tongue of Ptah, a god, spoke creation into being in Egypt in 3000 BCE, and the men who would be Lord God of the Romans in 200 BCE dittoed the Hindi Lord Manu's slave law writ in 2400 BCE, voilà, the beauty of intercultural exchange and eclecticism. Abracadabra: Male domination in creation is zapped in on the Absolute Truth of the spoken Word of Holy Alpha Males in the Sky. With so few knowing how to read and write from 2400 BCE to 1700 CE, and so much knowledge hidden, missing, and withheld from the masses, belief in Hu man Truth was consummated and the masses put their faith in Holy Alpha Males in the Sky. The L/lords laughed all the way to their cash boxes.

The Lords, men as fathers who assumed to be higher than the masses, controlling the masses as slaves, would force the re-identification of both the male and the feme. Named *fem* and *wer* in old Anglo-Saxon (*wer* from L., *vir*), were renamed *man* to denote "being *in manu*," a slave, and *fem* became w-o + *man*, slave wife of the slave, double enslavement. This is the original meaning of *man*, Manu's Law of subjugation in time renamed males as slaves! In time, *wif* → *w-o*-tacked-onto-*man* for expediency. Patriarchal scholars did not bother looking at reality to see what it was all about.

Hu, Ptah's marvelous phallic create-the-world tongue, is powerful fantasy. The male named *wer* became *man*, slave, to denote being under slave law, and *fem* became wo*man*, slave *wife* of the slave. Worldwide feudalism followed, the righteousness of slavery in Manorial and Ecclesiastical Lords made *man* and *woman* as hu*mans* the realism it is today, revealed in Holy Books by God-man-inspired men. Methodological solipsism complete and cosmic!

Manumission was a hierarchical *chain of control*, Lords controlling people identical to the biblical/koranic/torah holy chain of command. The categories were Lord owning man, woman, and beast as chattel. The feudal system blossomed; slavery went global. Rule by a few elite bloodline F/fathers as Lords went on for millennia. Lords, Kings, Emperors, Czars, Reverends, Barons, and the like, self-titled higher men entitled themselves to rule the masses of slaves classified as lesser men, sub-men and not men or women. Lords were Lords, they were male but they were not "men." The symbol "man" meant slave, and the Lord was not a slave. *He was the Lord*!

Why did Lords succeed for so long? Why did men, slaves, who far outnumbered Lords not revolt? Lords were clever. For the last 2,000 years, The Manus, the authoritative control of the husband over his wife, *had made every husband a lord. To lord* and *to husband* are equivalent. Wives addressed husbands as "My Lord." *Herr*, lord, is used in Germany to this day, *Monseigneur* in France until the eighteenth century. The House of Lords exists in the parliamentary system of England. Every man as husband was a lord in his own right in the Manus, with the rights of virility.

It took many years for lords to figure out that Manorial and Ecclesiastical Lords were superior to (hut) lords, inferior. The capital-*L* Ecclesiastical and Manorial Lords standing above lowercase lords had set up Q is and is not Q in kept-ignorant lesser/hut lords, the Lords laughing all the way to their cash boxes. By then money, power, and sex were inexorably linked in *higher* male = supernatural being, superior divine stud—complete with the right of "first night." Thank God for sex; worship of the Lord would not have happened without it.

Class structure: The hierarchy was Lords, the masses of hut lords, lesser men, poor disenfranchised men, and the *loerarchy* of w-o-men having little value and status below males. As lords began to see that the Lord saw them fit only for slavery, they saw that the Lord had rights that the lord did not. By the time ideas of emancipation from manu-mission entered his head, so much was already lost. The harm to general knowledge already embedded in language done in seminaries, he stayed on the Lord's side. The lords' first demand for rights: "The Rights of Man" (France, 1789) and Thomas Paine's defense of "The Rights of Man," dittoed in England a year later, paved the Lord's way for global *femic cleansing* cleared by the masses of lesser lords as if an evolution step had been zapped in by the Lord's "free will." Knowledge of our species came to a false standpoint. Belief in man's control of fem as w-o-man was total and global in magnitude. *Femulus*, L., domestic slave made the symbol *family*, "the *Holy* family" became a model and having sons a wife's duty.

Male rulers, male lawyers, male parliaments, male judiciary, male landowners, male developers, male doctors, male scribes, male philoso-phers, and male authority 4,000 years in the making devised systems of laws and designed languages to ensure that mothers, sisters, wives, and daughters should forever be excluded from everything that makes life worth living. Manu's goal in Sloka V was completed and consum-mated in the 1800s.

Every husband as *lord* of his wife is the one-on-one tactic neces-sary to subjugate fem. This one-on-one femic cleansing would achieve Manu's aim. M/men titled L/lord, King, Shah, Pope, Reverend, Baron, Bishop, Count, Marquis, Czar, and even small-*l* lord entitled H/him to rule. The *entitlement to rule* was in every man, even if it was only the small *king*dom of one wife. To husband → to lord → to control → to *man*age gave H/him total control through language and laws made to fit H/his right to control. *Fem and lesser men had to become ruler followers.*

Slavery has changed face, not structure. Today's control, econom-ical, social, and mental, is more esoteric. Higher men are privy to it. The masses are not due the information withheld. Fem as woman and "lesser" man are controlled. The Human patent "man is and is not male" is imprinted on the mind by Higher men with power. Today "Lords" pay laborers meager wages in a fearful job scene full of new fears, terrorizing dangers, and big risks, while paying Himself obscene salaries and bonuses, plus taking obscene profits skimmed off the slave's labor. Called the forces of "the market place," it is a heaven on earth for higher men, a global hell for the masses. Competition, a euphemism for the command that slaves produce more and more, is more of the same Lord-imposed law of control. What is so sad is that we do not seem to be able to see any alternative structure for society.

Indeed, slavery intensified as it changed face. Manu's Lordship is more with us today than in 2400 BCE. How so? The entitlement of "Lord" when privilege was at its highest peak became a threat to His life. So Lords started to call themselves men; *the entitlement of Man (in the Rights of Man)* gave them "the balls" to protect their power grabbing, greed, prostitution, and bullying through illogic, lies, and irrationality. That is, when Lords fell out of popularity, they started to call themselves *men*. We do not know today that His Lordship is anonymously hiding under the rubric of being a "man" formerly used only for slave. The new threat to Lords, a.k.a. men, is fem naming herself fem.

Manu's Law is in place today through "The Words" man, wo*man*, Hu*man*, and Hu*manity*. Higher "men" have personal autonomy without moral responsibility. Holy Father, special *par*ent, God, Santa Claus, Peter Cottontail take care of everyone's needs every day, everywhere, inflated with metaphysical attributes as cosmic provider, easily imposed upon the masses kept in ignorance by knowledge withheld for 4,000 years. Solipsism is a mysterious sponge, *solus*, "alone" + *ipse*, "self"; Manu alone named his self God and hundreds of other self-important men parroted.

Even to praising the Lord God in *wor*ship. Man/*u/s* covers, names, and protects male being, wo*man*, class status, sex-axe splitting of mind and body, autonomy, the W/*wor*d, magic, hand, mind, control, *vir*tue— *man* says it all. No need for any other name. So that it is in the sense of "man consists of man and woman" that Lord God-man exists—a magic *tour de force* through lies that grew to highly valued nonsense called faith in God, belief. The old Anglo-Saxon term *virschippe, vir,*

L., man, and *ver* in *verpa*, L., *penis*, v*erge*, Fr., penis, made The Word "worship." The very term *wor*ship means *manship*, having a penis. "Let us worship God" is literally "Let us *manship* God." I rest my case.

The tricks of illogic, lies embedded in symbols, self-contradiction, and dichotomy by sex justified by solipsism almost worked. But does this nonsense make better men? Does it help men be real, natural, or rational?

Sadder still, it harmed the mind of the species almost beyond repair. It damaged too many individuals in the species. Four thousand years of seminal hatred, seminal language, seminal law and femic cleansing, whoring using girls and fem, serial warring with other seminal beings, power grabbing using lies, false knowledge, dichotomy by sex, absurdity, aggressive sexuality, ethnic cleansing, and mindless cruelties did the species harm of such magnitude that it may not be repairable. Individually and collectively we are a very con/fused species of two irrational "men regardless of sex." Frozen *in manu* made being con/fused in 2 = 1 man and the love of irrationality, Q is and is not Q, our best attributes. No wonder man wars and whores a lot.

And no wonder we need to pray to G/god. H/he'll hear our prayers! We are not responsible for this mess. We are not the ones who make symbols that communicate lies, false knowledge, dichotomy, absurdity, aggressive sexuality, ethnic and femic cleansing, cruelties, and serial wars on one another. The devil, "our dark side," makes us do it. It is not our fault: *We have an innate flaw.*

No, we do not have an innate flaw! We did not commit any original sin. The competition to be First Lord among Firsts, like Hitler, Hu, Duvalier, Pinochet, Allah, Ciaocescue, God, bin Laden, Yahweh, corporations as persons—supporting lies set in tradition, the system of conventional false power. Right or wrong, "this is the way it is": The rights of hard-drive unaccountable virility call the shots on all the members in the species. The *system* Lords invented and made is evil.

Lies embedded in symbols we use every day, we all had to share in *the common evil* of belief in an innate flaw, original sin, the seductive SEX-as-division of mind and body born of slave law. H/he named fem "woman" to name the whole species "mankind." No alternative symbols for fem were left standing! She was "flesh as w-o-man in man the mind."

Such absurdity did not come from primitive minds, but from narcissist selfish men bloated with their own seminal and virile self-importance. Primitive minds are a hell of a lot smarter than this.

We can stop believing in the lies called Holy Truth. *We can refuse to share in common evil.* We can love and learn to use facts and truths. We can respect knowledge. We can make symbols that respect reality-as-it-is. We can make true-to-reality names and symbols. We have the capability to do it and do it well. We are capable of solving all of our problems using facts, truths, good reasoning, and the resources at hand and categorize correctly the specifics of issues.

Thinking is not nearly as hard as it was made out to be in 2 = 1 man. It was made to appear hard and fearful by the first scholars, priests, and holy men coming out of and believing in feudalism with its full-blown Lordships. The goal of semen producers in seminaries was to strike fear in ordinary people who did not know how to read and write, first as the unwashed masses, then as the *unread* masses. Seminarians for hundreds of years were the only ones who knew how to read and write. They fabricated seminal fantasies having no scientific or rational basis, no checks and balances, no rules and standards. They imposed the sex-crazed, sex-axed biased version of a mantasy-fantasy world that blossomed in Medievalism.

Life does not lie. Reality does not lie. Nature does not lie. Special seminal self-important men raising virility to sacred and holy heights lie.

Fem and man evolved with minds to develop rationality. They are the beings upon which the whole foundation of rationality stands. It cannot be the case that the purpose of mind is to do and believe in irrationality, such as supernatural Alpha Male Beings in the Sky telling two men-of-opposite-gender what to think, say, and do, using lies embedded in symbols.

Chapter 5

SEEING THE CON/FUSIONS
IN SEMINAL BELIEF

It is a theological tenet that semen is the first principle of everything. Before there was the cosmos there was semen, whence seminal. One goes to seminaries to learn about God. The *spermaticos logos*, Gr., sperm (is) word, speaks! The fantasy comes out of seminarians tucked away from society, male feudal scholars, monks, priests, friars, and Fathers who knew how to read and write, financed by the populace, poor and rich.

The sperm as "first" principle of everything talks, a fantasy that shatters all reason. But it fits into the notion of "first," "in the beginning" man, *special* in his hard-drive virility creator of all taught in religions. Rational people call this creationism.

That the spoken word uttered by sperm can do magic is from the ancient myth that the tongue of Ptah, *Hu*, 3000 BCE, created the world by merely *speaking The Word*. Sperm is special, giving males seminal power in speech. Historical linguistics is silent on what *hu*-tacked-onto-*manus* means. Adding "hu" to *manus*, neutral hand in male control by law, did not change or clarify M/manus. It cons the fusion of both neutral hand and male to make the name appear to be what it is not and imposes that that just is "the way things are." In reality "hu" does nothing. It does not change the meaning of the neutral hand of control given to man by law, the law of slavery, the Manus.

If it is assumed without proof that "hu" is from humus, then other animals deemed more animal than man (who is "above") should have brought about the names hulion, hutiger—this did not happen. It appears that only man is of the earth!

In medieval books there are drawings of man with two tongues, in his mouth and between his groins. Would one of these be *Hu*? Yet when the scientific attitude came about, this ludicrous and pornographic nonsense was not discarded. Today seminal books are written, seminal ideas are born, and seminal work is still being done. I've been waiting for an ovumal book all my life.

One truth not found in seminal work is that to be rational, symbols must reflect reality-as-it-is. Symbols must be in consonance with reality. Name one situation where irrationality is useful. Either we do good reasoning with honest emotions, or wallow in self-righteous, virtuous manure as irrational beings with sloppy emotions. "Since both a claim and its opposite cannot be true, contradictions are necessarily false" (Conway and Munson 1990). Fem cannot be a "man" and not minded. So as painful as it may be, we must look at Q is and is not Q, making 2 = 1 man's creationist claim "Truth."

Absent *fem* as w-o + man levitates *man* to being mind. This is a strange statement given the wild fantasies that religions make the masses believe. The belief that she is incapable of *mind activity* is still widely held: Two thinking beings are still one, man. Two men of opposite genders = 1 True Man is the secret in creationism, seminal subjectivism imposing faith-based fantasy as Truth. And the earth is flat. In reality, fem and man are simultaneous products of evolution on an earth that is round. But Adam as *first* and *man* is very important to seminarians in their fantasy of first "in the beginning …" Being first wins the game in naming, *upmanship*, language that gives men power over others.

Seminal, the "deep essence of being," is deeper than ovumal. Dissemination and insemination are what H/he does. A penis having neurons and synapses that speak is a handy tool to disseminate seminal knowledge into a body without mind. Yes, it gets this pornographic. The awesome *spermaticos logos*, applied to Jesus Christ, is at work in faith-based 2 = 1 man. Dualism displaces duality. Dual*ism* is 2 = 1, duality 2 = 2.

In dualism gender *divides* mind and body dictated by seminal word; in duality two beings each as feme or male self act to reach an inclusive objective. Dualism assimilates, swallows the *opposite* in the one entitling the one as mind. Duality integrates the acts of two different minded beings working together to achieve rationality.

When he-mind and she-body are *Special* Man, our nature, history, knowledge, and emotions disconnect in many ways from reality. Immaturity decorates the irrationality that follows. Facts get a bad reputation, for example, evolution. Creationism zapped-in on *spermaticos logos* is Truth. Fantasy becomes the stuff of belief, sticky because it is free. It is free from searching for facts, free from learning the relationships between facts, and free from the hard reality of having to face these facts and their relationships. The foundation upon which thinking rests is for all practical purposes destroyed. Immaturity loves irrationality.

Mind activity for the past 4,000 years has been and still is in the H/he-gear, the virile gear underwriting normalized aggressive behavior as "natural" in the male, violence in its many forms, including psychological bullying. The past is a record of the violence born from belief. But a biased and incomplete account of our species is not real history. The story of seminally special man is *historicism*, off track, off balance, and unjust, the story of *isms* all the way lies wrapped in niceties and euphemisms camouflaged as Truth.

Historicism began in 2400 BCE with Manu. Holy man out of touch with feme reality as fem, necessary to the team of symbol makers in reality-as-it-is, pushed the species off the rational road onto a runaway track of lies called Truth. Placing H/himself above all and first, H/he gave H/himself personal autonomy, the *entitlement* to the right to be unaccountable to no one but H/himself as a Lord—H/his supernatural dittoing double. George Bush cockily said "God Bless America" every time he finished speaking!

Above reality and first H/he is larger than life, the H/he-gear a potent bullying juggernaut. He/Christ/Mohammed/Savior zaps away the sin/innate flaw in the blinded/unread masses gifted with a deficiency in mind eons ago to support an unjust slave law by withholding information, causing the need for L/lords and S/saviors. H/he con/fused needs and wants in head-breaking repetitious propaganda. With effective knowledge-destroying pollution for 4,000 years, could global pollution have been far behind?

In 2 = 1 man, the F/father's *raison d'être* is hatred of feme cause. *Causality is the problem in fragile egos that would wage war against mind.* Who is to be *First* Cause/Prime Mover, Lord of Lords? Whose *semen* is The Supreme Cause? Whose tongue spoke creation into being first? Hu? God? Allah? Which Holy Alpha Male in the Sky is the First of Firsts in semen production? Banishing feme causality, male causality came up supreme.

One Supreme Alpha Male Cause? Above reality calling the shots on morality—to benefit virility! This fantasy harmed men as much as fem. Real causes such as feme matter and fem made powerless by lies = Truth; she-body has no right to say No to man's sacred hard-drive virility, yet hers is the duty of moral autonomy. The goal in *manurama*, making *in manu* global, was to make Manu's Law, being *in manu*, global: Mindless sex was to be the ground for sexual relationships. Today's free-sex movement is trying hard to get there.

The record of mind, civilization, and culture in the H/he-gear is the long, violent story of disconnects, dichotomous life lived in splits. As problematic as it is to fuse woman-flesh *in* man-mind, the whole *wor*ld of *Wor*ds is (was) in H/his hands, baby. The language he made says the male is both natural and supernatural cause. When and where He is supernatural, we must *wor*ship H/him. Man has supernatural materiality, and we must believe in the man-made world as the best of all possibilities. "God made man in His image" after man made God up in his image-ination. Solipsism spins off into *methodological solipsism.* "The masses *want to be fooled,*" H/he says, hiding the fact that the well of thinking is as easily poisoned as the well of water.

Fixed-for-eternity splits set up permanent confusion. A Fix-All Holy Alpha Male in the Sky necessitates big lies and lies to hide the many truths. So much illogic sustains dualism, 2 = 1; it overwhelms the critical faculties to stay consistent. Its depth and breadth confounds the unread masses, those who don't read much after they stop their schooling. Indeed, "Q is and is not Q" making 2 = 1 man Truth causes confusion and frustration of such magnitude that aggression and violence can easily be seen as normal creative forces "natural to man." The masses believe this. Yet the number of prisons to punish men is astounding—and in turn very confusing, since the 2 = 1 man system is designed to advantage all males. At least, so lesser men believe. Belief in the same lies is not the same for everyone.

The problems facing our species today boggle the mind. Drug abuse, obscene poverty, yesman re-legioning, mind bamboozling, unthinkable cruelties, basic dishonesty, gang terrorism, recycled frauds, international prostitution, parish theocracies, seminal rape, global mistrust, child pornography, laundered disinformation, femic and ethnic cleansing, large-scale wars, and obscene wealth in neutral hands of Lords-a.k.a.-men. The cause for this saw-bit society is *convergenital* mind abuse, abuse converging on irrationality caused by lies coming from holy neuron-filled penises of Holy Alpha Males speaking 2 = 1 man into being. (*Con* [as in, to con] + *verge*, Fr., penis, *verpa*, L., penis + genital.)

It is the "unread" masses who suffer most at the few neutral hands of sex-crazed Lords, higher men lusting to control others. The masses cannot see nor understand what has been done to mind. "Boyed" by their virile cocky immaturity in believing themselves first among Lords, special men make our species the least natural species on planet earth.

Dichotomy by sex is value severance, "is" against "is not," splitting by opposites—enemy making. Either you are male (good) or you are not (bad). Either you are rich (good) or you are not (bad). Either you are educated (good) or you are not (bad). Either you are white (good) or you are not (bad). What are deemed good are highly valued, opposite-wise, bad sides to evil. In 2 = 1 man, man is re-vered (*ver*, L., man), camouflaged by the quirky claim that the F/father having value of First One, it is the duty of the less-valued mother—opposite—to uphold the morals of the species. Fem would not create a symbol that would mean to *re-fem* a fem; she is as fem as she can be in reality (to revere = to re-man).

The underbelly of dualism is *unism*, the 1 in 2 = 1, forced unity. Unism is the mass-believing-in-man-collectively, precisely the *man-mass*. From here on I will call the "unread masses" the manmass, because missing information is not to be read anywhere. The masses had no alternative, no choice but to believe in 2 = 1 man, hence the manmass, the Greatest Social Engineering Project imposed on our species to make the masses believe in male fantasy and lies. The project changed fem and man, two as two individual speech users, into two illogical men of opposite genders into man making the whole species focus on man as *special*, creating the manmass, euphemistically the *hu*-man species.

One cannot "mass" people with facts and truths seen and found in reality, nature, and knowledge. Facts and truths do not have the characteristics that would mass individuals into 2 = 1 belief to control them collectively by "original sin." Knowledge does not make sapiens need the false comfort of salvation in a promised heaven.

Fem as fem is necessary to affirm and distinguish good reasoning, be a logic-affirming agent in her species with man. This irrefutable fact is knowledge. Once you think rationally (for yourself), you no longer need L/lords over your life to tell you what to think, say, and do to save you from original sin. The yesman groupies that re-legion their forces for mankind create a deep need for a Lord, because yesmen always need more yesmen. Belief in H/him has more value than the acquisition of knowledge that requires time, energy, and some pain. "Let any great nation of modern times be confronted by two conflicting propositions, the one grounded on the utmost probabilities and reasonableness and the other upon glaring error, and it will almost invariably embrace the latter" (Mencken 1922, 126). Why? Because the sum of mind tricks is unknown to the masses, belief is a hu-man right. Knowledge is a clear and present danger to belief.

H/huM/*manity/ism* is a game of Word politics, a house of cards. When Lordship lost its awe-striking luster in law, manor, state, and church, like royalty today, it lost its magic power to keep elite males above lesser men, slave males. So Lords started to use *man* as a name to identify themselves. The anonymity in using "man" gave Lords an unexpected benefit. It showed them that two men—slaves of opposites genders—allowed them to still be higher men, and have lesser men, and even disposable men, at their service. Left to do was find a clever way to stamp the injustice of this arrogance in metaphysical stone. Holy Alpha Male, Lord God *testi*fied: Holy testes (theological name, *livingstones*) reveal man in testaments. Upon Peter (stone, *pierre*) He built His church. In ancient times Patriarchs put their hands on their testes to show they were swearing to the Truth. Semen as first principle, sperm as word, penis with neurons, testes swearing to Truth—all sacred! Where were the unread to get this esoteric bafflegab? To impose such an inconvenient lie on the masses you have to deceive big time. Cash boxes, holy male sex, and seminal power do the trick.

Specials look down on all others-lumped-together as the insignificant kept-ignorant mass, manmass. Collectively, slaves of Him, Lord and Master, they cannot see themselves as independent thinking sapiens, individuals capable of rational and moral independence. They do not know enough: Crucial information is missing, replaced by silly *convergenital* fantasy and misinformation, the stuff of belief. So much stuff in fact that eventually it had to be organized, and religion, the religioning of groups of men believing in Allah or Emanuel or Buddha or Patriarch or Holy Alpha Male was organized and developed, religion now fully meaning the obligation to believe in one of these gods! The obligation to believe in and to submit to the Holy Alpha Male of your patriarchal clan is the stuff of belief.

Naming fem and man as gender-different thinking animals or sapiens puts consistency back in thought and presents five categorical truths that cannot mass people into legions of $2 = 1$ man believers. Continuity in consistent reasoning is on solid ground. Factual premises come to light: (1) to be man entails being male, and (2) to be fem entails being feme. These two consistent premises, equivalent facts in their truths, affirm (3) two individuals as thinkers = two sapiens as symbol makers. (4) Q is Q, and (5) $2 = 2$. There is no magic here, no deception, no need to mass people, no need to impose or indoctrinate.

Sapiens make the selves of both wise when the symbols they make are true to reality. Apfigs and women are false to reality. The very name sapiens holds the aim of making speech that makes the species wise. $2 = 1$ man as *hu*man shatters laws of reason.

The other necessary thinker, fem, with man, exists to achieve rationality, with the checks and balances this implies. It takes the two to achieve rationality. This discredits the assumed "theory" of man and shows why fem were kept out of the halls of learning for four millennia. The many truths discredit the false-to-reality $2 = 1$ man as sacred Truth.

Reality determines symbol making, not man. True-to-reality symbols make knowledge. The wisdom this brings is the foundation for moral behavior. Lords threw morality in seminal crevices of vice and evil. They did away with facts about the self, plunging individuals into deep ignorance. The ease to believe replaced the task of acquiring knowledge. Belief includes that it is better to believe in God/Holy Alpha Male than it is to look for facts and face them. A short-term pain leading to long-term good reasoning and balanced judgment for better psychological health is replaced by instant mumbo-jumbo gratification that creates much unnecessary strife, hardship, and suffering.

Being (cause) is related to doing (effect). Being bees—is—doing honey. Being sheep—is—doing wool. For four millennia historicism drugged the species to do irrationality by a backhanded command not to do good reasoning. Just believe in God. Do not challenge what man says is Truth. Do not use your own mind, just ditto man's seminal ideology and the sludge *wor*ds He made to fit it all. In 2 = 1 man, *be*ing is *do*ing abracadabra with a talking penile wand that spoke God into existence to speak man into supreme power as God.

It is important to know that symbol makers, cause, become symbol users, effect. The story of how a symbol is reached as a name and how it reaches every individual symbol user goes into the process. (1) Mind is mind in both feme and male, (2) both fem and man have minds, and (3) both fem and man make and use symbols. Although falsifiable, these premises cannot be refuted; they are self-evident truths.

Making and using symbols are the two processes in being and doing what a minded animal identifies with. We do not just have symbols and that's that. The symbol w-o-man fits *Manu's Law*, made with the intent to fit being *in manu*. I call this "fitting in" PMS², Pitched Manu Syndrome, using Power, Money 'n' Sex. Boys will be boys; girls "have the pussy!" Mind is sabotaged for *in Man/u*, the self-named Holy Alpha Male.

But the misconceptions about fem as w-o-man are rife and ongoing. Those who want to believe in Humanity concoct even more sophisticated fantasies laced with magic, willing it to "Be Truth!" In this way the convenient apotheosis of feme ignorance in knowledge, that which turns out to be false of fem as a "man who's not a man" is precisely that upon which the metaphysics of Holy Alpha Males takes off. It is because fem *is not* a man as wo*man* that sperm-speaks. H/he is both natural and supernatural at once. Q is and is not Q works in mysterious ways, dittoing God Himself.

Context does not fix nor repair "man both male and not male" in extension as is so often claimed. In fact, it muddles the already false and fuzzy issue. For here's the trick: It *is* true that one of "us men" with us—*Immanuel*—is not male. So treating each of the senses of man as male in one case and not male as opposite case involves the very gender-as-division idealism necessary to the One-man ideology.

This ideology assumes that symbols have discretely many senses, but that the entire repertoire of senses is fixed once and for all, God having given language to Adam. Thus, in gender-as-division, creature-mind and creature-body are *a priori*. Tricks plus tricks = what? So in H/him, w-o-man is a tempting axiomatic anti-concept, and the anti-concepts wo*man* and *man* both male and not male take a linguistic stranglehold on the mind, making it run the false track, belief in H/him Creator.

The logical sense of truths in facts is absent in predatory notions like woman. The extension of man, male half becomes whole-species-unto-himself. Abracadabra, part = whole proves 2 = 1 man. Once this formula is imposed, two are *transmuted* into One. Two opposite men = One man. *Man (and wife)* as Mr. and Mrs. His Name deepens belief. Read books written in the H/he-gear: Lords know that the *inclusion* of w-o-man is the *exclusion* of fem in His rank, status, and value. Man (and wife) is not man and fem. Why didn't George Orwell expose (true) exclusion = (false) inclusion in his brilliant book *1984*?

Because blinded belief commands absolutely: Thou shalt not analyze. This had horrendous implications for girls. Locked out of the halls of learning for 4,000 years and enslaved in domesticity like cattle, they lost big time. But the implications for boys were far worse. Kings, Emperors, Hitlers, bin Ladens, Duvaliers, Pinochets, Stalins, hundreds of wannabe Lords burst onto the scene, grabbing from a massive choice of lesser men for cannon fodder. Lords-alias-men have cheap labor fodder, prison fodder, cannon and cannon fodder, and even disposable fodder that few lesser men see and fewer understand. In March

2003, over 100,000,000 men were sent to the cannon-fodder mills in Iraq, ninety percent believing in the cannon fodder to submit to and worship God. It takes only a few of these supreme Lords to fragment millions of young minds.

Logic shows us that man cannot "extend" himself to include a not-male man. With this truth, we've destroyed a crucial chunk of religious/ seminal belief. What do we do now?

We look at intention. If creature-mind and creature-body cannot both have the same extension of being man, what does intention show us? Is intention the fully realized psychological state of man's ideology, taking in the psychological dispositions to accept, like sheep, the false extension of man? Or does intention now also entail extension like man also entails being not male? How far will solipsism go?

Oops! Being "not male," even if totally irrelevant, is a state that can be examined and described by psychology: *Feme* behavior is observable even when named false to reality as fe + male. Strangely, creature-body learns to make and use symbols and have ideas just like creature-mind, without having a penis. Deemed mindless, yet she learns to speak, think, and have ideas! What to make of this? What power doth the penis have?

Well, "great men" said that the existence of creature-mind was the only psychological state that could ascribe *to whom mind* was attributed! And, that no psychological state presupposes the existence of the subject's body! Pffft! There went fem's body—along with her mind— into nofemsland! Man's bodiless dittoing double Holy Alpha Male leaps to support mankind, and flesh carnalizes creature-body twice over! Solipsism is limitless.

Religion's battle of "man vs. flesh," gender-as-division of mind and body, is limitless. Creature-mind vs. creature-body, subject vs. object, penis vs. womb, production vs. reproduction—symbol maker vs. symbol user become an infinite chain of locked-in-conflict false divisions rationalized in methodological solipsism: objectivism, subjectivism, realism, existentialism, naturalism. How much more wrong could we have gone? Are we now to believe that a leaky pot does not leak if we do not know it does?

SEX *pre*determined who is mind and who is body in 2 = 1 man. A false restrictive method, it led to the destructive turn the species took because both the scope and the nature of both members were boxed in One sex-obsessed Truth, holy semen, holy testes, and holy penis for holy virility, the only sex drive named on earth. Thousands of symbols fit man's mental preconceptions of H/his ideological construction: Seminal magic conjures wor + k, wor + d, wor + ld, wor + th, wor + thy, and wor + ship. *Virschippe, vir*, L., *man* → *wer* → *wor* made worship— and warship. H/he is Creator Mind by holy genitals. The opposite one merely dittos/reproduces being flesh/matter without mind.

The pinnacle of seminal fantasy is penis envy. What degree does penis envy, or penis pride, overtake you? And psychoanalysis was born the link between penis and mind clinched. Any day now breast jealousy will be observed and *somoanalysis* will be born. God bless big breasts as advances in immortality ooze out of the sky.

For four millennia seminal fantasy—mental*ism*—is evidence of cosmic proportions that creature-mind does not think using his mind. He seems to use his penile neurons. Yet in man we must have *an absolute degree of causal closure*, allowing holy-man-based fantasy to be raised above knowledge and as higher, declared sacred—untouchable. The Bible, Torah, Koran, proving man is artificially raised to the superficial level called sacred. One lie covers another in methodological solipsism. Never doubt the sacred or you will lose your faith—and go to hell.

So if man (m) and man (not m) are different intentions, and man is used for both, then knowing that man$_1$ (m) is the meaning of man *is* a different psychological state from knowing that man$_2$ (not m) is the meaning of man. There cannot be two different logically possible states in reality and mind for being man. So it is not that heaven and hell exist, but that the world is split in two as a means to man's ends. So that man$_1$ in W$_1$ (heaven on earth) man is man (m), and man$_2$ in W$_2$ (hell on earth) is w-o-man (not m). But we are wallowing in virtuous manure. For intention in symbol is neither determined nor mediated by psychological states, only by what exists in reality-as-it-is. Neither extension nor intention justifies w-o + man.

"O'Grady," I said, when he had detached himself from the mob, "What can be done for them?" O'Grady said, "Forget it. They're the incurable poor. You can't do anything for them. A hundred dollars a week and they'd still be poor. This is the only society we have, the only one we know. It's a money society. So if they're poor, they're inadequate. If they're inadequate they're mentally ill, by the definition of our society. Their illness can't be fixed by effort or dollars. Only by will. Their will. And they won't." He smiled, pleased at being able to talk down to me. (Ireland 1972)

Nor do we need advanced physics or mathematics to see that there are two sapiens on planet earth. The femininity-causing symbol maker is not a half-baked man. To further sweat the seminal stuff, the causal relationship between male cause and feminine effect is not in reality. Male causes masculine effect. It cannot also cause femininity and feminine behavior. So when you consider that all symbolic animals are involved in knowing the cause-and-effect relationship in themselves for the purpose of self-identity, you see the magnitude of the Lord's carefully scripted innate flaw/original sin, inconvenient lie. In God's Plan, fem and lesser men must be controlled. They must not identify themselves as being thinking animals. To paraphrase, *"Forget it,"* say the Lords, *"They're the inadequate. A hundred books a month and they'd still be the unread. Patriarchy is the only system made for the common good, the only society blessed by God. It's man's world. So if they're unread, they're inadequate, mentally ill. Their illness can't be fixed by books and reading. Only by belief in man. And they won't. So it's their fault."*

The cleverness of methodological solipsism imposes that *woman* must believe in the identical thoughts, have the same sense data and dispositions as man. False or wrong, believe! Man is mind. It is The Word. Ditto and obey.

Like the labor gender divisions he produces and she reproduces, He put a gender division of labor in language development: Man makes symbols and woman uses (his) symbols. Creature-body cannot make symbols; she has no mind. Adam names and she reproduces his *wor*ds, like she reproduces babies. Boy must avoid feminization lest he lose the right to name all, including wife; he becomes larger than life as mind-possessing gender.

It is a blunt fact that everyone has to acquire the symbol system to speak at all. So that when you see the tasks in the symbolic system allotted according to gender, you see that fem had to be absent and invisible as a contributing partner with man in the process of making language and developing civilization. W-o-man (in man) and hu-man does the trick. Both false names carry the "hatred of fem as fem," hate mongering, morally reprehensible.

We see that the feme is neither umbilically nor phallically attached to the male, that each is its own concrete cause. *We are talking of concrete evidence here to two causalities.* Yet few have heard of feme cause. Thus speaketh absent symbols, *knowledge withheld.* Two causalities of mind! A One Cause-All Holy Alpha Male God (for each patriarchal bloodline), then, is more than nonsense; it is poisoned mind candy.

That feme matter is causal agency changes causality, its definition, and how we look at causality, evolution being one of many. It is not possible that femininity does not have its own cause, separate from any and all man. No One Holy Truth exists; there are many truths. No One Supreme Cause exists; there are many causes. Multiple causalities are useable facts, truths among many truths for sustaining rational life.

The conjuring of bodiless Holy Alpha Males as Cause-All Entities in the Sky is not only a grand delusion, it is also the biggest ego-inflating machinery that man could invent. As bull-sweet as it may sound to higher men, it is pure bull-tweet. Since God could not be wrong, how could man be? For as one hymn to him goes, "When you see man you see God." Bad psychology and bad reasoning impose *common evil* through verbal bullying, doing terrible harm to all.

Oops! (again). Fem is a minded being, a self-reflective being, therefore *she has the inalienable birthright* to name herself whatever she chooses to name herself. She could name herself *fim* if she wants. Being born into the sapien species gives her the full moral, social, and civic responsibility to use the more logic-based, more common symbols *fem* and *feme. Just like man, she has the birthright to name herself and do so correctly precisely because she has a mind to do so.*

I am a fem. What are God, church, religion, and man going to do with this truth? When you see one white crow you can no longer say "all crows are black." One fem stops hu/manity in its tracks. I am a sapient animal, sentient and self-reflective. As hard as it is to face the facts that make truths, welcome to reality! Q is Q.

The reason we ought not use man as fit-all-Name is that fem as feme has a certain structure, man as male has a certain structure, and it is good scientific methodology to use *fem, man, and sapiens* to refer to the sentient animals having these structures.

Extension must be determined socially by all fem and men to be moral, not in the elite man-as-Lord situation, since in the social and physical structures on planet earth fem as fem exists with man as man. And because it *is* true that there *is* a division of linguistic labor—some make symbols, others use them—it is not upon any dichotomy of man-mind and woman-body. In reality, speech making is based on (1) symbol making, (2) symbol using, and (3) both fem and man are capable of doing both.

Extension of a name depends as much on the nature of particular entities that serve as paradigms. In man, opposites define. Human, humanism, and humanitarian ditto doctrine-theory ideology and leave out the same two determinants: (1) The contribution of society made up of all fem and men, and (2) that of reality-as-it-is in which feme matter exists as feme and male matter exists as male only. Humanism, like parish theocracies, ignores both determinants, and as mystically centers on man being male and not male. Erase the false name woman, and humanism falls apart like the other religions. It is in being fem and man in reality that leads to being rational and wise.

So it is safe to say that a theory of mind—as mind—has not been looked at in a straightforward way since 2400 BCE. Since Sloka V there has been little, if any, sight to respect for mind, only 4,000 years of irrationality imposed by yesman re-legions and overwhelming unnecessary technological progress minimizing real life. For if you can hate mothers/fem, then you can hate anyone who comes in the way of your whims. Hitler knew seminal hatred. Where irrationality is valid, legitimating the false, what is to be expected? What irrational men of opposite genders do not grasp is that cause and effect relate in *common evil* as they do in common good; from hate and evil come hateful and evil acts. The unseen pure evil consequences in a living Q is and is not Q is that it levels the differences between rationality and irrationality, fusing them, conning the masses to accept a harmful cocktail of both = One Cause-All Truth, fatal to honesty, trust, and constant moral behavior.

If fifty-two percent of the species does not have a feature possessed by the paradigm members in question (forty-eight percent male), then the "not-male" paradigm *is* not having a penis. A negative is a paradigm! This has consequences far beyond its size, the geometric explosion in prostitution and child porn expose this. Entitled man looks at fem as bodies, w-o-men and girls dirty objects of his lust. PMS[2] gives him the privilege of calling the tune that degrades every member of the species. Error a.k.a. innate flaw a.k.a. original sin had to be invented!

In sapient reality, fem's features are breasts, ovaries, ovum, uterus for birth, lactation, and menstruation, none of which the One has or does. This makes the symbol w-o-man ludicrous, exposing the desperate superinflation of the *mentula*, L., male genitals. I call the inflation of male sexuality *studflation*. It determines value according to + male or – male. It is why real, practical, and nurturing fathering is in danger today. The macho motto in studflation, "He shoots, he scores"—Me-Tarzan-want-to-fuck-you-Jane-be-passive-'n'-shut-up. What a way to progress as a social species! 2 = 1 math studflates to 3 = 1, trinity in One God as basis for morality; so we now have seven billion and counting abusing the finite resources of planet earth. "Go forth and multiply." Lesser men are so confused that so many land in the poorhouse or in prison as disposable fodder! But this is just the way it is—it's God's plan. Seminal fantasy is brutal! Suffer!

In meaningful communications, speakers must know the facts about the issues they are discussing. The remedy, then, is not one of keeping traditional/patriarchal linguistic conventions that transmuted belief into "higher" knowledge. To believe is not *necessarily* to know. The minimum level of competence in symbol using demands naming the relationship between cause to effect correctly to make correct symbols to use. Manu's Law caused the reversal of this process, like one would reverse a river system.

Where gender splits mind from body, *valuation* is destroyed. The stereotype of low/no value fe/male passive, weak, non-rational, evil/slut stays the hate-mongering course for the stereotype of the higher-than-life value of male, active, strong, rational, and good—the studs-'n'-cunts recipe. Belief includes that humanity ought to allow the strong(?) to rule the weak(?), the assumption in *Manu*'s Law: free access to sex to satisfy his hard-drive virility. Let no little boy be "feminized" lest he lose his control over fe/males—his "natural power." A cocktail of lies and irrationality takes over in the mind.

The possibility of sufficient mind, a mind not needing God, goes unexamined in 2 = 1 man because correct and meaningful communications are lost. Power of mind is not having correct knowledge in a healthy body for self-identity, and an understanding of self through experiences, rational insights, skills, and talents through physical skills and talents having the strength to stand for what is correct; it is not having a good reason-based conscience to uphold honest emotions and having control over one's own mind and body—including one's sexuality for moral behavior. Unaccountability is in Q is and is not Q.

Power in 2 = 1 man is control over others using money, sex, race/blood, geography, intelligence, class, and status as divisive magic using—FEAR—to free *Hu*-men from sapient labor. Integrating the mind labor of different genders to nurture and develop rational mind in healthy body limited by determining laws such as Q is Q and 2 = 2 are not articulated in H/his seminal books. His books are on man = mind, man and his power to control nature, earth, sex, capital, wealth.

Power is a free-for-all studflated "Q is and is not Q" seemingly in favor of 2 = 1 man, a grand self-delusion of which H/he is a bigger victim of H/his illogic than the target gender. But fem carries a frightening burden in unlimited irrationality. Feminism, a desperate cry for truths did not call for "fem as fem" anymore than lesser men called for rights—with responsibilities—in "The Rights of Man" (France, 1789), which Thomas Paine dittoed in England. All bought into the Big Lie. All symbol users lost 4,000 years in developing *sapient intelligence.* But in its desperate cry for justice, feminism unknowingly exposed femic cleansing, even if it did not/could not "put a name on the un-nameable."

Femic cleansing is the causal mechanism for the incomplete understanding of our species as animals that make symbols, like sheep make wool. Instead, causality is One gender-as-division standard—too hard to comprehend. It spews out false information like "our higher-than-animal state," our need for faith/irrationality, our need to protect false beliefs to the death. Our "gifts" from God, such as "Q is and is not Q," that cons (the) fusion of meaning such that man *part = whole* species. Absurdities such as sex being "sin," blatant falsehoods such as fem being w-o-man, and L/lord-blessed lies such as God created man *abracadabra-style* are tossed in the seminal pot. In the cultural re-legions of yesmen beliefs are an enslaving chain of half-lies wrapped in small quarter-truths. The juggernaut of armed seminal hatred of mind bulldozes the brain. Our days of dignity as thinking individuals are few. We are a sick, dysfunctional species. *Manusclerosis*, the hardened belief of being *in Manu* for 4,000 years, and the common evil it caused, is our disease.

In manu H/he gives all of us a property that somehow accumulates male bias in all aspects of life by small imperceptible degrees, spread over 4,000 years. Belief in His Gift of free will predetermines our species accordingly. *Pre*determines? Both—free will and predetermined? Our species is and is not determined? *In manu* anything goes!

For four millennia mind had to believe in a nonexistent, illogical, and irrational outsider, what theologians and seminarians who study God call God. Relationships between causes and their effects were ignored, and semen being the first principle of everything, God's holy virility dished out free will to man predetermining what is what! How do ordinary minds see through such con/fused, seminally poisoned mind candy?

Logical relationships between seen causes and seen effects define the class having mind as sapiens and mind in sapiens as being a thinking organ. Logical relationships are a set of existing conditions in reality, such that because of their existence, show necessary truths to achieve sufficiency of mind. *Exclude one* and you exclude the limits of a real determinant in cause-and-effect relationships seen in reality-as-it-is. Exclude one and irrationality/nonsense fills the void. Limitless One brings on a holy host of hair-thin ideas, pseudo-facts, and lies, plunging mind into the chaos of belief in nonsense that overwhelms mind.

So it is not astonishing how weak the grip of facts has been in the 4,000-year *in manu*. If there is a reason for two irrational "men of opposite sexes" to have gone so far off reason with respect to what deals specifically with our species, it is Holy Alpha Males' supremacist end. Giving out far more misinformation than correct information connected *to the grotesquely split-gender level belief in being man as man-mind and woman-body fitting H/his cruel split-world levels of heaven and hell, H/he made it reflect the violent split-value standards of His master-and-slave paradigm*. Every split fit. In the sick logic of splits H/he treated mind and cognition as purely male-individual matter due His Lordship/higher man. Ignoring feme mind in the reality of mind and the social facts this imposed insofar as these show mind as consisting of more than male observations, the false became a sticking habit—firm belief in God. Splitting linguistic labor by gender, it hid the dual aspect of symbol *making* and *using* as He rode roughshod over the dual and social bases of mind and cognition, destroying the foundation of rationality. Parish theocracies to this day preach seminal man.

So today "the *in manu* code" is the only language in use. Patriarchal English is the only English we have. The code leaves out all fem, eighty percent of males as petty lords/lesser males, and the necessary limits set in determinants existing in reality impacting the relationship between thinking as cause and rational as effect. Belief in Lord God-man = knowledge of ourselves. What arrogance! How much more hypocrisy could be imposed *in manu*?

For once the very spiritual "Q is and is not Q" is internalized in both minds so it is in collective mind. The false formula cannot discriminate between the genders. Hitler and Melosovic, Diana and "Mother" Teresa are archetype victims, devoted role models to belief. *Manusclerosis*, the hardening of the multi-virus re-legions of men adhering to mantasy-fantasy, contradictions, skewed stereotypes, sacred absurdities, unique extremes, God-blessed races, beautiful hatreds, and eclectic falsehoods by higher Fathers brought together by the Lord's arrogant freedom-from-reality, the self-glorification of man as God is to be worshipped by woman, "the female in man."

The theory of being sapiens as fem and man comes without the fantasy assumption of the existence of God-man. The scientific and rational definition of fem, the feme animal that makes and uses symbols to communicate *with* male mind, is far too rational for mantasy-fantasy.

For after mind is disabled—made deficient—the gun can easily take care of bodies en masse without much remorse. And use the gun 2 = 1 man did, big time, and still does. Historicism is the story of serial warring and global whoring.

Fortunately, reason does not live by man alone. It necessarily lives in both fem and man as causes in relationship to being thinkers as effects. So like a disease whose cause is known when named, the cure for manusclerosis is *symbols restoring rationality, correct information, truths, and facts for the sapient species to use.* In this there is real hope.

The toughest virus in manusclerosis is the infinite "is and is not" dichotomies/splits justified in methodological solipsism, circular justification that looks a lot like reasoning, proving a thing by itself, proving man by The Word "man." Imposed on the manmass by Lords, powerful men backed by their blinded "real" w-o-men in the re-legions of yesmen "just know" in their gut of guts that M/man is what M/man says H/he is. Him Books in-the-H/he-gear are blueprints for the different/cultural theocracies/humanities; new "Q is and is not Qs" and differently posited 2 = 1 formulas will pop up. Sex sells. Lies sell. Manutopia sells. For the goal *in manu* is to make weak deficient minds dependent on Lord Father's gifts, the Santa Claus of empty comforts, false Truth, and nonexistent eternal salvation.

It is not going to be easy to get back on track. We've been forced to accept the given 2 = 1 man as God's gift. The manmass has a large vested interest in man. It loves to swing wildly on pie-in-the-sky phallic poles between split-fused rights, the right to believe in man as species *opposed* to the right and responsibility to know truths. So it is deeply in love with the conflict, contradiction, and the convergence of splits parading as ideas clothed in the *toga virilis* of warm, woolly seminal belief. The manmass does not ask for the right to know the facts, the right to correct information. How do we admit that a 4,000-year-old law giving men "free" will "determined" by God's seminal power would give birth to the belief in a purposeful error that would trump up an innate flaw to become the original sin?

A symbol communicates supernatural physics when it is not based in logic or mathematics, applicable to reality or associated with practical concrete procedure that enables seeing what is denoted by it. Where man is male, not male, and supernatural male, all "exist" as One man in Truth. Necessary inconsistencies and methodological solipsism proving "Q is and is not Q," for 2 = 1 man displaces the many facts and truths we ought to be working with.

An acceptable theory can imply few, if any, false propositions. A theory that formulates clearer definitions of its ideas and expresses its general principles openly and transparently so that they can be tried in the courts of evidence, nature, and reality provides a firmer, more rational basis for all discussion in which the idea is involved.

One of the reasons that compel us to reject a theory is *proof of its inconsistency*. A theory(?) imposing four contradictory premises all confidently assuming an identical "Q is and is not Q" is one that is not just trivial, but worse, the cause of *common evil* fatal to mind. Higher men confidently lying through holy bullying is not proof of what is assumed. A whole system of confident lying in methodological solipsism is even less proof. The doctrine-theory ideology that is man, life-in-the-H/he-gear is false and immoral. All Truth centers on and revolves around male omnipotence. Simply read theological books.

The *Hu* complex, "speaking creation into being," comes from a long tradition. Ptah was the Egyptian "Creator," ca. 3100 BCE. (Manu, 2400 BCE.) He "Created" earth with His marvelous tongue called Hu. Thousands of years later, other Lord-controlled cultural groups, parish theocracies, feudal territories, manorial holdings invented their own Cause-All Gods, Emanuel, Allah, Yahweh, God. Like Hu, the Christian God brought Creation into being by Spoken Word, in seven days! Thus, adding "Hu" + manus is a dead giveaway to monkey-see-monkey-do abracadabra! Hu!—when the *Manus* was law giving men control over wives is repeated twice in the Holy Book called the Bible. Abracadabra, "The Word" creates, and He/Hu who does this is worthy of being worshipped by the masses. All this nonsense—deemed "sacred"—challenging God was daunting!

Sound bites as symbols cannot change what exists concretely in reality. I cannot speak "Melt" at a stone and create liquid stone. In abracadabra if we say *apfig* three times, the apple *is* a fig; we believe and behave as if apfig is Truth. We believe words can do magic like change fem into a w-o-man. We cannot know that w-o-man is *not* a man because crucial knowledge is withheld. So we believe The Word can change concrete reality and we wallow in nonsense and irrationality. Worse, as dittoing parrots we are enslaved to nonsense and irrationality, a type of feudalism I call *esoteric*, underwriting evil, violence, aggressive behavior, and dishonesty as solutions, even leading to insanity.

The solution is not a case of *ungendering* the mind or unsexing the body. Splitting mind and body as opposites-by-gender is seminal fantasy. Truths entail getting the facts about the particular entities or issues we are examining and using these facts to reason correctly in relationship to them. It is highly probable that we can think rationally to make a society that is culturally user friendly to rational beings, sapiens. And it is possible through these probabilities to put behavior on a more sound moral basis, since it puts mind on a more reason-based foundation of thought and more moderate emotions.

Before we can learn to take this true, more correct and moral road, however, we must look at the petty, convoluted, false-to-reality road society was made to travel with eyes seeing reality-as-it-is for comparison. There is too much missing information to see all the harm done. Seeing real*ism* and comparing it to reality-as-it-is lets you see how each of us might undo or destroy a chunk of false belief imposed upon our species in Abracadabra Creationism. But this is neither a pleasant nor a clean journey. Belief dies hard.

Chapter 6

THE BIG PICTURE

What is there of importance in the behavior of sapiens, the animals that evolved to speak, that does not involve symbols? Not much! But before we can use symbols we have to make them. Making symbols is the first social activity that minded beings do, creating sounds and giving these meaning. We use these sound-bites-having-meaning that we call symbols to name objects, ideas, and concepts in order to relate to our reality.

Symbol making is a technology like any other, and like most technologies they have rules and goals. No one could make a car without rules for "making a car." In the same way, speech making, translating thought into sound in order to name reality is not done without rules. Ap*fig* and wo*man* break rules. The wisest goal for minded beings is making symbols to use that are true to reality, and this entails obeying rules.

A distinction in symbol making not found in most other technologies is that the resources, the raw materials, come from within the makers themselves, like making wool comes from within sheep. Sight, smell, touch, hearing, thought, experience, relationships, objectivity, chance, opportunity—seeing what is in reality to see—go into the thinking being's physiological and intellectual capabilities to make and use symbols.

The greatest danger in symbol making is having an overarching goal that one can create simply by making symbols fit it; *apfig* fits the goal of fig to be the "true *fig*." Symbols fitting male supremacy caused strife-ridden patriarchies, flog-wielding theocracies, cruel-Lorded kingdoms, irrational manutopias, and poverty-of-the-masses feudalisms. Force, aggression, and violence are needed and used to bring these into being, because they all stand on hair-thin bases in 2 = 1 man identical to *fig.* Their zigzag paths defy orderly explanation.

What the overarching goal is that took hold after Manu put into law that fem must not be independent agents is hard to say. But it led to fixed-for-eternity roles in gender stereotypes as criteria for who thinks and who does not. I call higher men who prey on mind as if it were a toy *patrists.* The genitals of *special* Father (*pater*, L.), sacred and arbitrarily inflated in importance, give H/him the entitlement to indoctrinate and control mind in the masses.

The goal in Manu's Law is male control by few men as Lords wanting to dominate the masses. So the rules for making symbols are ignored. "The Word" is made to do what patrists want it to do, name a species of men. This is supported by 10,000 Words listed in *Breaking the Patriarchal Code* (Gouëffic 1996). The goal had to be embedded in language as well as in statutes to show that male domination was the way things are and that it was "natural" for a few men to rule all fem as domestic possessions and the masses of men.

Law in "The Word" is formidable magic, claimed sacred and holy. The *doctrine of man* revealed by Lord God-man in Holy Books was dittoed in the secular *theory of man.* The dittoing ritualized the righteousness of hu/manity, for it is to be noted here that secular man did not (re)posit fem. He accepted and used the formidable magic in "The Word" of the doctrine. Church and state were never and are not now separate; they are wedded in "The Word" man as man and woman in hu-man. "The Word" creates man reality. This is why creationism is defended at all costs, The Word is all creationism has going for it.

Fem, named w-o-men, are ruled out as contributing members to the naming process. Thus the relationship between fem and man to achieve rationality as a team of thinkers is destroyed. Sexism, totalitarian by definition, forbids fem to be a partner with man in the civilizing process of our species. It denies fem even a sliver of self-identity as fem by forbidding her, by lexical law, the birthright to a name of her own. Lords null half the thinking agents, femkind, to create a species of "mankind" lauded as good-but-born-in-sin. We see from this that mankind has no checks and balances. No wonder he wars a lot.

The species is left to be run by only half of its agents, male, using only one-tenth of its brain potential—spouting lies. In the pursuit of dominance, mind is made deficient so that the blinded *manmass* cannot see the tricks. Then collective mind is judged insufficient, a fatal psychological blow. Hu*man* philosophers use the idea of *insufficient mind* as a building block in philosophy, and religions welcome it with open arms. Needing a Providing Lord somewhere in la-la land—to keep us moral—we are indebted to Him. We become His belief slaves; we must *wor*ship H/him who spouts lies, esoteric feudalism in full bloom.

The Enlightenment, a lie so debilitating as to baffle all modern psychology, did not save us from innate flaw/original sin/Human condition of being "both men regardless of gender." As both men "regardless of gender," patrists expanded and deepened the stranglehold on our minds. All movements toward emancipation were and still are toward deeper enslavement to L/lords of prey in *man*. Patrists still expand the rights and privileges of select and special males using the divisions of rank by gender, power, and wealth in the hierarchy of masters, slaves— and now spies—*in manu*. Verbal enslavement to "The Word" man, belief in word magic is alive. The unspoken command, do not touch H/his "virile and perfect" language! Thus the Lords of prey bed with the Lords of pray.

To be the species of fem and man that we are in reality is a truer goal. To see mind as sufficient, there is a transition from being deficient/irrational-loving hu/mans to being two fallible thinkers in the more probable thesis 2 sapiens = 2, fem and man. I call this transition the *Rofemtic Movement*. It reestablishes truths withheld from the masses for 4,000 years, including the fact of *fem*, the other contributing member in the species.

The *Rofemtic Movement* passionately seeks facts in probabilities in both as sentient beings, sapient species, thinking animals, rational feeling beings, and symbol makers. Our nature as beings-having-minds is sufficient to solve most of our daily and more difficult problems, giving a solid context in reality to the whole range of our emotions and a more solid basis underwriting moral actions. Sloppy emotions almost always arise from belief without evidence because they lack reality-based and rational contexts.

But we cannot address many issues about our species in historicism without repetitiously stating that the male is the basis, norm, and superior one. Male bias in The *Wor*d (in italics) shows that we cannot speak of our species as being other than male. For example, uni*ver*se, *wor*th, and *per*suade contain (1) *ver*, Fr., *verpa*, L., penis; (2) *wor*, Eng., from *vir*, L., man; and (3) *per*, *par*, *pere*, Fr., father, from the Sanskrit PTR formula that made *pater*, L., Peter as rock, Father. To "suade" does not need "per" to add clarity. The repetitiousness of male bias in *wor*ds *wor*ks because symbols naming the other thinker are missing. In the large code of male bias, "The *Wor*d" pretends to reflect reality. First, (lies in) language create (false) reality. Second, mind is made deficient by these lies. Third, individual deficient minds become collectively insufficient mind, and the whole process goes unseen, the sum of which I call *the common evil*. Yet humanity born-in-sin is sold as bill of holy goods, man is God's perfect Creation, believed by the manmass.

In embedding lies in names, other false goals "for the good of all" are hidden in ideologies such as "brotherly love" in mankind, when in 2009 mistrust, hatred, racism, and linguistic sexism are at an all-time high. Men war against men in almost all corners of the globe. Humanity "the good" doesn't work. Amidst all the warring and whoring, the rest of the species uses mind-numbing tactics to drown out the unnecessarily strife-ridden components in human life. Global malaise is blatantly evident.

Probabilities, on the other hand, build truer fallible plans among more honest thinkers and symbol makers so that mind can become the sufficient organ that we ourselves evolved it to be in the millions of years with evolution. Mind is not, never has been, and never will be an organ that can use a non-physical soul, homunculi, separate and apart from mind and body. Reality is the arbiter of what mind is and can do. As the reality of nature determines storms, so reality determines language and mind in our species.

The transition from $2 = 1$ to $2 = 2$ and from Q is and is not Q to Q is Q demands naming the phenomena in common evil *not* named in its 4,000-year reign of holy terror. This must be done in order to come up with antidotes to lying. *Studflation* and *manusclerosis* start the process. Common evil concealed in revealed "sinful humanity" striving as despicable "wretches" for the glory of God left just the things He wished concealed, unnamed, and unsaid, thus the hair-thin bases upon which He stands. So it is necessary to have "new" symbols, but the ideas are not new at all.

What was not named is *knowledge withheld.* Missing knowledge harms the mind; it causes a lack of facts and truths and lowers intelligence. When knowledge is withheld we cannot know what is being done to mind; absent symbols are silent. They have no voice, no sound, no meaning, and no value to anyone. When fem is not named, femity has no voice, no value. Manity is the only agency of mind we know; it is the only name in use.

So in *in manu*, irrationality is a strong habit of mind. We are to need God-man Lord to fix up the mess man-made deficient mind creates. We believe in Holy Alpha Males in the Sky who watch every one of us every minute, everywhere, all the time, for all time! This is the brilliant master-and-slave sub-floor of injustice unsurpassed in brilliance to this day. Select Lord-men split our species according to gender, race, and class to create a small hierarchy of highly valued men enslaving a large believing *loerarchy* of less-valued "men," the manmass. This is *esoteric slavery.* And Lord-men always knew what they're doing!

The capital of seminal power grabbed in "The Word" *man* by man socialized in w-o-man is the self-same politics of wealthy men as capitalists socializing the resources of lesser men and not men. Several hundred thousand higher men control and rule the six and half billion manmass on earth. Socialism wedded to capitalism, w-o/men and lesser men are socialized for the purposes of capitalist man: esoteric feudalism embedded in language. The Lord/capitalist/corporation plays with the mind of the masses, socializing them to be "paid" slave laborers for him, the large gap between the few rich men and many poorer masses exposing the sham, a system so imprinted on us that we do not know we are all *manning* it.

So what is Hu*man*ity? *Hu*manity has the aura of divine authority, the mystique of being "god born." But there is no mystery about "manity" spoken into reality by Hu. It is banal. When methods of analysis are applied to its tedious repetitiousness, its stereotyped paradigms uprooted and its falseness brought out into the light, the lies glare. *Hu* is manity's divinity, a divinity that changes fem and man into two men "regardless of gender" into one, man. Historicism's "whole man" is selfish man and his possessed selfless wife, woman.

(Hu)manity centers on man as ruling mind not mind as mind. "God made man in His image," genitals and all. The conformity of men to this central idea has the force of divine authority. The Word in revelation grants divine authority, begun with Manu, makes the unnatural order seem natural. The *Wor*d w-o-man hides the sham. So man appears to have divine credentials. In reality, Hu cannot and does not change the meaning of manity.

The magic: Hu apotheo-sizes manity to single supreme causal agency of the universe, uni, one, vers/e → *vir*, L., man, a unified *ver*ld → world (of men). Uni*ver*se, *wor*ld, and *fir*mament make man "the alpha and the omega." The *Wor*d makes Him worthy to be *wor*shipped. *Ver*, L., *wer*, AS, man, as in werewolf → *wor*, as generating morpheme made many symbols. *Vir* → *fir*, tree (consonant variation) → *fir*m like the tree trunk, like the state of the tumescent penis, made firmament the theological name for *heaven*. *Wor*, *vers*, and *fir* deify Him as the ALL. The first legion of believers in man—where in reality being man entails only being male abides—is born, re + legion (of men) → *religion*, a group of esoteric beliefs in a fantasy-pack of secrets. Then secret → sacred language is (ab) used to show male divine in nature, Hu conscripted to support the mystery of His divinity. Much linguistic abuse was seminally born in seminaries mostly between 600 BCE and 1350 CE.

Ditto-parrots of both genders, men, worship the Supreme Ones, from the Pharaohs down a long line of L/lords of Pray who Prey, G/gods, non-material invisible bodiless beings visibly male by genitals, beard, and deep authoritative voice—ruling fem out as thinkers, setting up irrationality and deeming the masses insignificant, unread, and stupid. *The masses were made into ruler followers*. One could have prophesied the *manmass*.

When fem are ruled out as thinkers, the claim is that ideas are fathered. C/creation is *seminal*. In this singular presupposition, deep in the 2 = 1 doctrine of man, the greatest tyranny of "The Word" is upheld in organized (false) beliefs, *religions*, in which the religio-secular Doctrine-Theory of Man having an innate flaw, born in original sin, is central.

That "ideas are fathered" tells us again that man is mind. H/he deemed matter to be mothered, *mater* → matter, roles *opposed* by gender, he-mind, and she-body. Splitting mind and body, man gives himself H/his divinity, His entitlement to call the shots on mind and body, life and death, heaven and hell, good and bad—solipsism is consummated.

Ideas fathered in "The Word" make examining presuppositions crucial. If word and what is being referred to are the same entity in The W/word, *man* then has violated yet another law of logic. In science, giraffe. The sperm in semen is word. Men stud/y "The Word" of God in seminaries!

Rational true-to-reality symbols reflect reality-as-it-is, and thus have no need to be defended. When has a philosopher ever written a book on giraffe-kind where one was not a giraffe? Symbols made to reflect reality do so when (1) both minds (2) are in consonance with (3) what *is* in reality. Respecting relationships seen in reality is more likely to lead to truths.

In fathered ideas, The Word is the thing so named, woman and man are the things so named and all hell breaks open into full-blown irrationality! Where fem is absent, "The Word" man is supreme, power-zapping in reality that is not reality. He pulls souls for salvation out of an immortality hat like one pulls a rabbit out of a felt hat.

The easiest entity to conjure is a supernatural double of oneself, man in God's image: H/he *are* L/lord of C/creation; H/he *speak* land, water, and man into being. On hair-thin assumptions—as easy as conjuring unicorns! Is this a failure of ratiocination, an ignorance of rules, or an intentional self-justified break from them? What is the difference between rule following and *special* man's make-his-own rules to create a ruler-following manmass? What laws, rules, and goals guide thinking beings as thinking agents? What "thinking" does 2 = 1 man do? What thinking do 2 = 2 fem *with* man do?

"The Word" in Holy Books is in every hotel room around the globe! With brochures offering sex as girls for men! Bad reasoning and terrorizing psychology that harms.

Once Manu* wrote Sloka V into law, Adam-born patriarchs of Jews, Arabs, Greeks as groups became "races," and in almost every one a self-appointed, self-important patriarch invented H/himself as the race's own True God. Two thousand years later the paterfamilias wrote the Roman Manus, dittoing Manu. Between the two laws that spanned 2,000 years, patriarchies spawned many Lords, Royal Lordships, Ecclesiastic Lordships and Manorial Lordships who ruled in step with church state and man in the grand theft of power.

Hierarchy and power *in manu* granted *entitlement* in status-giving names Patriarch, Pharaoh, Holy Father, King, Pope, Czar, Emperor, Reverend, Duke, High Priest—higher men, all Lords—The Lord was owner and master of the slave/lesser man, small-*l* lord and wife-slave w-o-man. The "purpose of life": *to serve the Lord*, the rock Father, Peter, the livingstones/testicles upon which He built His church. Symbol*ism* stands high in solipsism as it does in racism, sexism, class, and irrationality.

A harsh, cruel, and unjust system—feudalism—bloomed, lasting several millennia. The idea of *serving the Lord* stayed. The idea of "serving the Lord" was not struck down when feudalism broke down in the mid-1800s. *Fear* is a useful tool. Serve the Lord!

The Old English names *fem* and *wer* were in use when lesser males as slaves were renamed man to name them as being *in manu*. Belief in high-born Fathers as Lords, the categories were Lord, the slave man (as lord), and woman. In the chain of command all w-o/men and lesser men had a Lord whom they had to obey and serve, the Lord being His own God. The capital-*L* Lord was not a slave; that is, man. He was a Lord and His wife a Lady, not "men" because they were not slaves, class born in seminal Lordship.

Obeying and serving the Lord—the only way to be moral—is still belief today. Obedience to Lord God, Lord Jesus, Allah—most "races" having an Alpha Male Lord who must be obeyed to be moral! Obedience to the Lord = morality is still belief today.

Lesser males, small-*l* lords, had to give the Lord at least forty days of free labor per year *and* pay rent for the use of the Lord's equipment, such as His mills. The Ecclesiastic Lord made His own demands in heavy tithes for holy favors. These practices were not called slavery; the "legal" name was *mancipation*. *Manci* means "to guess"—in the sense of ordained by Lord God's mind, first ordained by Lord Manu, self-named God. To divine also means to guess. Big lies need a lot of guess *work*.

What is so astounding about *e*mancipation, officially and ironically called *manu*mission, the process from servitude-to-Lords to freedom(?), is that slaves had *to buy themselves out of it*. This refilled the coffers for a set of new Lords, while it took years for freed men/lesser lords to replenish theirs. A new class of L/lords, first as priests and Lords, passed manumission money to their sons, giving rise to aristocrats to whom "physical servitude"(?) was no longer owed. Well-moneyed new Lords put a new face on slavery as paid cheap labor. Today capitalists exploit the cheap labor of the unread masses already socialized for them. This God-in-the-machine working in the market place keeps money-sex-power going for twenty-first-century man. Full-blown *esoteric* feudalism!

Manumission freed(?) men and w-o-men physically from *in manu*. But no one was manumitted psychologically, least of all, fem. The Word man was not abolished; *fem* and *wer* were not restored. In fact, the hand of control lexico-graphically strengthened the word man as a fit-all Name. The name is legitimized in dictionaries and in thousands of other symbols. And taxation benefiting the rich in capital gains helps to uphold esoteric feudalism. The rich get richer, while the poor, who cannot escape poverty, get poorer. A cleverer money-sex-power scheme has never been invented to be so thoroughly and so well consummated.

Laws have goals that must be realized in all aspects of life, including language. In HIS Code, the feme is zero, held in contempt for not being a man, then con/fused to male as fe*male*. Between the Code of Manu, the Roman Manus, and thousands of years of feudalism, the control of mothers by the trinity husband-man-father spans 4,000 years. The Word "man" makes man controller—neutral hand. In this way, the word man *is* the entity named man; man is the neutral male hand of control by law in The Word.

The hand of control authorizes itself from Manu's Law and the Roman M/manus. It was only when Lords lost their divine mystique that they started to call themselves men. State manocracies and parish theocracies had hierarchies/classes of Fathers as Lords and loerarchies of lesser men and not men. Man in His sacred duplicate fused in *Lordship* became the foundation of its own science, theology, the *stud/*y of Lord God in seminaries where semen is the first principle of everything and *matri*culation (*matri*, L., mother) makes men *stud*ying God holy. What a grand fantasy! What a fantabulous delusion!

The Roman *Manus* performed the final miracle: Lesser males flattered as lord-of-his-own-wife paved the way for Lords. Millennia later, in 2009 Anno Deceptio, we've forgotten the cruelties and violence necessary to bring Lorded religions to birth. We believe in "obligatory man-being" for all; we believe in The Word: man, woman, and human, with all the concomitant nonsense and irrationality they carry. The insanity is deep.

The tactics used in Lord-based systems called religions are many:

1. Psychological enslavement to the fantasy "generic man," Adam, primogenitor, Mr. #1's Rib made w-o-man. H/he as mind named all things. "In the beginning was the word" spoke all into being. Therefore, man consists of man and woman; we accept the nonsense *man* is and is not male. Not only is this a deadly false principle to teach the young, it also teaches logical absurdity, while the stud-flation of man for worship as Lord goes unseen.

2. A "man" that does not entail being male. When "he" is woman, we accept the nonsense that there is a man who's not a man. We teach a second deadly false principle to children, a falsehood that not only neatly fits the first one, it even proves it as well. Two non-facts fit the neutral hand-of-control doctrine-theory, something highly dangerous to teach to children as a system of thinking. In this nonsense, all of the following are equated: man = hand, man = mind, man = male, man = sole naming agent (Adam), man = whole species. Magic is conjured through context, *when I say man, I mean man and woman* brings the fallacy of equivocation to success because man *is* the only *wor*d having lexical status. *Fem* not in any dictionary makes it plausible and makes the sham hard to challenge.

3. Magic by context, waving the seminal wand of meaning; one moment Adam is generic man who did all the naming, next he is the first male being—who created woman. Myth makes good mystery. Context hides one-half of the equation just long enough to hide that the false equation is being made, while semen being the first principle of everything theologically makes it divinely correct to wave the seminal wand. When *at all times, in reality, being man entails only being male abides.* Context is bogus in this issue.

4. Revealed man in The Bible is only one of many blueprints of culture-differentiated parishes/theocracies on earth. The Koran is another, the Torah another—cross-cultural eclectic Holy Father Lordship in "races," patriarchal territoriality.

5. As evoked in Holy Books, if one cannot get the facts from being male, one can use being not male to conjure "evidence." But this irrelevant, nonsensical presupposition is never articulated, it is never overtly formulated because it would display excessively blatant lies such as "man is and is not male." And like God, whose maleness cannot be seen, *common evil* is (was) not a visible crime to the mind. No reality check is superfluous considering the constant repetitiousness of $2 = 1$ man's *special* details.

6. A deficiency in mind is imposed. *In manu* has for millennia been suffered by fem and men. Revelation conceals esoteric slavery in the Judeo-Christian Emanuel. Subtle, simple, magical law in The Word imposed for centuries as religion was so gradual that the species did not notice it being done. Man-mind names the "not male" like any other passive non-rational object, naming it w-o-man. By force of indoctrination, we believe "w-o" makes her man-reality Truth. Not only is she effectively shut up and rendered passive like an object, she is also rendered incapable of seeing what is being done to her mind: She cannot recognize the nonsense in theory. This bamboozles her thinking: Girl and mind are hit with excessively hard blows to her reasoning capabilities. Not able to *see* the issue in question, *her mind is disabled and claimed deficient:*

Claim of Deficient Mind #1.

7. Boy and mind are hit with the same violations at the same time, but seemingly in his favor. The game is higher men, Lords having "the controlling hand" over lesser man, making lesser man a loser in His society, where he cannot see the issue in question. *Mind in him is made as deficient as hers: Claim of Deficient Mind #2.*

8. Progress is violence to women, rape, child porn, prostitution, femicide, wife beating, fear of other men, and war. But with time, indoctrination and the socially embraced belief that "Father sees, is, and knows all" defines authority. Seminal virile Truth 2 = 1 man takes over; the lust to control satisfied. Everything is turned upside down and made to walk on its ear. Evil expands two individual deficient minds to collective mind being insufficient to solve problems: *Claim of **Insufficient Mind**.* The *need* for God is created. We the species/society/collective/manmass have insufficient mind.

9. Therefore, we *need* the Lord to lead us to green pastures. Too few see solipsism at work.

10. The "yoke of servitude" owed to higher man in worship and labor keep us too busy to see false-thinking man leading his cultured non-thinking man. The archiparadigm in mankind = species. Father, Subject/name giver, ruling Mother, Object/the named one, looms larger than life and is so overwhelming and powerful that it addicts the critical faculties to belief in man. From H/his dualism, splits flow like a swift river: He is objective, she is subjective; he is rational, she, emotional; he is autonomous, she, dependent and deviant; he is mind, she, body; he is sacred, she, of earth; he is publicly individual, she, privately possessed; and so on. The yoke is heavy, cumbersome, and false, but worship Him we must.

11. Living the splits in gender-as-division is obligatory. The "universality" of our (hu)manity in tradition, Higher Man Lord has us believing

that capitalizing manus/hand to hide the Manus/Law, His *neutral* hand of control shows that word and reality are one and the same in God-man. It is no surprise that *in manu* Lords would invent *mer* + d, Fr. (*mer*, L., mother), the *wor* + d for shit. God-men always knew that twisting symbols off their rational basis would give H/him *seminal* power to bring mothers down in value.

Sound (in names) makes a subconscious impact on the mind, setting the stage for image. *Mer*ge implies the mother in the identity of the father like *apfig* in fig. (cf. *ver*ge). Com*mer*ce implies mothers as wares, traded for sex, prostitution; *mer* + *x*, L., means "wares." We learn about words through the sound first. But few know that *mer*, from *mater*, L., → *mere*, Fr., *meter*, Gr., → *mare*, Eng., that man would see the mother as object, more animal. Few people learn what linguistics means to their lives. Using gender-biased names to split he-thinker from she-non-thinker was not visible to the ruler-following manmass.

12. Indoctrination method: authoritative repetitiousness. The politics of repeating the Truth man as man, woman, and human in thousands of other *wor*ds. Jews divorced wives by repeating "I divorce you" three times. In Patriarchal English, there is only one *wor* + d using the morpheme fem! The lexical item human is law, period. Claiming that an accident is a "human error" is propaganda. It can't be a giraffe error! Hu and *w-o* whirl around man repeating man, in reality male only, supported by a cast of thousands of *wor*ds confidently assuming male superiority to be Truth in manpower.

13. Obedience to the *Lord*, smoke and magic in the belief that the purpose of life in perfect humanity-born-in-original-sin is the lofty moral goal of salvation. Souls for God achieved with lies and ideas in opposition, a pack of contradictions and the hatred of fem as fem are means/ends in man. The Doctrine-Theory of Man is the cleverest bamboozling of the intellectual faculties of all time! It has no precedent, nor rival. Where obedience to Alpha Males = morality, lies = Truth. Studflation does its magic: The name Lord exists, therefore, the Lord exists. Obedience to laws in reality, nature, and logic

are nowhere in His agenda. He makes His own rules for the kept-ignorant to obey.

14. The word-law/lexical item "human" distorts and falsifies the common attributes in both genders. Thinking activities such as symbol making and using, building self-esteem, seeing what is in self-reflective abilities cannot be harnessed to make propositions that would challenge His lies—too many names are missing. Thus the *infallibility* of doctrine-theory in The *Word* of God is guaranteed—Absolute. This is beyond clever.

    Probabilities are always vulnerable to fallibility. Show me one being, thesis, or entity that is infallible! Science, reasoning, and experience all laugh at infallibility. Infallibility exposes the need for absolute certitude to assuage minds made deficient, which is why faith-based fantasies are valued above reality-based, scientific, and reason-based wisdom.

15. Accepting lies as principle of thought, the young uncritical mind cannot see what is wrong. Instead, the young uncritical mind lands in a fluffy-puffy seminal nowhere-land when it tries to think about its own species as two that ought to make symbols reflecting reality, *the foundation of thinking and rationality*. Thus "he" finds himself relying on generic miracle thinking in the H/he-gear, Q is and is not Q and $2 = 1$, instead of following rules seen in reality and nature important to doing critical thinking. The twisted mass of high-voltage false wires/gender-loaded lies in $2 = 1$ man, are *per*fect carriers of irrational energy for belief. Infallible, 2 men of opposite genders = 1 *man* is repeated *ad nauseam* by mortal and supreme immortal Lords alike to the believing manmass.

16. The consequences in $2 = 1$ miracle thinking are the large number of beliefs that *The Word* creates as if by the magic of free will. Mystery is injected in the details of false definition, repetitious methodology, far-fetched parable, relentless-from-the-top preaching, and indoctrination having divine authority, deification in The Word passed off as Truth. *Word*s, thought, acts, and speech reside

in H/him. This magic is with us today in dictionary entries having lawful force in science, literature, culture, society, and scholarship. Their relentless use formulates anew and repeats every day the laws of subjugation, slavery, patriarchy, and feudalism hidden in "The Word"—of the G/god that is man.

17. In F/fathered belief, conformity is obedience, a virtue. As w-o-man, fem not only supports false belief, she also strengthens it in her obedience to man as the submissive thing she is made to be. She is the man (not male) who hoists the Lord's ascendancy to G/god. W-o-**man** makes M/man a monolithic omnipresent sound, **an archi-morpheme**, the most used morpheme of all time. The species stands in thralldom to man. We believe en masse that (hu)manity is holy, above all animals, including women and idiots, bound to return to heaven *sans corpores*, wings 'n' all and holding his trusted sword, where man corporeal as lord goes to Lord supernatural, like manus (hand *neutral*) goes to Manus (law of control). So that everywhere and at all levels social life displays the daily spectacle of miracle thinking. Sold as a bill of True holy goods, it is all lies, a bill of *evil goods* the source of *common evil*.

Our species is made into one that it is not by *wor*d alchemy. To make the fig appear supreme, I simply rename the apple *apfig* and abolish *apple* and *fruit*. *Apfig* is unassailable—*infallible*—when fruit and apple are out of mind. The greatest tyranny of "The Word" is in 2 = 1 man—Truth making the species believe that humanity came from a consensual contract. It did not. Special man/Manu, grabbing power, imposed it, a root religion imposing mandatory worship of Him, whence the social aggression "natural" in man. Why do these men so need to be re-manned, re*ver*ed and *wor*shipped?

Solipsism is clever. *Apfig* is half-lie wrapped in quarter-truth, a form of lying that sucks on reason. The quarter-truth in apfig is that, yes, there is an entity existing to be named. But as apfig, I could write twenty 600-page books on the *fig*ness of the *apfig* and it would be impossible to falsify my foolproof arguments all centering on "The Word" fig in ap*fig*. This is what Holy Truth is all about! In the process, the fig is studflated far out of proportion in reality, and in time becomes Fyg, God of Figs, and that's the trap. But I could write only half a line on the apple being a fig—in the fruit category—and rules of logic seen in reality and nature and rational argument would stop me dead in my tracks.

Sound, voice—*sonal*-ity—"The *Wor*d" is the tool used to make Patriarchal English. Lords claim per-*sonal* autonomy: What he says as F/father is Truth. But the defense of half-lie-quarter-truth needs hair-thin arguments, large verbosity, seminal profundity, pedantic footwork, and the extremely subjective objectivism of male centrality.

The Word (of) man first appears hard to refute because critical information such as fem is missing. Critical thinkers are not aware of the large dose of miracle thinking injected into the symbol system used to defend belief. The high-voltage dosage of lies and falsehoods in language short-circuits critical thinking, disabling the mind.

Few individuals are trained to see the artifice of miracle thinking; like the feme sex drive it is not named, so it is not discussed in psychology, sociology, linguistics, or any social science. Thus we cannot compare critical thinking to miracle thinking. So it is easy to become addicted to the belief that all mind activity is thinking. Thus thought is and is not thinking mimics man is and is not male and w-o-man is and is not a man cuts the force of indoctrination in paradigm repetitiousness. The species is seminally gang-raped by "The Word."

Conformity/obedience to man as man and woman is dangerous to everyone's liberty. One cannot choose from correct information to act morally. Imposing belief in deficient mind by falsehoods, it transforms individuals into believing masses. The deficient mind posits the collective mind to be insufficient, a psychological practice so destructive it defies naming. The insufficient mind obviously needs G/god-man to help it solve its problems. When the media, for instance, decide what the public can tolerate to hear, they collude with the belief in insufficient mind: They assume the public is not strong enough to hear and bear truths. And it is true that the mind has been dangerously weakened!

Deficient mind is self-fulfilling in the face of lies and pseudo-facts. The Lord/Higher Man *is* the One-and-Only individuated mind. H/his books in the H/he-gear do not admit methodological solipsism. Fem not being individuated, w-o-man in man's name is thing so named. In

solipsism, doctrinal man and G/god's plan are one and the same com-
posite belief imposed on the masses, 2 = 1 Absolute man. Imposed on
the manmass as "knowledge," it imposes that all culturally differing
organized beliefs centering on *man*, that is, religions, are to be tolerated. Tolerance of multicultural half-lies-quarter-truths, mind candy, is
thrown out to believers like candy to children. Tolerating each other's
nonsense and irrationality is the archetype model for morality. This
is insane.

It is not hard to see that people are masses/herds/mobs to be tamed
and controlled by Lords as rulers and told what to think, say, and do.
Unknown as individuals, they are massed on sight and made to conform, obey. Then the adjectives stupid and ignorant are ascribed to their
collective status. And as the stupid, conforming manmass, individuality
and thinking correctly *are* quashed. This is how clever solipsism is.

For individuality as such is very dangerous to Lords lusting to rule.
Such self-praises as "the greatness of man" and "the perfectibility of
man" cannot be understood by the stupid masses. L/lords know the
masses are not rule-following beings: They are fully *ruler/Lord-follow-
ing heaps of (kept-)ignorant flesh*. Mobs are "sisterhoods," reflected
in The Word *sorosis*, Gr., sister, meaning fleshy heap or mass. Not individuated, she is an attached-to-man, dependent-on-man glob-of-flesh
made to ditto man. What Patriarchal Language does to our species is
so evil it takes great effort to keep one's equanimity.

Individuality is as dangerous to *in M/manu/s* as fem, logic, science,
and knowledge. Potential rule-following thinkers must be forced into
being *massed, ruler-following, blinded believers*. H/he sucks everyone
into it until he and/or she conforms, obeys the Lord, while its *wo*rds
conceal the fact that humanity has double standards, false laws, and
immoral phallic-based aims and values. Conformity, obedience, forces
individual*ism* of every deviant expression possible to fester. Pedophiles
are good individualists. So too pimps, pornographers, "free"-market
capitalists, dictators, and go-it-alone leaders.

Homo manus, the man-man species, is a tangled mess of addicts
to the convenient short One-Name-Fits-All Man, a drug-word more
debilitating than crack cocaine. The drug has collective rights in battle-
ready conflict with individual rights. The psychological malaise, cynicism,

and discontent around the globe are witness to all the falsification.

Patrists never thought their *words* revealed what they were concealing. Even Holy, Absolute, and cocksure certitude have no guarantee. But Esoteric Feudalism is harder to see than Medieval Feudalism, and harder to eradicate. Those who would deny that you cannot achieve control over others through mere language and make piles of money unheard of in Medieval Feudalism without real slaves to help you climb the ladder of fame, fortune, and power over many others are the most enslaved. Lords—a.k.a. men—are the fathers of Aristocrats whose sons are today's obscenely moneyed higher men of influence applying clever cosmetic changes to slavery. Esoteric Feudalism differs from Medieval Feudalism in face. Capital*ism* in social*ism* and vice versa is its political face. Today's Lords, Dictators, and Corporations as persons go it big, global, and alone!

The name *manmass* is apt. *The social element necessary to care for the capital of mind in as many individuals as possible is totally out of the picture. The capital of independent thought is not welcome as a social enterprise in 2 = 1 man, human society.*

Esoteric feudalism is nothing less than the socialized servitude of the insignificant, unread, stupid masses created over the 4,000 years since Manu's Law. H/he withheld knowledge and concealed it in revealed half-lies-quarter-truths capitalized in H/his higher hand of control. Revelation conceals that the mass prostitution of fem as woman and wares for commerce gave Lords their first taste of ownership and wealth. Capitalism was born from the socialism of sharing possessed w-o-men among men for wealth making and reproduction. The idea of *manu*-factories came from this process much later.

There is no name for the clever "concealment in, with, and through revelation." So I call it *concelation. Concelation* is the seminal underbelly of revelation. For this is the law in H/humanity: *For every item of revelation there is an equal item of concelation.* Solipsism justifying Q is and is not Q makes the constant re-legion-ing of Lordly forces to impose the belief that select males as Lords, now under the rubric man, have value over and above all others on planet earth. Reality, existents, including the feme self, have no independent existence outside the Lord's mind. Lords having the virile passion to control others, impose this mantasy-fantasy, common evil for all to share, a socialism unnamed until now.

The seminal power in common evil is the lies called Truth. The Truth and truths are now two different concepts, like Manus, law and manus, hand and man, Lord and lord. And the Lord, the wolf in man's clothing, mingles among the ignorant sheep, the believing manmass, without being seen or recognized.

We will know when this slavery no longer exists. Attitudes will change. Money and w-o-men will no longer be currency in man. Fem and men will have the capital of their own thinking life and the knowledge of their sufficient minds the moment money, power, sex, rank, and fame change in importance, and sapient life becomes a balance of real capital with real social values again. Climbing the ladder to be Lord in heaven on earth will be the silly, futile exercise of seminal obsessed Lords. Respect for facts, mind, reality, scientific research, planet, nature, and all of life will be central to life and morality.

In hu-man "politics," being left, center, or right holds no meaning. They are the same viewpoint. The maze of disconnects in Patriarchal English is so large and confusing that it causes behavioral confusion and chaos. The result is always more of the same. Where people are tamed to believe in Q is and is not Q to impose belief in $2 = 1$ man, the chain of contradictions embedded in symbols that all must use every day as basis for action, we see the spectacle of behavioral chaos every day.

Chapter 7

DESTROYING WHAT IS NECESSARY
TO ACHIEVE WISDOM

This is the problem: One-half of the species, fem named as w-o-man, cannot identify herself as a logic-affirming agent in her species. The Father, having grabbed the voice 4,000 years ago, is himself an illogic-affirming being. Therefore, mankind is/are two illogical men as one irrational mankind of opposite genders. The foundation upon which thinking rests to achieve rationality and wisdom is destroyed. Whatever concerns our species is conjured by the neutral hand of man's control in the rubble of muddle.

Irrelevant details, half-lies, and information withheld do not show the *opposite* half, the male half, to be logic-affirming agents. Poisoned Truth about our own species is what we have; mankind makes poisoned language. Bees do not make quinine-laced honey.

Muddling is easy. Fathers extend meanings in concepts such as *husbandry*. To husband is to manage and control stock. Manorial Lords possessed cattle, sheep, and wife/slave as *chattel* → cattle: stock. "Go forth and multiply," in the Holy Book fem became a husbanded ewe (Eve) to breed, needing a shepherd, her lord. (Eve is ewe, like vine → wine; in Latin, *v* is a *w*.) Small-*l* lord, the ram, and his "ewe" are sheep, chattel, the Lord *owning* the chattel. Capital-*L* Lord used the lord and his eve to breed more slaves for Him.

In manu domesticated husband and wife as rams and ewes, sheep, needing Lords. Sheep need to be led to green pastures. Patrists wielding pastoral hooks and authoritative crooks put *man—and wife* in pastoral herds needing "the Lord is my shepherd, I shall not want." In His lust for control, we are farm animals "domesticated" into being ignorant herds and masses. Blindsided *a priori*, we need pastoral guidance. This "hardwires" mind *to need the Lord as shepherd*.

As lower animal, ewe (Eve)/mare (mere) needs her #1 Ram of Rams, Stud of Studs, and Lord of lords to breed her and give her value. Esoteric slavery is subtle mind control done through thousands of biased and foolish traditional seminal fantasies.

In manu coupling is called marriage. To beget sons, the sexual union must be wisely husbanded, that is, *man*aged. The husband manages and controls the commodity called "the fruit of the womb" to beget sons. *Mari*tus, L., *mari*, Fr., husband, head of wife and womb, marital rights address the husband. His "conjugal right" is to access and manage the womb to beget sons: increase his stock of males, rams, and studs. Wife is a field to be plowed by the penis. Farm metaphor: (Lesser) man/ram and wife/ewe are mind-less animals, sheep. This suited both Manorial and Ecclesiastical Lords.

The Mark, *bar*, Heb., son, *begat* in the *wise* management of the womb is the aim. Pastoral imagery invokes barnyard animal copulation. Yet we are to believe mankind is/are "above" animals, *special*, made in the image of God! Q is and is not Q lies between the sheets of the bed in "The W/word" of God. *Lit*, Fr., bed, from *lect*, L., bed, made The Words lecture and literature, sex prescribed by sacred seminal authority in seminaries, where semen is the first principle of everything. Seminal lectures in bed are vital in 2 = 1!

Mind soon disconnects with the goal of being a critical thinking agency. Patriarchal language stopped fem and man from being on the same plane to grow emotionally, create knowledge, exchange facts and truths, and experience both pleasure and procreative sex. Over 10,000 symbols, words, and most family names contain man, son, and father. Few matronymics exist. She cannot do naming, the mind's basic activity, to identify herself as fem. And man's identity is now an inconvenient lie, the liar leading the lied to.

Partnerships of fem and men as good thinkers are not in pastoral aims imposed by pastoral Lords. Feme mind is not wanted by Lords.

Man-and-wife, Mr. (and Mrs.) John Human is the husbanded social unit. Yet this did not stop divorce!

Pastoral imagery is the birth of pornography. With his penis, husband ploughs the vagina/field of possessed wife, revealed in *matri*mony, to make a mother of, through the husbanded social union, *matri*, L., mother (cf. patrimony—testate money, from testes). This fulfills pastoral ideology; "biology is destiny." Subjugated to her husband, the two are One in his name, the womb used for breeding sons. Yet no historical linguistics or etymological dictionary admits or denies that *w-o* in *w-o*-man means "womb of man."

In M/manu/s, every man is by law a lord by marriage. The husbanded social unit is the one-man-one-w-o-man social state in which every husband can legally lord a wife. Like God Lorded Mary to beget Jesus. *Mar + d*, SK, (*mar, mother*) means husband as *head*, the one-on-one strategy that serves femic cleansing. The husband, petty lord, administers *in manu* for the Lord, control over w-o-man, superior, as husband. The 2 are 1, him, in "man—and wife." They are not 2. *In Manus* mathematics is seminal math.

Moreover, homosexual coupling between priest and God in seminaries is higher than "sinful" homosexual coupling. Lesser homosexuals are not in the position to wield control over a womb to beget sons, a secret reason why gays are lesser than lesser men. To procreate is outside the contract of lower homosexuals. The neutral-hand-of-control by higher homosexuals in seminaries conjured most of this 2 = 1 ludicrous mantasy-fantasy.

Femulus, L., feme slave → *family* extends to implicate "fem" as domestic slave. Patrists are OK with this! In pastoral ideology, boys are to believe men to be Creators, pope → population, and girls are told what their place is in God's scheme of things as muted vessels of procreation. The Lord is subject to no laws but His own, accountable to no one, since God created man in His image. In this conceit, the One-Name-Fits-All belief-in-man as whole species must satisfy thinkers and non-thinkers alike.

I was only nine when I heard a priest in the pulpit say, "A woman, that's nothing. Fill 'er up, men." Many obeyed and became poorer. Four thousand years of *in manu*, the mystical magic power in The Word and the re*ver*ing (re-manning) of priests and clergy, massed the population into blinded believers. Add to this the *Hu* complex, the belief that Spoken Word creates reality, when a Higher Man/Lord speaks, it is Absolute Truth, and "The Word" is consummated. If highly intelligent thinkers have not seen through this, how is an ordinary mind to do so? How would the kept-ignorant masses ever do so?

The inconvenient lie as Absolute Truth is corruptive and evil. Fem misidentified as w-o-man overidentifies #1 man, appealing to phallic pride. The right to control wives brutalizes men; lust for sex power makes ditto-men of the inconvenient lie and spousal rapists, the politico-religious privileges of controllers as tempting as the apple of blame. Blame Eve. What weak man doesn't want to be L/lord, Jesus, Mohammed, Emanuel, Krishna, Mithras, or Yahweh—standing above her in phallic splendor?

In manu belief in "the womb of man" is not a big stretch. *Manushyayoni*, SK, manu + *shya*, womb + *yoni*, penis. *In Manu*, yes, it's this wild. Manu needed both genitals to give birth to seven Manus. The mantasy-fantasy in manusclerosis drowns the *credo ad absurdum* of senseless noise in the conned holy fusion of red-green mumbo-jumbo. *We are our genitals*! Mind be damned! The sad part in all this is that we use these "words" as if they were Truth. This is the horrendous terrorizing crime against the mind.

In prewriting time, no one could hear the difference between Truth and truth. When the development of oral speech evolved to written speech, the masses were mostly uneducated. It was easy to impose True lies on them.

In 2 = 1 man, then, change is and is not change. One reason why we did not see the change from Medieval Feudalism to Esoteric Feudalism is that it was too much in our face, squatted in the "pastoral holy family," big and bold and in the Bible. Man and w-o-man changed the face and method of feudalism from physical and legal to lexico-political. Mere *wor*ds impose "neutral" control as if (1) L/lords exist as divine beings, and (2) are necessary to moral life. Mere Words, patriarchal lingo, give "divine" aura to Absolute Truth! But "The *Wor*d" is not truth; it is pure and simple L/lord-imposed masculinist symbolism.

Symbol*ism* is not grounded in reality. Few know the complex art of linguistics. When clergy/males in seminaries, the first ones to read and write, caught on to what language could do, a lot of seminal fantasy exploded onto the scene. The Word *mentula*, L., male sexual organs → mental. The ones with penis and testicles claimed the sperm to be word, *spermaticos logos*, Gr. Those who do not produce sperm are dumb animals to be bred. From this pornographic House of Words, where semen is the first principle, seminarians broadcast male divinity.

Many linguistic scholars insist that the language of man is perfect. The Jews claim Hebrew to be perfect. Sanskrit, from Samskrit, from shemitic, Shem *father* of the principal nations speaking this language → *semitic*. Is *semitic* seminal? Language is fathered, from the theological tenet that semen is the first principle of everything. Unscientific and irrational phallic-based symbolism raises male genitalia to divine: The Word says so. Divine because symbolism is a picture game of masculinist ideology in The *Wor*/d, destroying the wisdom that ought to be reflected in true-to-reality symbols.

Ba'al, Hebrew, and *Herr*, Ger., lord as title of husband gives men the right, entitled as lord, to manage all. H/he tames *Mother* Nature. He constructs *mother* ships. He navigates the *mother* sea. He builds the *mother* plant. He directs and fights in the *mother* of all wars. He presides over the *mother* country, he chairs the *alma mater, he studies daughter cells, he directs sister factories*—there is no area where "he" does not man(age) or control her—as object or animal. In symbolism, objects are feminine, she-body without mind, people are male, he-mind. Splitting mind and body by *gender* is morally right in patriarchal language.

Thus celestial bodies without flesh equipped with the same but invisible *mentula*, same "beard of wisdom," same deep voice and virile gaze as man, exist. The centric role of god's genitals need never be mentioned; He is a "neutral" male! Mysticism par excellence! Lies embedded in symbol making to a perfect deception. Symbolism fits solipsism to a T.

What is the reality-based evidence that L/lords exist as supreme non-fleshed male beings? Is it the political high jinks of power grabbing done in and with The Word *as Truth* through self-granted titles as L/lords? Sheep believe body and mind are divided according to gender because blinded false belief blinds absolutely. The masses believe men are rational, that she-as-object is not. Knowledge withheld does this effectively. The wisdom of fem with man as partners in the civilizing process in making and using knowledge for rational ends is for all practical purposes destroyed.

All is in H/his name. "Our Father, hallowed be *thy name*" invokes absolute mind control over fem as powerless earth-bound mother breeder. All the while, the prayer appeals to the pernicious mystifying moonshine of Divine Right *in manu*.

The Lord of Authority has Almighty God on his side! And lesser men partake in his control. Bafflegab! Men believing in such empty promises get hooked because they are as blinded by knowledge with-held and bold-faced lies as fem. They believe the nonsense imposed by the weakest, most fragile studflated male egos that walk on planet earth. "I want $$$. I want power over others! I want free access to sex! I want to be boss! I want everything in my name!" evangelistic baby-men shout.

The rationale behind H/hu-man actions is not reality, facts, evidence, critical thinking, or any trial-and-error experience; to the contrary, it is a holy pile of childish fantasy and falsehoods signifying nothing. Manu and his evangels and clergy knew what they were doing when they made gender-as-division—he-mind, she-body—the split that makes the fiery burning phallic bush of absolute contradictions "Truth" in the mind of the species. It would make the Doctrine-Theory of Man implacable. To doubt the religion of man, for it is a religion, constitutes the biggest heresy today!

The human octopus of the religion of man has many tentacles:

- The false identity mill putting all thinkers in H/his-One-Name-Fits-All, sustaining esoteric feudalism, a type of slavery understood and enjoyed only by Lords-alias-men.
- *Manusclerosis*, the hardening of *in manu* falsehoods in the mind damaging *all* minds, violating both fem and man individually and sapiens as a species collectively.
- The necessary violence used to impose the inconvenient Lie = Truth on the family plays itself out differently and similarly in the state.

- The gross imbalance in the *common evil*, causing any and all social contract between fem and man as equivalent thinkers and rational agents to be poisoned even before any negotiating about facts and truths concerning thinking life as life can take place.
- The deadly edict of *original sin* imposed by neutral hands of control. *Infidelity to the Lord's seminal in manu doctrine, the rejection of H/his control over mind, and the analysis of H/his false system are the real "sins."*
- *Sheepgate*, the pastoral fraud of being "lambs of God," making people believe in deficient minds no better than sheep, then needing a higher male mind for moral guidance.
- Necessary inconsistencies in symbols as well as $2 = 1$, Q is and is not Q.
- *Argumentum ad feminam* via seminal words concealing truths, making refutation of $2 = 1$ man look foolish and futile in the face of solipsism due to hair-thin realism, w-o-man, making evidence non-existent, argument impossible, and "man" *infallible.*
- The re-legion-ing of many forces, including industrial, commercial, academic, and military, into branches of the religions of seminal man having no checks and balances.
- The crime of knowledge withheld concealed in revelation.
- The unseen transmuting of fem and man into a believing flock of sheep dittoing the trick of transubstantiating a cracker into the body of Christ, a male who saved all men for all time in all places from all *sin.*
- Belief in the morality of seminal immorality as higher and holier morality,
- Belief in the magic of tricks, such as capital letters, w-o, Truth, H/hu to make manity the only named state of being, where femity is not named.
- Heap on this the politics of relentless rituals, the self-righteous repetitiousness of lies, the global magnitude of its consequences, and the many cultural and eclectic versions of the religions of man bamboozle and effectively reduce the reasoning mind. The foundation of thinking and wisdom based on reason in true-to-reality symbols is destroyed.

- Morality and the emotions giving one the energy to be moral are indefinable in the face of religio-politico-lexical $2 = 1$ M/man. Appended to the penis-with-neurons by seminal-cord the *choice that is not choice* is to believe in God—for eternal salvation. The $2 = 1$ doctrine-theory of male-control ideology destroys choice when choice is the very training ground for and the very ground of morality. Sin-ify the foundation of thinking and morality goes down with the sin.

That faith-based fantasy is "higher" than reason-based truths is the pinnacle of *credo ad absurdum* precisely because there is *no choice*. Either you believe in Holy Alpha Males, the source of *common evil*, or you go to hell. Choosing to behave the right way has nothing to do with the phallic way of seeing the *wor*ld! Nonetheless, believe in God, say your prayers, don't experience pleasure, and don't challenge the holy system, abracadabra, you are moral! Theology is the highest *stud/*y for divine *matri*/culation (*matri*, mother), and the first principle of every-thing, thus *stud* and *matri* in The Word preach the studs-and-cunts idealism justified in methodological solipsism. Mind is thrust in seminal-land, holy pornography.

The $2 = 1$ doctrine-theory-religion-ideology of man is the root of much evil and violence on planet earth. *Manusclerosis* has the masses *wor*shipping man-mind (to hate fem and her mind) Hollywood-style in Hero *Wor*ship and loving irrationality. It portrays a faith-based fantasy world where fundamentalist religionists push hard for a world in which any sin (please be a sinner!) goes in their la-la land; war, seminal rape, and violence are all OK just so long as you believe in God-Male Savior, and show it—publicly.

The thinking that one thinker does can affect all lives that come after. Louis Pasteur found that boiling milk kills harmful bacteria in milk. Pasteurization is almost global.

Manu's wrong, unjust, and illegal law of feme subjugation in India made slavery legal, almost global. Where a hierarchy of men lord-ing it over a loerarchy of fem is put into place, wisdom is irrevocably lost. No one can be consistently rational. Irrationality/faith in institutional lies mixes with a smattering of rationality, and then frustration and violence follow. Warring becomes the norm with soothing whoring. Massive con/fusion in mind imposed by gender-as-division he-mind and she-body affects gross imbalance with its pie-in-the-sky extremes held up by the silenced "unread" manmass of blinded believers. The species could not have been put on a more self-destructive track of phallic *progress*.

The Rofemtic Movement, the movement to reestablish true-to-reality symbols and truths, aims to cut away the sky-ropes to be on planet earth where earthly fem and men are born and live. Its mission is to assert and affirm the more probable reality of fem and men as seeing and reasoning agents working as a team: rational fem and man working together. It is much more likely that thinking life done in, with, and through sapiens doing good reasoning in true-to-reality symbols made by both fem and man who evolved capable of doing logical thought and being rational is better than God-Male Creationism imposed by knowledge withheld. I see no medium through which respecting Q is Q can be undone in a wild and woolly, phallic, sky-hooked transcendent *wor*ld, creating "heaven" for Lords—and "hell" on earth for the rest as the stupid, insignificant, unread manmass.

Granted my hypothesis is not nearly as virile nor as mysterious nor as seductive as the goal in man's manifest destiny to control all as L/lord. But it is more practical, more natural, more probable, more fun, more achievable *and much more moral.*

There is a clear choice between good and evil here: Either you call fem as being fem and give the world consistent, sound reasoning, the name that identifies her as a logic-affirming agent, or you call her the derived man as w-o-man deviant and sin, a crime against the mind harnessing irrationality and heaping violence onto the world. Yes, Virginia, you can (almost) fool most of the people most of the time—when you conceal knowledge in purposeful error, that is, revealed "original sin" that we are all made to share in even when we had no role in its making! It's as easy as creating the apfig.

When "The *Wor*d" changes 2 = 2 reality into Absolute 2 = 1 realism, it is obvious that language abuse causes injustices. The 4,000-year-old Social Engineering Project to change two thinkers, fem and man as sapiens, into two men of opposites genders as mankind is proof.

Cocking, warring, and whoring are out of control. The problem of the twenty-first century is this: Four millennia were wasted on the seminal sludge of irrationality, religions, contradictions, and confusions assaulting the mind. *We must undo the mess in a much shorter time.* We must reestablish *sufficient mind* in the societies of fem and men.

This means destroying the massive verbal infrastructure of L/lords, clergy, prostitution machines, faith peddlers, select male wealth-making machinery, and sacred secrets kept in churches, temples, synagogues, industrial and corporate CEO offices, and the inner sanctums of monopolies by their predatory seminal balls. Do it, we must. Or lose all. Mind, reason, truths, knowledge, and wisdom are at stake.

Chapter 8

FEMIC CLEANSING
DENATURALIZES THE SPECIES

The manu-factories of Islam, Christianity, Judaism, Hinduism, and others take their cue from the patrix, the fathered board of man-words in *de manu in manu*, global in scope. M/man is titular holder of what the species is, as Hitler was titular holder of the German state, evident in the Law of March 1, 1933. In this way, One-Name-Fits-All supports the social, state, and church Patriarchies, a.k.a. Humanities, on earth.

In 2 = 1 man, right and wrong are determined by gender, the gender that determines mind. This means unbridled, unaccountable hard-drive virility determines mind. The board holds lies because the seminal idea that gender determines mind breeds lies that harm and damage the mind of the whole species, making violence a solution to solve problems as well as calling up God.

In manu the role of mother is that of object, meter (cf. L., *mater*, like L., *pater*, Peter), car, plane, university, nature, church, industrial plant, ship, and she-objects he makes and manages, the *meter* measuring his rise to wealth and divinity. As meter, the mother's role calibrates the mirror by which the F/father, Peter, measures his image as ruler. He has to know how effectively the mantasy-fantasy 2 = 1 man works to keep faith in man.

What He does not see is that the meter also measures the extent to which men are brutalized in the process of silencing, pacifying, and objectifying fem. I call the mother as "meter in man" the *manumeter*.

It measures revolving-door belief in M/man/u since Absolute-Man male and not-male is and is not what H/he seems.

Revolving door belief is measured by the *manumeter*. Tolerance, the catchall slogan excusing any and all belief, tells us that you must not judge individuals by their beliefs, that when you judge beliefs you must not judge the one who so believes. The principle for excusing belief is that you are and are not to judge. It allows free speech to those who do "Q is and is not Q" mind activity to claim the right to believe anything they claim their right to believe. Pornographers believing in ugly, twisted sex claim the right to free speech for sex with children. Others claim free speech to believe in their favorite phallic God, the same claim held by pornographers, prostitutors, pedophiles, and the manmass.

Tolerance gives everyone *the gift of not being ultimately responsible* for the things believed. It is as if belief, as specific as airplanes, had nothing to do with choice, choosing one's beliefs for behavior and action, as if one were born with belief like one is born with arms. You are not to say that the beliefs one chose to hold have consequences; that one's belief practices, and the behavior based on these beliefs, are related. So if someone believes the lie w-o-man, it is OK because he believes it. Revolving-door belief supported by tolerance dictates excusing individuals for their choice of false thought, since belief contains the belief that belief itself has no consequences. Witch burning? Slavery? 9/11? Hitler believed the world should be free of Jews!

Is it true that beliefs have no consequences? Belief is most often confident certitude in the irrational for action! It is seen in the protest against abortion: I am a Christian and act accordingly, I have Christian values. Believer, belief, and action are as inexorably related as thinker, knowledge, and action.

How do you excuse the thinker or believer—but not the thinking or believing "he" chooses to do? Here again, mind is split from body, creating a freak of nature; $2 = 1$ man with H/his irrationality, porn, prostitution, sin—the whole masculinist box of violations to impose having faith in God who forgives sinners, that is, believers—*but not thinkers*.

Smack in the middle of tolerance are the goodie-two-shoes *Hu*manism and *Hu*manitarianism, solutions that are not solutions. When you analyze these, it is seen that both feel-good ideologies are colossal failures, more of the same religion-of-man rhetoric. Conquerors and colonizers feel sorry for the conquered and colonized robbed of their riches and resources. Throwing aid to the robbed, their hu and man souls are saved!

Although the criticism is a linguistic defense, as it clearly is in this book, judging "belief in man" to be false is taken as a direct offense against man himself. Mr. #1 man in 2 = 1 is *Hu*manism's central thesis, a religion not to be challenged. The legion of *Hu*manists, like religionists, does not like to have its secular sexist God exposed.

Linguistic violence to fem, wife, sister, girl child, and mind is tolerated through lexical law, making men more violent than they are by nature. *In manu* brutalizes men in H/his competitive hierarchy and fight for power and control, denaturalizing them by small degrees along the way. Many say, "I'm a feminist. I believe in women's rights." What can possibly be w-o-man's rights? More lies? In humanism, man is central to "order and good go*ve*rnment." What is her right here? Fem wants sapient reason and fairness to prevail for everyone, not lie-infested patriarchal aims and objectives embedded in language.

Revolving-door minds invent, alter, and arrange information in clever ways through pseudo-facts and false premises willy-nilly. Partisan minds, using the manumeter, measure the success of their *idée fixe*, man imposes presuppositions as superior sentient being and being right. Seminal "logic" is taught at all costs so that patrists and Lords cannot be seen using the revolving door. O. J. Simpson has himself photographed going to church. Presidents have to be seen going to church to be elected. Indeed, "Mother" Church is the biggest manumeter of all. Through her vagina the *common evil* that is *hu*manity can pass as "good"—and tolerance boosts the fantasy. Going to church, wearing a cross, holding the Torah, reading the Koran show that the one doing this is moral. No proof needed. No hard labor needed to seek out the facts and truths to choose wrong from right!

A name that is not true to reality is symbol*ism*. W-o + man add to *ismitus*, the disease of *isms'* deadly track of deceptions. When you do not have symbols that reflect reality-as-it-is, symbol*ism* does the job even better, belief results. "The right" to embrace belief for belief's sake, faith, is deemed good, right, and correct. So why is the cross but not the swastika tolerated in Christianity? Why does the Star of David arouse hot emotions in Islam? Why do fem in Islam wear the burka, while Muslim men have free choice in clothes? When Q is and is not Q, belief is willy-nilly and the zigzag road is tricky to navigate. When things go wrong, enter human rights and the human rights hero!

The "'human rights" hero is a savior. In hu/manity, power begotten from opposing poles "is" male and "is not" male is brutal in its final decisions and punishments. This power sits mostly in rich white men as Lords and self-anointed G/gods leading the sheep to indoctrinate sacred-male ideology, theology. Touted as good, it brings mind control to global success. Like the genitals of God, the violence, aggression, and force needed and used to impose the package of irrational belief and make it succeed need never be admitted. Evil and good are con/fused in humanity, a *word* that excludes half the species as fem only to "include" her as w-o-man, using lesser men as pawns and cannon fodder.

So *H/hu*manity is a war machine like no other. It is a politico-lexical-supernatural machine *manumetered* in not-male millimeters, a machine indicting reason, nature, reality, fem, and lesser men through the brainwash of original sin. Sacred secrets go deep!

The irrelevance of being "not male" blanks out everything that is relevant in fact. Being feme animal having mind is the fact of fem as a thinking agent *with* man. Instead we must believe in a rope of false divisions, dual*ism* 2 = 1. Thus all kinds of violence made necessary are tolerated, then claimed *natural* to men's natures. We do not understand the principle of boomerang victimization in the zigzag of methodological solipsism.

Millions of men killed in wars, millions more imprisoned and tortured as war prisoners, millions slaving for higher men, and what is inexplicable to me, millions of men languishing in prisons around the globe for criminal offenses, when the system was made to advantage males. This is hu-manity! The seminal trough of gender-as-division imposing 2 = 1 man hit the targeting gender as much as it hit the target gender. Femic cleansing hit and damaged the whole species, denaturalized it. It is no longer a species of thinking animals.

A major reason, then, for the 4,000-year longevity of $2 = 1$ man set up for mind control is the *cultured* ignorance of fem and lesser men. Half the species plus the masses of men were purposely cultured to believe she was a passive, mindless object, over and above her cultured dependence on her L/lord for financial support, linguistic information, psychological definition, and the identity of her social role, twisting with it the characters of masses of men deemed lesser. Culturing brutality in lesser men, these serve to do the dirty work for highly selfish higher men of prey—Lords, owners of the world's wealth and power. Huge numbers of prisons are built for lesser men who don't comply with His rule. Like w-o-men, many criminals are *manu*factured in the $2 = 1$ ditto machine of man.

The "is and is not" core makes individuals go in hundreds of opposing directions. The con of fusing opposites, is and is not, embedded in Patriarchal Language creates a need for the *hu*man rights savior, superman, spiderman, ironman to fight *enemies*. How we love belief in enemies! Hollywood loves making block-buster films about Fantabulous Alpha Males saving the world! When $2 = 1$ is Truth, violence (in lesser men) is part and parcel of "the *Hu*man condition," secretly making higher men look good. The masses of lesser men are brutalized and denatured in $2 = 1$ man, and then "man" is said to be "naturally" aggressive and violent. *As you believe, so you behave.*

*Hu*manity is not only an epistemological fraud, it is also the Greatest Social Engineering Project on planet earth. Fem's biology is *exploited* as *w-o-man*, forced to collude in the fraud. Limitless man above accountability for his beliefs has personal autonomy, like Enron's CEOs. *Hu*man rights heroes fight for the rights of man to believe in male saviors who save oppressed womanhood from brutalized, denatured manhood. Methodological solipsism works in mysterious ways. Violence pays! Lies pay big time!

The exactitude of a theory is judged on the facts upon which it is established and developed, and what these facts do to theory. A theory running on seminal ruminations of "is and is not" is not a theory. We are to believe that the great "*manu* (factor) in us," the neutral hand of control, is good by virtue of its being male—neutrality. This allows patrists to rule supreme as higher men who appear to have grasped reality. Imposed by knowledge withheld, it fools the masses. And after imposing "Q is and is not Q" for millennia, he tells us that the manmass "needs to be fooled." Needing a need that is not a need? Now that's talking the talk Q is and is not Q! And so the Lord made us all walk the walk.

Born under the star of the lust to control half the species, the chain of contradiction/isms proselytizes a grand delusion through lies in The Word, phallic bafflegab, and verbal mystification. The ideology does not depend on the distinction between true and false, right or wrong, but on the *finking* (false thinking) done between and among *special* self-studflated males, weak, self-praising, self-named gods. To stand against divine self-valorization is to be judged evil until there is an almost-not-there hair-thin distinction between good and evil. "Let us do evil that good may come" (Romans 3:8). And giraffes may yet give birth to elephants. Who knows? Just believe.

Today, O. J. stands "forgiven" by Mother Church, the *manumeter* of His goodness and morality. The mix of sloppy emotions in our thrall-dom to generic man and the simplistic idea of being both men regardless of gender in the "brotherhood of man" are good. Good because all the while H/he excludes half the species included, abracadabra, as not men. Twisted nonsense so compelling! Just FEEL that it is true and believe! Accept and ditto.

The indifference to the setbacks imposed on psychology, science, and reason is smuggled in under the rubric of "*vir*tue," a religious value in man's name to keep thinking, science, and reason at bay. What is *the common good* in the femicidal ideology of man evident in The Word woman? Don't ask. Just feel it to be good and true and believe.

Patrist ideology in the violation of reason gave itself three dispensations from truth: intellectual, practical, and moral by dressing *common evil* in the garb of *common good*. This is why the phenomenon of *common evil* was not named in 2 = 1 man. H/his idea of and interest in mind go in opposing directions at the same time. Commitment to nonsense is not named sloppy emotions, bad reason, pure subjectivism, or even insanity. In fact, brazenly seminal, faith-based fantasy fornicates with the belief that mind is insufficient. It needs God. Which means that there is a lot of "*vir*tue" that is ugly fuck'em-hard-and-hate'em big vice. Both fem and man are denatured by such ugly ideology.

The dispensations are self-given. It is not only to the privileges and status of higher men that one should impute the problems afflicting our species. It is also to the thoroughly confusing Doctrine-Theory of Man that came out of H/his chain of contradictions causing confusion. For theory ought to use critical reasoning, science, and evidence to reach its conclusions; phallic-central*ism* is not a choice here. Phallic centralism throws away the building blocks to do good reasoning and science to arrive at morality.

Intellectual dispensation is begotten by hiding the single fact favorable to rational thesis—***omitting*** the proposition ***being man in reality entails only being male***. In my thirty years of research I did not see this proposition spelled out as a premise in man. Having divine *mentulae*, he had the right to withhold this information. The stud (stud-ent) is valued for what he does to broad/en his knowledge of the *matrix* (mother) by penetrating the object of his stud/y after which he *matric*-ulates. The arrogant, pompous bluster in phallic lingo by which lesser men are brutalized and fem nullified is degrading. *Stud*/ent and *matri*/culation is a telling pair of W/words: If you fuck her you are a man, my son. So when God gave Adam language, did He also give him The Word "fuck"? Withheld information "fucks"!

Practical dispensation relies on suppressing the criterion of effectiveness in judging premises by depriving the examination of valid premises, *premises withheld*, like the one above. In this strategy one can be made to believe in deficient mind. Patrists fabricate super-hair-thin details, absolving unarticulated premises *guaranteeing failure of refutation*. It took me thirty years to see the "is and is not" poles in man, which I now see as elementary. Keeping fem out of the halls of learning for 4,000 years gave H/him a great advantage!

Moral dispensation is stolen by studflating maleness as superior. Good is in male, *vir*tue (*vir*, L., man). What is a crime for lesser men and women is not a crime for patrists/Lords. Indeed, the big crime of femic cleansing is absolved in ideological self-absolution. Man = virtue. But beliefs being sacred, tolerance commands us not to judge the believer, only the beliefs. The Lord, Supreme, divine, unaccountable for his sexuality, impregnates Joseph's wife, the *Virgin* Mary, *telling her after the fact* via an *angel* that she is "with child"—does not constitute rape. The Lord's right is the same right that first-night manorial Lords gave themselves. Seminal rape is OK. What a role model for morality!

Belief in Man-superior, man-inferior, the archetype social structure parallel to Lord superior, lord inferior, no beliefs were to be judged. But no archetype lives in isolation: It is meant for the whole species of symbol users. Sexism, racism, class, and irrationality operate on the "me-superior, you-inferior" paradigm, the *archi*paradigm 2 = 1 man, because The Word *man* in man, woman, human is the archimorpheme in His lingo. Thus Allah is superior to God, Emanuel is superior to Allah, God is superior to Manitou—baby-man politics, *common evil* shared on a massive scale.

In the end, we are and are not responsible for our behavior, including thought. The Lord especially is not. Nothing is straight in hu*man*ity. But we are held responsible for murdering someone because "he" possesses a soul that Jesus G/god-Male wants. Abortion is murder; femicide is not. Murder is wrong; the electric chair putting disposable men to death is not. Femicide is not in law books. All murder is *homicide*: We are all men regardless of gender! Tolerance is free speech for the select few who dis*semin*ate hate covertly in "The Word," the open-sky policy for intellectual fraud and massive deception. How does an ordinary mind see through the convoluted maze of the grand fraud that is 2 = 1 man?

The ideological split of he-mind (male) from his she-body (not male) and tolerance of false belief exempt patrist scholars from having to appear before the tribunal of exactitude, accusing anyone that it is to bow to narrow mindedness—to believe otherwise. Reason is denigrated as "rational*ism*" or political correctness, while Hu*man* ideology clothed in its *toga virilis* puts the stamp of objectivity on patrist subjectivism. To subject "The Word" to a reality check, logical analysis, or critical examination is mortal sin in 2 = 1 man.

Do patrists have the right to pass falsehoods as duly tried facts? To yoke science with embedded hocus-pocus creates a glued-together-collective-kept-in-ignorance-by-the-Lie only to abuse their ignorance. The terrorizing evil *of making procedures of critical thinking and science almost useless* concerning minded animals in the face of faith and belief disables the mind. It destroys the criteria for doing consistent reasoning in thinking, knowledge, and science, destroying the reality of multiple truths easily grasped by any average intelligence having the correct facts and information. The Lie succeeds because the zillions of little lies are hair-thin excuses that fit one into the other that hit you in the face relentlessly day after day in its puzzling zig and zag method.

A global false ideology disguised as Holy Truth is a black hole of seminal slime allowing every form of thought mutilation and crime. It creates the massive maze of false belief and confusion best called *common evil*, causing behavioral chaos, individual*ism*. It is so massive that it is hard for the common good to walk on its four rational feme and male legs burdened by the overweight of its nonsense and poison, verbal land mines and its lead blanket of real*ism*. The strength in individuality to stand up for what is real, true in reality, and good is for all practical purposes killed.

The violence *in manu*, born in law and imposed by social bullying using lies embedded in language, is the power-money-sex Trinity using guns, rape, prostitution, child porn, disinformation, and outright lies to keep intimidating the manmass. Concealing facts, devaluing critical thinking, and derogating reasoning invests the mind with a *convergenital* appetite for messiahs, prophets, gurus, or supernatural heroes who solve *all* of Humanity's *insoluble* problems, the cosmic know-it-all All-Powerful Higher Alpha Fathers made necessary. God takes care of all things. God Bless America! Allah is great! *Let correct information be damned!*

The reaction is apathy, indifference toward fact, resistance to evidence and toward knowledge, correct information, and even ruling bodies. Cynicism and fear of facts—the masses hate the politics in them. Weakened disabled minds need special crutches, fictional salvos, strong booze, golden strokes, mind-numbing drugs, mountains of food, divine supermen, and synagogue/church/temple supports to face the stressful conned fusions of strife-filled human life every day. The massive confusion in the conned fusion of opposites making all One-in-Truth makes violence a necessary solution.

(Necessary) mystification in the Social Engineering Project $2 = 1$ man is valid. High priests in business, church, and uni*ver*sity dole out in seminal catechism and lecture the equivocal ManG/god as author of life and death. The kept-ignorant manmass helps to protect this original kernel of deep lie-inducing irrationality, where "flesh-feminine-sin" enslaves fem as woman-object serving man-mind, subject. *Sheology,** the great mystery in theology yet to be exposed, is the staunchest guardian of *concelation* in revelation taught in "Mother" church. Father Priest and Mother Church copulate in the Sanctuary.

The most evil injunction, *tolerance of suffering*, "being God's children-cum-lambs" hides *concelation*, makes revelation appear to be real. Mind activity adjourned, irrational, cruel, and contradictory in behavior, no problem; Humanity is the highest good. Harming mind is not a crime; homicide is. In Catholic Brazil, wife killing and femicide are small potatoes. After all, Christ was subject to his Lord God, who existed for Him only to be nailed to the cross of his Superior. Be nice Lambs of God! Suffer *all* ye little children!

Everything is backward and upside down in phallic ideology. Having no checks and balances, it institutionalizes immorality and calls it *vir*tue. The seminal edict: Men must make fem into w-o-men, something she cannot be, brutalizing males in the process. The problem is that, like oaks cannot stop being oaks, the feme cannot stop being feme! So they will eternally be the cause of sin in $2 = 1$ man Truth! Fem can never be a man who's not a man: *the enemy.* She will eternally be a second-class, half-baked man as cause of sin—until the species suffers enough nonsense to stop the Social Engineering Project.

The violence in man stops fem from being herself; critical thinking and good reasoning in her are denigrated as "the ridiculous exercise of self-serving purists." Then the claim that F/faith cannot be put under the scrutiny of reason is cockily made on the verge/penis of Man as Absolute Truth. So much is relinquished to patrists that to stand up for the fact is a fearful look inside one's inner motivations and the extent to which one's *belief* in the legitimacy of the irrational has taken hold. Good correct thinking is put down by frightful accusations, such as political correctness, inventing neologisms, or feminist depravity, predisposing one against rational reforms. Team this up with tolerance, enhance it with free will and free speech, and you are whiteballed into silence and keeping the status quo.

Man is Absolute Truth! Amen. God bless Man. All the while, evil breeds more evil, violence more violence. Methodological solipsism rolls on and accumulates *vir*tuous lies, more she-objects, and mystic con/fusions.

In the iconography of woman/sacred cow protected by the iconography of holy bull/virtuous stud born in original sin is *gender-as-division* of mind and body. Original sin is she-flesh in man made in God's image, bodiless mind doing battle with flesh. Take one lie away and necessary Christ the Savior goes up in seminal smoke. Take another lie away and Allah stands on quicksand. Take another away and Emanuel crumbles. Expose the sacred secrets of organized mantasy-fantasy beliefs, the relegions of higher men and their religions disintegrate into the phallic peacockery that it is.

The curate in seminal knowledge disseminating revelation in theology does not elicit demands that H/he show the facts proving His thesis of he-mind-superior, she-body-inferior, and lesser-man-inferior. The mind is so disabled by obligatory belief in man being *in manu* that it would never occur to believers to ask for proofs, clear and forthright explanations, overt—written out—premises and propositions, missing information, and omitted concepts. The bias *in manu* is too perfectly executed. For instance, racism today hides under the cloak of etiquette as good manners toward one's fellow *man*, and profound sexism hides the hatred of fem as the love of woman in man and his tokenism. This helps immortalize the class of learned L/lords in philosophy, men in academia, such as Otto Weininger—who should know better. They know better! The motive?

No one dares to say fem is fem. No one dares to say that two exist in the species to contribute to knowledge. No one dares to proffer the definition of being sentient, thinker and speech maker as sapiens. No one dares acknowledge that there are more than two sexualities in nature. No one dares admit that we are as animal as any other animal species—but more fragile and vulnerable because of mind. Tolerance of nonsense is law. Tolerance of lies, belief, substitutes the responsibilities to find and respect facts based in reality, true-to-reality symbol making, real differences, and critical thinking. And name-calling gags the rational voice. The violence in common evil, the *manusclerosis* in the whole species terrorizes us. We *man* all the grabbing, warring, whoring, and pornographing of children around the globe. Let's be proud!

There is little left to lose in ridding the species of the verbal infrastructure that houses the Lie. Being a flawed/sinful species, the Grand Identity Theft of fem, the Global Social Engineering Project of changing fem and man into two men of opposite genders as one man, the Power, Money, and Sex global privileges in mankind denaturalizes the species.

In sapienity, truths are based on the probabilities seen in reality, and morality is based on *choice* from among the possibilities in them. Relating facts and actual truths make knowledge. Knowledge helps to relate reality correctly and is the path to wisdom. What is correct is right, and thus conducive to lead to moral act. Q is and always is only Q in reality and cannot also be not-Q.

We do not need *common evil* ejaculated from a trumped-up seminal "original sin." We do not need evil born of necessary inconsistency imposed by lexical law. We do not need the Lord in the pasture—we are not sheep. These made insoluble problems we would not have had if it were not for the obsessive penis pride of select weak and envious higher men entitling themselves with the lust to control mind in the rest of us.

We are sapiens with good sufficient minds. We can use any correct information that we possess at any one time creatively to solve our problems for the common good.

The power of the concealed in religion comes from the belief in the revealed as Truth, innate flaw-cum-original-sin "in man," a covert deceit to studflate man to being whole species. This belief in innate flaw/original sin protects the Lie that the species is mankind, and this stops it from being challenged. *Necessary inconsistency imposed made Q is and is not Q valid, an innate flaw was **purposely implanted** in the species, then named original sin, showing that the tail of solipsism turns back on itself, its head, as final and Absolute proof.*

In reality, no flaw or original sin is true. Manu subjugated half the species to the other half by law, the law was then used by Lords to develop language. The myth of Christ/Mohammed/savior saving souls makes the masses believe that Fantabulous Alpha Males in the Sky are so fantabulous in kindness and generosity that He would sacrifice Himself to be our savior from "original sin." The long convoluted code of solipsism at work in $2 = 1$ became *methodological* solipsism, binding us all in irrational duct tape.

Sacred belief, "The Word," is not about reality. No void happens when you leave false and myth-based ideas behind. Children do not believe their imaginary friend exists. Reality is so full of marvels and solutions that you will hardly be aware that you have left behind the infantile behavior of pretending a savior exists as we do a transition from arrogant phallic pretensions in sacred-*word* secrets to symbols giving correct information, the *Rofemtic Movement*. The structure of knowledge is based on hard-won, true-to-reality symbols. Knowing is the deepest satisfaction an individual can experience.

WITHOUT ANY SENSE OF LOSS

*Women are not bound to their names
with any strong bond. When they marry they
give up their own name and assume that of
their husband without any sense of loss ... The
fundamental namelessness of woman is simply
a sign of her undifferentiated personality.*
— Otto Weininger, Austrian Philosopher
(1880–1903)

Otto Weininger published *Geschlecht und Charakter* (Sex and Character) in 1903. He believed that all people have elements of both femininity and masculinity, that logic and ethics are one, and that logic is tied to the principle of identity, A is A.

But for him the male aspect is active, productive, conscious, and moral, and thus logical, while the female [sic] aspect is passive, unproductive, unconscious, and amoral, and thus not logical. He argues that the female [sic] life is consumed with the sexual function: both with the act, as a prostitute, and the product, as a mother. In contrast, the duty of a male is to strive to become a genius and to forego sexuality, for an abstract love of the Absolute, God, which he finds in himself.

Otto Weininger committed suicide in 1903. He was 23.

Fem received this seminal knowledge and wisdom since Manu's Law in 2400 BCE! Maybe it is rational to say that such deep confusion causes deep depression that leads to suicide.

Chapter 9

FIRST STEPS TOWARD REDUCING
THE COMMON EVIL

The first step is seeing both genders as having minds. Two exist to affirm logic through the symbols they make to provide checks and balances in naming reality.

But select (self-elected), power-grabbing Fathers entitled themselves as Kings, Popes, Emperors, Czars, Priests, Dukes, Rabbis, Bishops, Lords, Reverends, Gurus, and Monks. At the same time, these learned men paraded their en*vergure*, Fr., fullness of intelligence (*verge*, Fr., penis, *mentula*, L., male genitals, mental) conjuring Supreme Cause-All Holy Alpha Males in the Sky. He stood on heaven-high scaffolds of The Word in H/his phallic splendor above the masses.

Few realize how much Latin and French influenced English. Greek and Hindi also injected cultural eclecticism into the English language. The masses do not see this. The French pronoun *le* denotes masculine, *la* denotes feminine. Everything in French has a gender, similar to the Hindu tradition. There is no neuter pronoun in French. In English the pronoun "it" is going out of usage; "she" is used almost exclusively to denote objects and things.

Le verge, m., means penis, *la* verge, a yard in length, replaced by meter today. *Les verges*, pl., means the whips! *Tête*, Fr., head, from *testes*, L., made testify, testament, and testate; seminary and seminal are based on semen. The Truth con*verges* in the *mentula*, L., male genitals, vowel variation → *mentale*, Fr., mental. Seminarians were the first to catch on that *doing linguistics* to favor males would give men a great advantage, that there was political gain to be made in male-based names. Few people know or are aware to what extent even one linguistic formula can do to spread an ideology like being *in manu* (see Gouëffic 1996). Language imposed the reality that power, money, and sex vested in priests, ecclesiastical Lords, Manorial and political Lords as "the way things are" in reality. Slavery had to appear as "the way things are." There was no better way to do this than embedding the aim in language to be used for centuries; it would create *belief*, the hardest addiction-to-irrationality or *common evil* to reject in order to start healing the mind.

The linguistic secrets imposing Q is and is not Q in gender-as-division of mind and body are sacred in "The Word." Serial warring, global whoring, mass poverty, harsh punishments, and ongoing conflicts for 4,000 years among *special* men stopped the species from doubting The Word of man, a.k.a. God. But doubt we must. Doubt is the second step in the walk toward reducing the common evil in order to clean it out of the mind.

The extent to which we use The Word spawned in, with, and through *in M/manu/s*, and act upon it, is the extent to which *in manu* is law and keeps being law. To destroy *in manu* as law that went from physical-legal to politico-*lex*ical in "The Word," *the genetic origin of sapient mind in both fem and man must be general information again.* Upfront forthright truths must underwrite attitudes in our species. The sapient mind can make the correct relationship between cause and effect. This is not hard to do.

The path to maturity and morality is seeing the harm done to sapient mind in *manuology*, the logic of *in manu*, now called theology. Here are some suggestions to help you reduce the unnecessary harm, strife, and suffering done by imposing *manuology*.

Do Not Accept the Abuse of Tautology

Man as two opposite genders are/is man. 2 = 1 is false. The tautology in reality: Man (male) is man (male), Q is Q, 1 = 1. Fem affirms fem— with man as man.

Do Not Accept the Original Necessary Inconsistency

Body/w-o-man-in-man/mind the original "innate flaw" came to be called original sin. The chain of not-male → physical male → supernatural male determining the value of being man makes her *enemy* of *special* man. Enemy making built into the flaw makes warring and whoring natural in 2 = 1 man! Virility politics praises the phallus, virtuous staff, no penis = distaff. Doubting such divisive politics reduces contradiction, confrontation, and conflict. In reality, gender does not divide body and mind, lies do.

Commit to Being a Rule Follower

Rules are and are not rules in *in manu*. "Q is and is not Q" is the rule. In reality, Q is Q and 2 = 2, always and everywhere, on Neptune too. Rules exist in reality for consistency to make facts of equivalency: Fem → feme and man → male follow the rules seen in reality to see and state correct cause-and-effect relationships.

Know That Special Rationalism Is Not Rationality

HIS, the Holy Integral Solipsism, patrist in the image of God, who cheats, lies, plunders, steals, rapes, pimps, whores, murders, and wars, nonetheless exonerates himself in the creed that God made Him is His image; perfect, High, and Holy circularity proves the divine authorship of man done in and with The Word. This is not about reality-based premises and reasonable argument, so they cannot be not-knowledge. Symbol-*ism*, 2 = 1 man, embezzles with relativism, subjectivism, existentialism, positivism—off-balance thinking, isms all the way. "Isms" come out of the hidden dogma that semen is the first principle of everything, seminal authority imposing what is and is not to be believed.

Do Not Allow Your Mind to Be Controlled

The "unnecessary inconsistency" imposed to claim an *innate flaw* in our species came from the lust to control the masses. It causes massive confusion in zillions of lies, the *common evil* to be rejected outright. Now that we know how and why it was invented, it will be easier to reject the mind-disabling concept. We can apply critical analysis and independent thought to the tricks used. Losing Lord-imposed deficient mind will not be lamented and regretted. In fact, we stand to gain truths, sapien dignity, intellectual honor, and long-term serenity in rationally balanced selves. Moreover, *correct information* and truths require fewer books and fewer legislated laws, fewer regulations and restrictions and less bureaucracy.

Keep in Mind That There Is a Relationship between Cause and Effect
Relating cause and effect is the cement in reason and wisdom, doing so correctly and consistently is to be wise. When *fem's birthright to name herself as a logic-affirming agent* is taken away by force of male divinity in The Word, the cause-and-effect relationship between her mind and her body is broken. No choice exists for her but to support Q is and is not Q, common evil, the choice is not choice. Male divinity creates *givinity* in the feme, the giving-in characteristic obtained by making her believe in her weak, passive nature, w-o/man submissive to man. *Givinity* has her give in to *special* man because his divinity needs this from her (give in, v., → givinity, n.).

To illustrate an aspect of givinity, in 2000 I was in a major world city. My fourth-floor hotel room looked out on a main intersection. A big stone gate opened to a "red-light" district to the left of my hotel. On Saturday night I settled down to read in front of the window. At 6 p.m., I saw a trickle of white-clad men heading to *the gate*. By 8 p.m. a white stream of men were going to the privilege of virility, going on to well after 3 a.m. "Sex for men" was advertised in a glossy brochure, with the Bible, in my room—boasting of "girls" from every corner of the earth. How did so many *girls* get to this place of prostitution? On their own? At their own expense? Did they *choose* this life? *Givinity* appears "natural" in girls abducted and imprisoned to give sex to men. These girls who "give in" are "just sluts"!

How do not-males deemed to have no sex drive (it is not named) come to want sex so badly that they would *choose* to do it with many strange men every night in a strange country? Do "girls" really choose this life? Is it not rather a case of abduction, no choice of good employment, and the religion of man imposing the unspoken phallic law of *givinity* for unaccountable *virility*? The *no choice* these girls have is to commit immorality as the seductive objects men claim them to be—they're just sluts!

Be Aware of Gate Keeping

Man, both male and not-male, has only two possible directions: (1) To fully return to Father-head authority to keep H/his esoteric feudal system going, pushed hard today by extremists and fundamentalists, or (2) to have a weak, arrogant, penis-proud man proclaim himself a new Alpha Male/Father-Lord—a new True God—and create a brand *new* religion. Both of these are more of the same mind-controlling strategies; He would use all the same lies to grab the neutral hand of control over the mind.

Realize That Lambs of God Are Sheep

In $2 = 1$ man, all unfortunate accidents, all misfiring, all impositions, all pain, all injustices to mind and body are boxed in the gilded world of the sacred and untouchable, where no limitations to "Q is and is not Q" exist. Above and outside of reality, H/he treats adults as sheep. "The Lord is my shepherd" is clear evidence of this transmutation. Shepherds watch over sheep: The masses are animals. The divine Lord is not! Illogical, false, and immature at core, the Lord stands above the masses in phallic splendor.

It's marvelous being a child. My childhood was serene, carefree, so filled with adventure and the wonderment of learning that I would give anything to return to it. I had few responsibilities. Reality pushed me to adulthood. As an adult I found that our genetic purpose of mind (our *sapienity*) was to aim at our intelligent *self*-determination to grow to full maturity. I shucked off the idea of being "born in sin" and found myself needing to use my mind. I found thinking for myself exhilarating. I did not want to stay at the immaturity of childhood once I became aware of the power in my mind.

Those with minds cultured to be deficient suffer from overwhelming seminal magic and are let out of taking responsibility for their emotions, thoughts, and actions. Adult immaturity yearns to regress to the past, to the unaccountability of their youth. As children/*lambs of God*/flock of sheep, this is granted to them. In 2000 Anno Deceptio, the pope reiterated that the God of the Roman Catholics was the One and Only True God/Shepherd. A pope globally stating Q is and is not Q with divine authority is impressive; it keeps "deficient minds" immature and too busy to ask relevant questions and doubt lies.

Now, popes and religions know the mysteries of life and the *wor*ld. They know that the biblically known world is 6,000 years old, that earth is flat and stands still, that God created man and his world in seven days, that Adam named everything, making men superior to w-o-men. God revealed seminal $2 = 1$ man because they know with Absolute phallic certitude that Q is and is not Q; embedded in language, it is made to last for eternity.

But along came Galileo, Newton, de Beauvoir, Mill, and Darwin with usable facts and truths, fatal blows to seminal ruminations. Fem is fem in reality, a premise that cannot be refuted, a fact affirming Q is Q and $2 = 2$ are true to reality. So truths are not scary after all. Truths are life enhancing and thus interesting, creative, and exciting; they reduce the *common evil.*

Are there yet more forms of violence that can be unleashed, and more virulence that can be foisted on the species? Are there evil acts worse than ethnic raping and mass killing? Yes. Germ and nuclear weapons can destroy all in a few minutes. Man is not *manu*-factoring nuclear weapons for nothing; killing products are meant to be sold and used! "Progress" has lost meaning too. The *mysterium tremendum* in seminal lingo not only lets War Lords off the hook, it also needs killing machines, a compelling reason to doubt man Lords.

Accept Calling Fem, Fem, and Using the Name

What would we lose if we accepted fem as fem? Air? Water? Forests? We have already lost these, plus mind, knowledge, rationality, and wisdom. *We have nothing more to lose.*

Understanding doctrinal *neutral* control is neither easy nor pleasant. Why is serial warring, international manning of global whoring, genocidal events, seminal worship of H/him, and massive false belief still going on? What do we stand to lose where the false thinker controlling the cultured non-thinker H/he imposed in His Social Engineering Project? Understand we must, or irrevocably lose all.

Understand the Obedience Factor in the Targeted Half of the Species

We could ask where fem was when w-o-man was made from the rib of "man's loins." The Bible makes silence "woman's greatest *vir*tue," and her *givinity* in his divinity kills her intellectual initiative. The fear of going it by her insights as fem is now endemic to fem. She fears her own insights, making H/his neutral control of her perfect. Well, not quite.

But where was fem when the *in manu* became law? Did she see the degradation of reason and fem coming? "When you see man, you see God," says a popular hymn to Him. Beloved lies—beliefs—do not make knowledge: They take over the mind.

Yet she is not blameless. She will plead lack of knowledge. But what is it that she did not know? That being man entails only being male? That generic man cannot be both male and not male? That *w-o* cannot do magic? Balderdash! She let babymen get away with the deception so that she too could escape "God's wrath"! She believed in the romantic mantasy-fantasy of Alpha Males! She too gave belief primacy to get into man's heaven to be in *the arms of Holy Alpha Male in the Sky*! The Zen of Romance! Belief is far easier than the pain, energy, and time needed to find the facts and then to stand up for them.

When language determines and *makes* reality, the Lord can do what H/he jolly well wants to do! H/he conjures grievous wrong done to him by fem to blame her. This excuses his weaknesses. This burning bush of phallic blame dumped on the man who's not a man is very harmful. In fact, surprise! It boomeranged on H/him. We are all suffering equally the harm it hailed upon the species. The cart of lies was pulling the heavy horse of His Truth.

To see and posit fem as fem is to assume responsibility for one's own thinking. One has to mature to commit to known facts. Belief is from be + *lief*, OE, pleasant, love, but "beloving" lies do not make facts for knowledge, only seminal comfort for weak men. This is where lesser men can take comfort; they now know they are not weak like higher men.

Realize That Being Rational Does Not Go Against Anyone

Doing good reasoning does not make rationality "the all." Good reasoning elicits better emotions, making more possible a self-directed integration of our feelings and emotions with our reasoning and thinking abilities to achieve maturity.

No one knows this better than fem from her experiences in giving birth. Nurturing and monitoring new life has astounding implications for language. The belief that Adam named everything turned men into life takers, death makers. Life givers see that minded life is life that ought to make language that is friendly to life.

The UNESCO Constitution, 1946: *Since wars begin in the minds of men, it is in the minds of men that the defenses of peace must be constructed.* This is a good example of Patriarchal English. Written in the H/he-gear, man as Savior of the *wor*ld makes war to defend peace to stop war! A rofemtic constitution would read something like this: "Since *belief in man/u* puts *fatal errors* in the minds of fem and men, it is the defense and constant use of consistent reasoning that must prevail in both *with* their commitment to have real knowledge taught to young minds. *Peace* can come no other way."

Almost all sapiens can reason and think. One does not need to be a rocket scientist to see that $2 = 2$. Both fem and men are necessary to the process of good reasoning to achieve rationality. When feme rational thought and male rational thought are integrated in consonance *with* one another, "all the Lord's priests and all the Lord's higher men couldn't ever put Cocksure Father God back together again." Reasoning enables us to get out of the grip of Absolute False Truth touted as *faith* in $2 = 1$ man fantasy concealed in revealed man. Knowledge is public, useful, and has no information to hide from anyone.

Need and Want Correct Information

We do not suffer from information overload. We suffer from overwhelming false information and lies. Libraries full of books explain the hair-thin false, Truth *in manu*. Books on theology, manuology, make you feel as though you are inside a sacred testicle full of holy semen, never clear or forthright because so much crucial information and facts are missing, replaced by seminal fantasy. *We suffer from missing necessary information*, knowledge. Life needing seminal fantasy is in the same boat as "fish needing bicycles."

Know That Manuology Kills the Process of Valuation

Devaluing femity to overvalue manity, the game of upmanship in *valorization* is grossly imbalanced. Midas hits gold semen! The male is *wor*th more than the feme, sons are the child of preference around the globe. Does hydrogen have more value than oxygen? Does air have more value than water? Why then is male of more value than feme? Just *believe* and shut up—or else.

The whole false exercise did away with the concepts of sapient, sapiential, sapienter, and sapience, with the goal in these being reasoning to make symbols true to reality. Concepts that name, define, and explain our capability to do naming and make true-to-reality symbols are missing too. Instead, we are all men, slaves to the (Hu)man lie! Discarding concepts that would have us aim at *following rules* in symbol making, and respecting what is seen in reality and nature devalued reason, concrete evidence, cause-and-effect relationship, fem "with" man as partners, and logic, all important to our species. Beloving God comforts minds made deficient by lies as Holy Truth.

Patrists devalued (1) the cause-and-effect relationship in fem to bring down (2) *the probability of multiple causes*. This would help to impose the idea of the monolithic Lord, a single Cause-All, Know-All Alpha Male. Strangely, many humanists, rationalists, secularists, and scientists do not see feme cause with male cause in reality—yet tout multiple causalities—*and the monolithic Alpha Male Cause*! Q is and is not Q is quirky and unpredictable.

Higher men consider femity, feme causality, sapienity, reason, consistency, independent thought, and analysis dangerous. They fear ideas that are *ratiogenic*, rational at source, and thus a source of further good reasoning, anathema to belief. Instead, the anti-concepts woman, faith, belief, *mysterium tremendum* (thrown at me once to make the mystical appear concrete and make the person who said it seem extremely knowledgeable), immortality, resurrection, and tolerance of beliefs are preferred, apotheo-sized in self-induced trances, pompous rites, magic rituals, and individualistic flakiness.

Understand That *In Semino* Rationalizations Are Deadly

That being man entails only being male, that he is both male and not male, that w-o-man is the man who's not a man are never openly stated. *In semino* rationalizations by virtue of the *high value of start-up semen*(!) in the *wor*ld is the theological/manuological stuff of first beginnings. "In the beginning was *The Word*," the *spermaticos logos*. Belief in this nonsense is to accept that the manipulation of knowledge is OK. A real mind killer!

In semino rationalization is a divine art. The human condition, being born with an innate flaw, sin, is treated as a serious idea. Knowledge on the other hand has no purposeful error embedded in language to host a grand intellectual fraud. There are no secrets in knowledge, the facts are forthrightly articulated, on the table for all to see, thus capable of being put through the most rigorous court of reality for their truth or falsity. Names and symbols reflecting reality are the key: Their *fallibility* can be tried.

The average sapien has little knowledge of linguistics. Like sing sang song sung, vine ↔ wine, secret → sacred, vowel and consonant variation are methods used to make new, different, and/or related concepts, a fascinating technology. Children would learn it as easily as they learn mathematics or economics. But children are taught nothing about *making symbols*, because they would learn the rules of logic, cause-and-effect relationship, evidence—in short, critical thinking, and that manipulation is easier than naming truths.

Be Aware of the Granting of Official Manumission

Psychological *manumission* has not been officially granted. Laws, constitutions, and statutes globally address men as rulers. "The Word of God'" in French is "le *Ver*be de Dieu," *verbe* → verpa, L., penis. An organ that erects is *ipso facto* a ruling organ. Emmanuel Reynaud (1981) says that "the destiny of women is invariably death or submission, rape, prostitution or marriage." Constitutions could easily include fem as full civilizing agents *with* men! We make constitutions, we can change them. Why is fem not in constitutions? Because of the belief in the nonsense that 2 = 1 man! As long as this belief persists, there is no *emancipation* for fem.

Know That Seminal Crypto-Messages Are Hard-Working Underpinnings

In manu lingo is esoteric (*linga*, SK, penis lingo). The Latin name for man, *vir* → *ver* made *ver*nacular. Acts done when the sun's rays (son, Ray, Roy) light the day, *di*, L., from *di/eu*, Fr., god, le Verbe de Dieu/ God, phallic act of day is respectable. The vagina is dark, night! Dark is evil. Sex (sin) is committed at night. Did Eve *evil*? Like Manu *man*? Zap! Man has a dark side, a not-male object seducing H/him to sin. Light and dark, day and night, white and black, good and evil split in gender-as-division of body and mind. It brought out many Holy Alpha Male prophets, big profits for *special* men. God's 2 = 1 man corrupted and poisoned everything in life.

Seminal crypto-messages make control of mind appear OK. Exposed they let us see studcraft forcibly normalized and godfatherheads hoisted to divinity on their own phallic petard.

Understand the Inalienable Right of *All*—*Yes, All*—Speech Users

Sapien law respects mind, good reasoning, fem, man, all life forms, and nature as it is. One very crucial item in sapien law blatantly missing *in manu*, important to all thinkers, is **the right to correct information with the responsibility to transfer it to the young**. Real knowledge is knowledge we can use because it is based on facts. Q is Q for everyone. When Q is Q, 2 = 2 for all, self-evident *cosmodigms*, patterns both quantitatively and qualitatively balanced existing everywhere in the cosmos, scientific and rational in basis. Respecting them is the way to achieve peace, wisdom, serenity, and honest emotions.

Know about the Law and Creating Truths

There is only one scientific law practiced in humanity by default. For every action there is an equal and opposite reaction practiced in *for every revelation there is an equal and opposite concelation*. There is an item of necessary knowledge concealed for every item of nonsense revealed by God. The grand delusion holds in Theory: thesis man, antithesis not male, therefore, synthesis *man*. This method is untenable as soon as knowledge withheld is exposed. Therefore, ***it is not only about naming knowledge withheld, but also of doing theory integrating two thinkers who by definition evolved capable of***

making and using symbols as the foundation upon which all rationality stands.

Cocksure antithesis brought out every kind of Truism under the sun. The main law in *hu*manity could be called "the *Ism* Law." Patrists had us zigzag from hu*manism*, propaganda of no small stature to positivism, verbal mentalism of no small stature. To subjectivism claimed "objective," a phallic humility of no small stature that took us to limitless liberalism, a treadmill of no small stature to virilism, virility of no small stature to $2 = 1$ *manism*, divine realism of no small stature to feminism, a tour de force of no small stature—until we ism-ed out. Few caught in the tsunami of *isms* could see the candy-coated destruction of consistence in mind activity being celebrated by faith predators.

Life-in-the-H/he-gear has God, wealth, language, law, social institutions, and the kept-ignorant, believing manmass on H/his side. How could H/he lose? Yet Holy Virility in man did not succeed to get free access to the vagina as Manu God intended. Nor did men get polygamy rights. Why did man not achieve freedom from his sexual responsibility? What is free sex? What is *control* by the neutral male hand?

When you cannot reason nor do scientific looking with false premises about your species, you cannot achieve true goals for the species. Using true-to-reality premises in sapien science is to be *in consonance with fem and man realities, both feme and male causalities*. Consistency leads to consonance of mind and body, leading to balance. A leaning $2 = 1$ man-train on a biased-for-man track derails itself.

Premises based on facts lead one to *do* thinking, to *be* a thinking being using all the valid and sound premises necessary to the project. Fem is capable of doing thinking and being a thinker. Lord Manu wanted to break this in her and destroy it. He failed. Even with zillions of lies and linguistic tricks using 4,000 years to succeed he failed. This is why I say that the Social Engineering Project, "humanity," is a colossal failure.

Manufacturing words out of mantasy-fantasy to fit a pet doctrine bamboozles thinker, thoughts, reason, science, and goals. Science acknowledges no higher authority even with its fallibility factor. Apfig is fiction, w-o-man is seminal mantasy-fantasy, neither has anything to do with reason, science, correct relationship between cause and effect, and no respect for reality. Respect for reality is the foundation of right emotions.

Honest scientists no longer believe that bodies fall due to gravity on Galileo's say so, but on many trials to find probabilities. More looking, more trials, more experiences convince them that Galileo found a truth. Although many scientists are, science itself cannot be, and therefore is not addicted to *in manu*. Scientists are trained to see the small difference that makes all the difference on planet earth. But scientists are not science; many are human, bred with deficient mind! Probabilities in facts make science fallible. Fem is fact. As a fact, it is fallible; it can be tried in the court of reality for its truth. That fem exists as fem is highly probable, so the fact of fem as fem *as it is now* is not refutable.

Like science, reason acknowledges no higher authority. We must put on trial for ourselves any presupposition in premises stated as antitheses. This is what we call being reasonable and using our own reason. Independent thought uses consistency in logic consonant with scientific thinking. Morality based on and communicated in, with, and through concepts doing good reasoning puts choice for action on reality-based alternatives. There is no other way to arrive at the bases for moral behavior.

Be Aware of the Minefield of Mantasy-Fantasy

Doctrinal Neutral Man is a minefield of falsehoods clinched in Holy Integral Solipsism. The deadliest aspect: the Lord as possessor of Truth. Thus, the knowledge of *good* (man) and *evil* (woman) must not be knowledge, says the Bible! H/he treats himself as God in the sense that He is not prepared to allow the justification he accepts for H/himself as God to be used by anyone else. No one is *to know* the truths in reality and nature, only H/his Truth, built-in guaranteed success for His Lie!

Antithesis *in manu* is to posit man; *argumentum ad feminam* is the *deus ex machina* that motivates H/him to withhold knowledge. Morally and intellectually reprehensible $2 = 2$ becomes $2 = 1$, pulling "original sin" out of the seminal trough of he-mind and she-body to do the trick. How can ordinary minds see through such low trickery?

Know That to Be Moral Is about *Choosing* to Do a Certain Act and Not Another

To make intelligent choices we must have the smallest distinction of difference brought out clearly and forthrightly so that we can discern what the *difference* means in and to the *similarity*. This is necessary for good judgment. If a snake has venom that can kill you and an almost identical one does not, is it not good for you to know this small difference in their similarity?

We cannot choose truths for moral behavior when covert/embedded lies are all we have. Even the smallest differences in similarities help distinguish the good from bad. No one can get the ability to discern differences and what these differences mean when man is the Name for all categories. What are the differences between man in man and man in woman when being man in reality entails only being male? This muddies and dulls *the skills to discern* fine distinctions that may be a matter of life and death. Not all mushrooms are created equal, some kill—instantly! False misleading names harm the mind.

Concealing vital information such as fem makes discernment almost impossible. In man, difference is man. Difference = similarity—well, not quite. False similarity (not male) is false difference, one (gender) mind, the opposite not mind. Difference-is-opposite = division-as-opposite-gender. Difference = division—well, not quite. Blinded in-sight, lost skills of discernment, and large conned fusion loom big, harming the mind.

Two distinct categories, two gender-different beings in reality show differences in their similarity that all sapiens can use to hone the skills of discernment. Both evolved with brains to be logic-affirming animals, name facts missing in man. Thus any discussion about our species, culture, language, and society is inadequate. One-half is missing.

Know the Effect of Losing the Skills of Discernment and "Free Will"

Loss of discernment does not let you see that higher *value* is given to non-existent entities/Holy Alpha Males than to existing beings. The sum of falsehoods in the 4,000-year Grand Identity Theft of fem has more value than the truths in being sapiens, better than what 20,000,000 years of brain evolution could ever do with mind.

Even the oxymoron "human error" is good propaganda, when *hu*man as a symbol is a crime against mind. It excludes fem, makes her a man, validates fantasy and magic, and lets everyone in the kept-ignorant manmass off the hook. We shadow think, fink, and believe, and treat these as serious enterprises.

*Hu*manity speaks realism into existence; the *manu*topia is a perfect-imperfect *man* as species, perfect in that he is created in God's image, and imperfect, *deficient*, born in original sin and thus needing God, all *infallible*! How does one try perfect-imperfect man?

A perfect-imperfect species does not exist except as a model for irrationality. Imperfect/sinful *hu*manity is perfect for being created by God? M/man is *determined* by an original commission of wrongdoing, sin, not of his making. W-o + man flesh is to blame. Hate her! Evolution be damned! What good camouflage for seminal bafflegab! What an alibi to get out of the responsibility to do correct thinking! What a weak excuse from weak men to escape from being accountable for their own sexuality!

Determined? Whoa! Back up the doctrinal machine for a minute! 2 = 1 man does not admit being determined: God gave him free will! He can instill "Q is and is not Q" for all to share. H/he is not determined by reality. *God gave man free will*! Well, not quite. In man H/he is predetermined by put-into-place inconsistency—zap—original sin!—zig—he is free to do as he wills, zag—Q is and is not Q.

As reality-as-it-is determines language and language affects thinking, thinking is anathema to the doctrine of man. Rule following is not what God wants. Man is not about to let reality get in the way. God gave H/him (self) free will. H/he determines reality and nature by The Word. H/he made language! Free will is so bandied about that the sense of what it means is lost. And if you are totally con/fused at this point, I'm glad, because I cannot go beyond man being given *free will* by God Himself and being *predetermined by original sin*. I am too tangled up in limitless dichotomies split even smaller by free will = being predetermined. When confusion of this magnitude takes over, guess what? *You have a deficient mind*. Everything is self-justifying and self-fulfilling *in manu*. Solipsism10[100]!

Religion and man abhor the idea of "man" being determined. This is the highest idiosyncrasy in the *pre*determined fatherdigm $2 = 1\ man$ born in original sin. God gave man free will, to do what? Violate reality? Oppose nature? Falsify knowledge? Ignore the rules of logic? Rape fem seminally? Tell science to go to hell? Create false emotions?

Q is and is not Q puts all minds in the seminal nowhere-land of hundreds of ises and is nots. Anything goes in $2 = 1$. For instance, every spring in my youth, married pillars of society, Knights of Columbus, put crisp $20 bills and whiskey in their pockets to go and *have* the 12-year-old virgins on the "Indian" Reserves. None were ever arrested for statutory rape. Higher men can do no wrong! Free will is so wonderful—for some.

What is free will? In my view, it is "I want. I *want*. I ***want***" seminal lust, free sex, wealth, power, title, status, all in my name. The irrevocable fact is that there cannot be "a more" to the will we have naturally within each of us. There is only *will* and it is clearly a *sapient* issue: correct information to use for the initiative, motivation and fortitude to use the will to make moral choices. There is only the will that can be used to choose to do what is right. False information, like the big piles of it in $2 = 1$ man, makes citizens do the wrong thing and breeds more corrupt and criminal minds than we can dream of.

But looking at "free will" shows us that the first consideration of patrists is the *linga*, SK, penis → lingo, *ver*pa, L., penis → verbal, verb, and vernacular. *Vir*, L., man → *vir*tue → *wor* → *wor* + d, *wor*-ship. *Mentula*, L., male sexual organs → *mentale*, Fr., mental. *Tête*, Fr., head, from *testes*, L., → testate, testify, and testament, the *spermaticoi logoi*, Gk., the sperm as *wor*d that speaks creation into being. Owning a penis having brain cells one need not bother with facts or mind. Let's hide facts, withhold knowledge, and claim free will.

Know That the Will Is Not Free to Go Against Reality or Logic

Will is not *free* to break the laws of reality, nature, logic, and thought. Breaking laws results in misinformation, even disinformation. Breaking one of man's man-made lies now parading as laws may not be such a bad thing, but lesser men get thrown into prison by the thousands for doing so! Doubt free will we must!

Seminal thinking, free will, is taught to children day after day before they are critical enough to analyze it. It is hammered into their head—as *faith*—long before they are able to do critical thinking. Pseudo-facts are taught to children at the age when acquiring thinking habits stays with them for life. Indoctrinated with saving his *soul* in the *mysterium tremendum* of divine edict commanding wife to be submissive to husband couched *in manu* is the import of seminal thought, the virus for porn and prostitution, filthy, degrading, and evil. In this, free will appears to be such a glorious gift from God! Doubt we must!

What is so shocking is that the holy pile of irrational nonsense is not seen as *insanity*. Indeed, it is considered sane to have *faith*. *Cleanliness* is applied to split-by-gender mind and body in *sanity*. The son is clean, non-self-polluting; he does not *menstruate*. Mental (mentula) health and sanitation (non-self-polluting) link *sanity* in *sound (mind)* Fr., *son*, made sonality as in personality, male child—son (of the F/father). He does not self-pollute; he is sane, clean, perfect. San, sanity, sane, *sain*, Fr., → saint, Santa Claus, Father Christmas—*son* of God—divine in so many ways! We must doubt The Word!

W-o-*man* menstruates: She is not clean. How evil she is! The Zenith of this mantasy-fantasy is the mathematical unit 10^{-15}, which is called *femto* (divided by 1,000,000,000,000,000) and is registered in dictionaries. Ironically, it is the only other symbol using "fem" in English that is registered in dictionaries! A fem is much less than zero: *Hate her*! They are mere placeholders between man and man, like zeroes are placeholders in numbers. *Between Man and Man*, the title of a book by Martin Buber, implies as much.

Know This Other Fit-All Name!

Finking, false thinking, causes confusion of cosmic magnitude. The tragedy is that because it is not labeled *finking*, there is nothing to compare it to critical or good thinking. Thus finking goes unchallenged. We must believe that any and all activity of mind is thinking. Few thinkers who sincerely want to commit themselves to thinking critically do not know the extent to which *finking* is injected into their reasoning habits, causing failures in thinking. It makes many of their problem-solving skills fail, like faulty wiring makes electricity fail. Finking has you believe in individual deficient mind, making the collective mind insufficient, the manmass churning out believing individualists.

The $2 = 1$ man seems to favor men. But males have so many questionable privileges of control that they fail to see that they are as controlled as fem, that the harm done to them is "equal but different." It imprisons them in the controlling mode, demanding eternal vigilance, continual policing, conspiracy, spying, violence, and wars. Finking cowards lie, falsify, hit, grab, push, bully, rape, and—violate any which way they can. It makes criminals out of lesser men that higher men use to show off their "goodness."

Few sapiens are educated as sapiens. Few are trained to recognize finking because *finking* was not named, it is absent. Thus we believe that all mind activity is encapsulated in One-Word/Name-Fits-All, like man in the seminal is-and-is-not strategy. *Thinking* encapsulates all mind activity like *man* encapsulates the whole species. Thus thinking that is and is not thinking rolls on unchallenged without our knowledge. *Error* just keeps on disabling our minds kept-ignorant-by-knowledge-withheld, and we all partake in this *common evil. Finking*, doing is and is not trickery, is what $2 = 1$ man wants.

Undertake the Task of Eliminating the Lie and Its Supporting Lies
We must rid ourselves of the deadly "is and is not" strategy *in manu*, first imposed in "man is and is not male." As shocking as this is to the believing manmass, I am talking here about *de*-hu-*manizing* the species, taking down the orgy of *seminal* mind activity. Human/seminal free will does nothing for our efforts to evolve toward being right-feeling and reason-based thinkers. *Bias and lies do nothing for maturity and morality.*

A real comfort here is to know for the first time that it is neither hard nor scary to rid ourselves of harmful lies, disinformation, violence, and slavery. It is necessary that we do so or we will lose our planet, ourselves, and all life.

■   ■   ■

Whatever it was that fem as "primitive" thinkers did in society before 2400 BCE, when historicism began, could not warrant Manu's Law.

That she evolved *estrus* out of her sexual system was not enough for him. The chain of false dichotomies the law brought about imposed obscene disproportion: a hierarchy of men—a loerarchy of "opposites." The equally obscene disproportion of punishment divinely ordained, for example, God's infliction of "pain" in childbirth in spite of her pro-creative contribution to the species is revolting. God did not decree that "hard-drive virility" was a punishment for men! Why? The whole seminal exercise *did not make men better beings.*

The serial warring between and the shared whoring in patriarchies expose discords among men. Faith and irrationality cause necessary violence; poison air, water, and the food chain; and pollute mind where the hierarchy of higher men in class-gender-race splits abide. The scape-goat, *the love of w-o-man in man* hiding the hatred of fem, is simply a luscious feast of phallic "good conscience" for higher men, a feel-good seminal lust. In making fem his expiating victim, his society soothed its cultural hatred of feme mind in fem, and through the hidden worship of H/his virility in semen as Prime Creator God, all had to accept the sacredness of pornography and prostitution embedded in H/his religions. We lose nothing in getting rid of purposely created error, obscenity, and large-scale evil.

What does it do to a girl's mind when she learns that there are thousands of large brothels, each holding hundreds of girls like herself as sex slaves in every city on the globe for the use of their vaginas to service ten to twenty penises a day to make megabucks for their own-ers? Humanity "in its goodness" doesn't concern itself with the mass disposal of young girls' lives. Men need brothels—or, as the telling goes, there would be that much more violence on earth! 2 = 1 man is the only animal on earth who prostitutes the feme by imprisoning her in large, dirty institutions, keeping her mind untrained, unskilled, unlearned, inexperienced, immature—free/paid sex to enrich the Lords of Broth-els for their Brothers. (Hu)manization denaturalizes the species on a grand scale.

Chapter 10

RETRIEVING IDEAS
TRUE TO REALITY

Truer-to-reality symbols exist. They show that our forebears, preoccupied as they were with survival, had no aim to prejudice language to favor one gender. They made symbols to name things and events with their belief in the *forces in nature* as gods, whom they believed controlled their harsh lives, none was the Supreme Cause-All One, such as *Thor*, thunder; *Ceres*, cereal. Superstition and beliefs, lack of knowledge, drove language.

Today, we know language ought to reflect reality. Manu's subjugation of one gender by law 4,000 years ago resulted in naming Supreme Alpha Males in the Sky, Hu, Brahma, Manu, Ptah, God, Allah, males who spoke all into being by "The Word." As Gods they controlled the clan, the patriarchal ends of higher men.

So it is not surprising that in his preface to *The Ghost in the Machine*, Arthur Koestler (1967) would say that man "contains some built-in error or deficiency predisposing him toward self-destruction." "The proper study of Mankind is Man," Alexander Pope says in his poem "An Essay on Man." The total entry under *woman* in the First Edition of the *Encyclopedia Britannica* (1771) is "the female of man," all believed as gospel Truth to this day.

Aristotle, Aquinas, and Rousseau said that from the true nature of *man* the true nature of education follows logically. If we know what man is, then we can lay down the essentials of adequate education for all men everywhere and always. And so God made planet earth the greatest little whorehouse in the cosmos.

The sapient approach is to discover the logic-affirming *purpose* of mind, both feme and male, using their skills and talents to make true-to-reality symbols, not in duping terms of "H/his essence" as all mighty being. Sapience includes by definition every developing mind in concrete time in relation to all that exists in all societies in which *ut* (he and/or she) is part of and on the same plane with all other life in an inclusive story of life. (*Ut*, pronounced with Continental European *u*, linguistic /y/, as in *musique*, Fr.)

The sapient approach recognizes fem and man as finite, not only for premises from which to deduce the aims of education, but also as a set of *determinants* that show the limits in probabilities to extract their possibilities for the species. Discerning and electing the correct, more rational premises from among probabilities that both logic-affirming animals agree upon is the basis upon which knowledge is developed. Fem and man are the thinkers upon whom rationality stands. *There are no others that develop speech, and so there is no other way to arrive at sound premises, valid knowledge, moral educational aims, and healthy psychological balance.*

But to go this way we must *choose to make* true-to-reality symbols to use. We must change the way we look at reality. Dual *seeing*, sight, and insight make for greater awareness and intelligence. So where an entity or phenomenon exists that is not named in the 4,000-year $2 = 1$ reign of terror, it must be named. And let boymen call these neologisms!

The development of the thinking animal, both physical and cerebral, needs as its end a desirable rational-and-emotive education that only sapient education can bring about. We must see two contributing interworking minds balancing practical rationality with honest emotional experience for moral behavior. This aim is dead in the finking waters of doctrinal life-in-the-H/he-gear. For forty centuries education was for boys. Girls were minimally educated at home; they were not allowed in the halls of higher learning.

I call true-to-reality symbols *rofemtic* because fem exists in reality as thinking agent. The symbol fem names her existence *consonant* with her reality as contributor. Rofemtic names restore rational, logic-affirming symbols. It is patterned after "romantic," because there are thousands of man-based *wor*ds in patriarchal language that we cannot change, and fewer than fifty fem-based ones. Language after 2400 BCE developed to make male dominance. Rofemtic names restore balance in language, important to good reasoning.

Symbols consonant with reality is not a new idea. It looks new because reality sets limits, and limits are not wanted in historicism's 2 = 1 man. Many true-to-reality ideas in pre-Manu times were suppressed, left out, or concealed after Manu's Sloka V. These will seem new because of knowledge withheld for so long, but they are "as old as the hills."

The difficulty in retrieving ancient true-to-reality symbols such as fem is that there was no way to develop fem-based speech. Restoring an old idea makes it look like a neologism, a newly coined symbol for the sake of coining a new symbol. This gives a sense of the magnitude to which *concelation* in revelation made irrationality valid. *Ut* (she and/or he) must see the seminal tactic of hiding true-to-reality ideas.

Tribal loyalty, feodal, faithful → feudal ↔ foi → faith, set up absolute *faith in the manorial Lord*: He was God on His large property. Fem lost *the right* to do her own naming *in manu* as wife of slave. Using the name *fem* reduces "male slave" to mean male only, freeing him from the injustice and violence in having faith in the Lord. Being man entails being male, being fem entails being feme. The two premises reflect reality.

The 2 = 1 (im)morality hinges on feeling Truth in Higher Male/Lord dictating to male-slave man and w-o/man. This gave rise to sloppy emotions in two infantile, irrational men, two "men" kept ignorant to keep them believing in their slave status. I call sloppy/sleazy emotions, *slemotions*. Not all emotions are good. Sloppy ones plead for the false to be Truth. Slemotions are *manu*factured feelings, not genuine. They transcend reality *slaves* "love"(?), the manorial *Lord*, the patriarch. The experiences of the well-balanced self-identified as fem and man have upright feelings to other sapient-identified selves. Soul-feelers make bad actors, almost always superficial and artificial.

It is no surprise that reason; nature, including feme nature; reality; and independent thought are so little valued. Missing ideas, absent data, and false information make it hard for sapiens to be true to themselves, others, and reality. True-to-reality symbols are rational and forthright, not wanted in "man." Truths are inconvenient because facts determine limits and influence truths, the *evidence* of limits in reality are not wanted in infinite 2 = 1 man by infinite 2 = 1 man. Man gifted himself predetermined free will!

The *rofemtic* symbol raises the devalued feme animal that makes symbols, thinks, and does good reasoning to being *fem*. This frees man from being identified as *enslaved-to-the-Lord*. Fem as fem true to reality is more probable, *probabilities* being a characteristic element of scientific and critical thinking. Thus rofemtic concepts restore ratiocentric and *ratiogenic* processes for a more natural, correct, and practical plane for thought and names. This gets fem and man out of the seminal gutter of infinite false language, because the rofemtic attitude reestablishes the factor of *limits*.

Determinants set limits and show the natural fallibility in facts, they respect that critical subjectivity *is* to be balanced *with* forthright, critical objectivity. *I* am a *fem* is both objective (*fem*) and subjective (*I*). The rofemtic attitude achieves balance using the limits set in determinants. *Two* thinking beings are necessary for *balance*. The One does not have the possibility of balance, imposing illogic instead. Determinants are necessary to symbol making because they limit thought.

Restoring duality as two, then, opens the field to fem *with* man as a team. This field does not tolerate "woman *in* man." Two avenues of respect open up for being a thinking animal: respect for body and respect for mind *by definition* necessary to the integral self. This dual basis of *self* for developing self-respect makes possible the *balance* in an integral body-and-mind duality that I call *selfual*, also the source of respect for *other* thinking *self* (objective) *with* respect for my *self* (subjective). Duality is more creative than dualism. Two members = two truths = the possibility for balance. Two in duality opens to diversity and plurality. Duality is the basis of plurality. 1 = 1 = 1 for eternity.

In 2 = 1, the only possibilities are selfish and selfless, both undesirable. When feudalism was being torn down, priests in the pulpit preached to their captive audiences that "the negro had no soul." Manorial and Ecclesiastical Lords had *the right* to own slaves. Soul is not about mind and body. And "spirit" is suspect since it is derived from the same root as sperm, Gr., *speiro*. Selfish and selfless are patriarchal prescriptions for the gendered roles of fathers and mothers in being loyal to the Lord; this fit the aims of slavery.

Selfual includes the *other* self and *my* self, two *by definition* in respect for my mind and my body, fem with man two *by definition*. *Selfual* names the dual basis of respect for myself *with* the respect for other self, inclusive by definition and by intention in the symbol *selfual*. This symbol is more fully explained later in the chapter.

In 2 = 2, the problem-finding question is, "What are fem and man as thinking life?" In 2 = 1 romantic belief, the big Solve-All Question is, "What is man?" The answer: Get better control of the masses or declare war on the enemy. So what follow are symbols that we likely had forty centuries ago and should have now. This is why they look "new."

Ut is a third-agent pronoun for "she and/or he." The term *uter*, L., means "both as/of each," and/or "each as/of both." Since much of English is based in Latin through French, *uter* in *utervis, uterque,* and *uterus* denotes two by definition. Since the English tradition often does the chop-chop on foreign symbols, I shortened "uter" to *ut*. The base morpheme "ut" carries the concept of each as both or *both of each,* affirming the logic of duality as two. *Ut is an inclusive pronoun based on solid etymological ground working for the common good of all.* It is inclusive *by definition* and consonant with reality.

Ut, third-agent singular pronoun for he and/or she is short and economical, like "it" and "us," useable and effective in all situations where necessary. From here on I use "ut" to show that it is better than the awkward, tedious, long "she and/or he" that has the mysterious quirk of crawling back to the exclusive "generic he."

Ut includes both fem and man, each as gender-different, logic-affirming agents. It is the only other pronoun we need. *Ut* has an affinity with "us," initial *u*, and with *it*, final *t*. Ut is economical since it denotes "each as both or both of each," where duality is the case. Ut respects both thinkers by including both. This breaks the patriarchal embezzlement of being the superior One by generic "he."

2 = 2 is a law in reality and not new. Laws abide in determinants. Duality exists and ought to be so *by definition in symbol and name* for intellectual economy, showing limits. We need and ought to want inclusive concepts that set up truths as guides to elicit moral behavior.

2 = 1 tells us that laws are to be broken when it suits One's whims. Lesser men who turn "criminal" put this into practice.

First, the feme animal that makes and uses sound symbols to communicate, think, and ratiocinate in reality is fem. Her reasoning mind is now respected. Second, this rofemtic concept stating fact *and truth* calls for the respect of every *other self* with a mind, and thus by definition includes respect for male mind by the law 2 = 2. *Selfual* respects both selves by definition because it includes both thinkers: It respects the limits in the law 2 = 2.

Selfual, adjective, goes to *selfuality* as noun. Like sex → sexual → sexuality. Selfuality is strength of mind to do independent thinking using true-to-reality symbols and ideas acquired through the development of respect for both minds. Where fem (feme) respects mind in man (male), respect is forthrightly given to both by definition. Fem and man each develop a definition of *self*. Ut cannot have a soul, spirit, or homunculi as a part "higher" than the self that goes to heaven, illogic and irrationality that justifies patriarchy.

The wisdom in *respect for the self* of both can only be named *sapience making ourselves wise by the symbols we make* that elicit respect. Sapience does not embezzle propaganda for anyone. It appeals to the wisdom in obeying laws seen in reality and nature.

In the probability that two gender-different members exist is the possibility for balance and justice. Balance is a possibility where fem is *with* man in the enterprise of developing the mind with the body and what the self can do, *isonomy* being necessary here.

Isonomy (registered in lexicons) is to name the respect of using logic in naming. Where there are two, both feme and male must be named in isonomic terms: fem, feme, and man, male. Mind common to both is named in both its different and similar aspects, each having its own value in name, *iso*, equal, *nomy*, name. This is being true to reality.

Isonomy uses gender as a category for classification, not as a division to split man-mind from woman-body. In isonomic definition, both have mind and body energies to be integrated in a *selfual* and mature femhood or manhood. Both fem and man have minds and bodies to be developed as sapiens, wise selves, selves neither good nor bad in themselves. Both have energies to bring the self to reflect the originality born in each individual being living life in the collective identified in ut's own name.

Selfual originality comes from reason, ratiocination, and honest emotions, for selfuality needs the knowledge of and about our selves to feed the common good. It is to develop skills of good discernment so necessary in a cosmos so full of small, important differences *for sapient innovation*. The fact of selfual originality lets us see that mind ought to be educated with correct information to bring out its originality.

Dittoing in patriarchy brings out masculinisms, Jim Jones, Conrad Black, George Bush, Enron's "higher men," bin Laden, Koresh, Stalin, Madoff.

The honest emotions invested in 2 = 2 are such that balance is possible because ut's reasoning capabilities are educated to be in harmony with ut's emotions. The attitude to harmony in the integration of body and mind in view of self and other self for self-identity raises the value of reasoning in individual minds where both minds are on the same plane and in the same playing field on planet earth. Where there is no fair play or justice, slemotions explode on the scene.

The value of good reasoning to mature self-development goes without saying. The human propaganda machine so distorted issues as "The Truth" that there is no name for "in praise of good reasoning." Another absent symbol! Historicism even called reason a whore! Name one situation where unreason or irrationality solves the problem? Neither faith, slemotions, nor irrationality ever solved a problem. We need reason-based symbols reflecting reality-as-it-is, *ratiogenic* symbols. Anything else is useless.

Ratiogenic means the source of further good reasoning, *ratio*, proportion, balance + *genic*, source, origin. Symbols based in reason, true to reality, are the source of further good reasoning. Opposite-wise exchanging *irratiogens* such as w-o-man in man = species is the silly futile exercise of swapping favorite lies. But ratiogenic does not exist in 2 = 1 man speech. This explains why we do not also have irratiogenic, even when we have effeminate but not feminate! (Cf. carcinogenic, cancer-causing, coined decades ago.)

Reason is determined by the laws that determine logic, what is in reality, the relationships in nature seen by our eyes, in the mind, and felt in our emotions; experience in circumstances, time, place, chance, and so on, all determinants. Reason is not only logic or logic going it alone. Reasoning respecting determinants also helps us to see and name things correctly to make ratiogenic symbols.

What exists in nature and reality, the laws of logic, inference, relationships between cause and effect, hard evidence, experience, and our genetic make-up as mind-body selves are not infinite. What is limitless? Maybe numbers are—but most things in the cosmos are finite. The fact that science arrives at *probabilities* shows that things have limits determined by rules and laws in the nature of their matter: Multiple causes cause multiple effects, few of which are infinite. There is no such thing as a One Almighty Cause-All Male in the Sky causing an Infinite Split-by-Gender Effect, *special man* above all other life.

Ratiogenics by definition are symbols that name determinants, the finiteness of things showing the limits in reality. Even abstract ideas such as *in* are finite, determined by reality. W-o-*man* "in" man confounds limits. Fem *with* man does not. Like reality, ideas have limits because they are determined by the logic in reality in spite of reality's apparent chaos. Fem with man has much more creative potential than w-o-man in man.

But determinants are not welcome in 2 = 1 man; they limit Him too much. Limits demand accountability. Accountability demands maturity. Determinants place limits that determine a criterion for objectivity. In limitless 2 = 1 special man, belief and believer are seamless, above law, why you are not to judge both the belief and the believer. But determinants and limits exist and must be reflected in symbol. Fem and sapience posit limits that exist, positing the respect for limits at the same time. Respect is a multifaceted emotion, and developing it is a long, steep climb to sapient maturity.

What is in reality and nature determines that we reason according to the limits in them, and this is what helps our species make ratiogenic symbols, names to use to further rational thought. *Ratiogenic* did not become a symbol in humanity because it is about making true-to-reality symbols that cause further good reasoning. When the isonomic equivalence in speech using male, man, with speech-using feme, fem, communicating duality existing in reality, it causes a further ratiogenic effect, *balance.*

The repetitiousness in the ideology 2 = 1 man in "The Word" cannot even begin to do balance. It rides on extremes of man split into two opposite men, one having limitless value, and w-o-man having little value as a man who's not a man.

Limits and determinants are related like form and matter. The giraffe and the squirrel both have organic matter, different. Both have form different in size, shape, skin; it is important to see how form and matter operate in reality. The key to understanding the multiplicity of life forms is also in the duality of matter *with* form, both finite.

The limits in our matter and form containing our minds that put together sight, insights, laws of reasoning, relationships between cause and effect, and material evidence determine thinking life, limiting the self in reality. The thinker as individual in the collective is determined by limits set in the reality of being both (1) individual and (2) in the collective. Sexual, physical, and cerebral energies, finite, limit what we do. Limits are central to *the common good* necessary for the survival of thinking life; seeing Q is Q, ut sees 2 = 2. This gives ut useful knowledge limiting the integral energy in *sapienity,* the synergy of two *different* sexual energies in, with, and through two *similar* cerebral energies. So the responsibility to see reality-as-it-is invites ut to (1) want and (2) need to mature into a moral selfual being, because in reality the sapien, like everything else, is neither good nor bad in utself. Ut contributes to *the common good* by being a ratiogenic animal: To *do* good thinking is to *be* a morally mature individual, a sapien in the full sense of the name, wise.

Oppositely in hu-manity, two men of opposite genders born in sin are perfect-imperfect creatures of God. This is a source of limitless irratiogenics and nonsense.

Sapienity leads and takes itself to *wisdom* by respecting limits, since it is rational to reason to arrive at truths. Isonomy makes the members in sapienity by definition wiser in naming the limits that exist *in themselves.* The inference in acknowledging that two finite speech makers and users—who must obey the rules of logic—different in gender, posits sapient synergy that comes from the integration of sexed-body energy with mind energy, neither of which is limitless.

Isonomy, ratiogens, and selfual are not named in Doctrinal One. How do you integrate One limitless mind? Limitlessness imposes total assimilation of the not-one "in" the One—not integration defined by "with." Providence/predetermination/free will displace reality's determinants because belief displaces knowledge—like w-o-man displaces fem.

The rofemtic true-to-reality symbol respects mind. Few if any symbols define *sufficient mind* in 2 = 1 man. Hatred of mind is embedded in 2 = 1 man's lingo of the *soul*, a name that allows H/him to ignore mind. Ideas respecting mind must be named after their 4,000-year-old sabotage. So these are the words that may appear "new" but are not:

a. **Selfual**. We *need* a name for balance in the relationship between body and mind. The extremes, selfish and selfless, do not do the job. Selfual allows ut to talk about the self-determined, self-defined, self-limited body and mind defining the attributes in *self* and *other self*, each as indivi/sible dual/ities, individuals. In reality, mind and body do not divide into body/fe + male—selfless id and mind/male—selfish ego. Selfual development is *to create an identity* using ut's self-interest *with* the other's self-interest, a rational empathic method creating balance imbued with fairness. *No self develops in isolation.*

Aware of the limits in the indivisible *integer*-of-*self*, the roles of both subject (I) and object (me) are respected with *the other's self-interest* also as both I and me. Consideration of "other" in selfual identity aims at balance in ut's indivisible duality *by definition.*

Dual*ism*, selfless wo*man*/body *in* ego-possessing selfish man/mind forces disparity and injustice. The One has a *soul* that rises to heaven at death, his body now three parts: mind, body, and soul. It is bad enough to split mind and body by gender, splitting *self* into holy part—soul—higher, and sin-based part—flesh—lower, expands *the common evil*. This is why we badly need the concept selfual for *the common good.*

Selfual respects mind with concrete body in indivisible self. It respects both feme and male bodies having minds to develop integral selves who consider their animal duality, rationality, morality, and mortality head on, not afraid to do so.

Seeing two where two exist in reality respects natural limits. The respect of limits, facing the truths in limits is the biggest measure of maturity. Ut cannot walk through a table or on water. *Sapience* is the conscious energy/will to be practically good and morally mature by choosing to obey limits, rules, and laws in reality.

Free will, the unaccountable right to make life an intellectual, psychological, and physical hell via the magic of providence, determined that "lower" beings be dictated to in phallic slogans such as Protagoras's "man is the measure of all things," where being man in reality entails *only* being male abides. Language praises men as superior.

Selfual works at balance, mature individuality sensitive to other selves. Ut's differences from others and others' similarities to one's self are respected in the *process of integration*. This road to real maturity uses limits creatively. For one, logic limits thought, which, by the way, almost always surprises us in its capacity to help us innovate, create, and invent. Moreover, mature individuality is always more interesting than quirky individual*ism* oozing preboxed beliefs in fantabulous faith-based mantasy-fantasy.

The respect for other self is in the symbol selfual by definition. Dual self-interest sees male and feme as subject and object in mind and body, giving everyone the real possibility to mature to moral individuality with less strife and confusion. *Selfual* is as necessary to sapient mind as food, air, and water are to body. No *self* lives in isolation of others; therefore, no *self* develops in isolation of other *selves* and this process is now named, we can now talk about the selfual fem and selfual man.

b. **Gynility**. Gynility, from *gyne*, Gr., fem, the feme sex drive, *gyne* too is underused as a generating morpheme. Virility without gynility is bullying, aggressive, unaccountable sex drive, violent, like water without oxygen is hydrogen, undrinkable.

To take the lie, the anti-rational or irratiogenic Word of Higher Man out to reinstate missing information and restore as much factual data as possible, we need gynility, the strong sexual-drive energy and will in fem, named and made public to see feme strength in her mind and body. Gynility makes fem forge ahead in the search for truths, necessary to the relationships between fem and man for drawing up a *sapient* social contract *to create a history of balance-in-truths and truths-in-balance to further the project of integrated truths and correct information for the purpose of civilization.*

c. **Gynobase**. Gynobase is not new, but it was used only in relation to plants. It also concerns sapiens as the basis of investigation into sapient problems and doing better *problem finding* that leads to problem solving. All species problems involve fem, half the species, as much as they involve man, the other half of the species.

What problem does not affect the whole species? Problem solving by asking, "What is man?" is damage control. Man excludes fem. "The perfectibility of man" as man and woman is not achievable; the dual*ism* of man-mind controlling wo*man*-body is immoral at the start. "What really is prostitution" is not asked in 2 = 1 man. "Who is to blame," the biblical "she," the mindless object of H/his phallic desire "to know woman"? He *stud/*ies the "hu*man* condition" and *matri/*culation tells H/him that he must ask, "What is man" to solve man's thorny problems—back to solipsism and Manu.

d. **Gynex**. Gynex is the point in thinking development where rational and objective energies *with* the emotional and subjective energies relate fairly in fem and man, sapiens. The four-feet-on-the-ground view based on the integral thesis of fem's feeling-and-thinking *with* that of man's feeling-and-thinking, each valued as utself, is set in down-to-earth practical theory transparent to the average mind. The thinking species *can* name rationally and *can* classify correctly and *be* emotionally committed to the truths of their animal nature as sapiens.

The point achieved in integrating fem's and man's emotional and intellectual theses in a *consonant* thesis is *sufficient mind*, the ground for thinking. Oppositely, limitless finking-in-all-directions-at-once centering-on-special-man is imposed on the species.

e. **Kinethics**. Kinethics is the dynamic interactive ethics that includes all life forms related by fem and man doing what sentient-minded animals evolved to do: make *sound-bites-reflecting-reality*—on the *same* natural physical plane with all other animals and other life forms existing in reality. Kinethics by definition is respect for the equality of non-symbolic and symbolic animals to hold a moral kinship with all of them. All life forms have systems of communication specific to their kind or species. Man as "higher" is a violation of ethics that causes programs of extinction, species genocide, programmed mass pollution, global waste, the irrational manmass, and serial warring.

Kinethics are the relationships sapiens make with *the multiplicity of life forms* on planet earth. Multiple causes, multiple life (forms.) A rational symbolic system furthers ratio-emotive ethics in fem and man as animals *with* other animal life and life forms. The preposition is *with*, not higher—or "in" man. Morality demands no less.

Ethics that include all life forms considers life in its plurality and multiple causes. This cannot be denied. But murderous saints, preying angels, and higher men of god, special, not animal, find it hard to see how ethics is related to what *being competent, rational, speech-using animals* really means to *animal* life such as w-o-man.

Psychological, moral, and social advantages are brought to all life by the mutual respect done between *selfual* beings and non-symbolic, communicating animals. Kin, related, + ethics replaces the false religio-secular, from-the-top-down (immoral) "ethics" preached by higher-than-animal Lords—who make mind *deficient* in order to control it. When ut speaks of law or medicine, ut speaks of ethics; when ut speaks of life, ut speaks of *kinethics*, the all-inclusive relatedness of life.

f. **Matrimorphosis**. Matrimorphosis is the changing of the patriarchal religio-secular-politico-lexical paradigm of Father Subject/Lord/Ego and Mother Object/body/id to two equivalent inter-*in*dependent, fallible thinking beings, fem and man, in sapienity. Reality facilitates the integration of the mother as mind-and-body *with* father as mind-and-body in common knowledge and society. When the mother is subject, fem speaking for herself, respect for mind is a constant aim, and this is to the common good of all life, including non-symbolic animal life.

g. **Egorithm**. Egorithm is the natural rhythm in *selfual* egos developed in the full awareness of ut's own duality *with* that of other aware selves, action done in reason-based emotions resulting in *sapient* behavior. It is the balance of critical thinking and upright emotions done by fem and man. This natural rhythm is destroyed in 2 = 1, "opposites" are on separate planes, the minded One higher, selfish, and the opposite, lower, mind-less, selfless, and thus enemies. Enemy making destroys the rhythm of possible selfual egos in fem and man as two empathic thinking, feeling animals *natural* by fact of evolution.

h. **Egonomics**. Egonomics is the emotional economy in the dual-based development of the self (saving fem and man time and energy misspent on ideas in opposition set up in 2 = 1) to do what is necessary to achieve balance to be a natural species, sapiens. Integrating the egos of isonomically defined fem and men in their relationship with each other and other animal species to achieve balance. This is a *new* task, demanding *new* skills. But limits set in duality 2 = 2, is the basis of measure for maturity. Because selfual individuality includes *other selves* by definition in the making of a *self*-identity, this makes the skills easier to learn. It is an exercise of twos in consonance with one another and reality, like two front wheels *with* two back wheels do the act of balance to make a car run.

Limits make egos stay in proportion to their mind and body self-reflective capabilities, natural. Egonomics, 2 fem and man who feel = 2 egos for measuring egorithm, include empathy for and mutual cooperation with others' *good*, necessary for an orderly society. An ego based on selfual being, upright emotions, and rational thought is more likely to behave in a forthright and clear way. Where split-by-gender is the rule, big egos rage in irrationality and non-egos suffer in manned ignorance.

i. **Ratiogenic**. *Genic*, source, *ratio*, bearing related proportion. Ratio-genics name cause and effect correctly logical and are the source of further logic, since logic and straight thinking respect the limits in reality and nature in minded animals.

    Respect for mind in body with respect and use of ratiogenics is the heart of the rofemtic concept: making and using true-to-reality symbols. The romantic 2 = 1 man loves irratiogens and psychesthenia, the weak mind. *Psychephisis, strength of mind* is not named in Patriarchal English. Strength of mind and strength of fem are unnamed in 2 = 1 man. Ratiogenic symbols will heal the insult of psychesthenia, weak mind, and replace it with *psyche-phisis*, strong mind. Mind is strong where true-to-reality symbols, ratiogenics, abide.

j. **Siology**. Siology is the science of *see*ing the same thing with the objective eye that ut *sees* with the subjective eye. Where consonance exists between the objective and the subjective, the consonance necessary to truths is more likely to be present, then and only then can an actual consensus be achieved regarding problems concern-ing the whole species. Problem finding leading to problem solving helps to see the contradictions, disconnects, and confusions embed-ded in the insolvable problems of 2 = 1 man. Ut needs to find and see the relevant issues and evidence in problems that help to do better problem solving.

    We name the cosmos. We create *the common good*. Being objec-tive-by-purpose must be proportional to being subjective-by-nature. Respecting reality-as-it-is makes us as objective as we can be with being as subjective as we are by our nature in making symbols to use. *See*ing what is there to be seen, not making up something that cannot be seen or is not there, arrives at useable knowledge. See-ing through the intellectual "eyes," (I) with what ut sees through ut's physical eyes (me), puts in*sight* in consonance with physical *sight*. *Siology*, from "si," in sight + ology names the science of sight *with* insight. Pronounced see + ology, *siology* is the science of *see*ing reality-as-it-is in both perspectives to make correct symbols. (Vision, *vise*, Fr., to aim sight → wise, like vine → wine.)

Siology lines up what the physical eye sees with what the mind sees. Consonance and consistency, the hallmarks in dual seeing, Q is Q affirms $2 = 2$ to avoid passing off any further $2 = 1$ cryptic formula. Siology sees and uses the limits in being feme and male thinking animals and what fem *with* man can do. Limits highlight the possibilities in the probabilities in being fem and man.

■　　■　　■

I would venture to say that few achieve healthy long-term self-esteem in $2 = 1$ parasitic life. The "ises and is nots" do not enhance life of the self. They fill it with strife and *un*necessary violence, because "needs" such as outside-of-nature Lords abide. Naming missing information puts truths in sharp contrast with the lies in mantasy-fantasy ideology passed off as theory. Anyone passing off *special* subjectivism as man's objectivity is being thoroughly disingenuous. It is necessary to restart the rational-with-emotional capabilities naturally existing in sapiens committing to truths for solid life-long self-esteem.

Ratiogenics and siology further this aim. What sapiens need and must want as thinking animals are ratiogenics, true-to-reality symbols that advance all minds in slower, more even-paced natural steps toward being a thinking species. I see no other purpose for which the brain evolved. *Living thinking life is the most fulfilling adventure of all.*

Unfortunately, the totalitarian *in manu* ethos penetrated the species. A species bred on irrationality lying to guard it is not about thinking. When moral choice is between lies embedded in language, it redirects *sapient* behavior into *hu*man behavior, silly, nonsensical, and immoral at the core. It is the incredible case of Manu, one man, in his unjust law, sending mind racing off in the wrong direction for 4,000 years! It is the biggest crime against the mind ever committed.

If you think a repeat performance is not possible, simply look at the wave of fundamentalisms, conservatisms, and traditionalisms camouflaging new violence between religions, sweeping planet earth. In 2 = 1 climate, there is always another free-will loophole. Dean Hamer wrote a book called *The God Gene*. He claims faith is hardwired into our genes. If that is the case, then we also have a Jolly Green Giant gene, a unicorn gene, a missile defense gene, a war gene—the list is limitless—back to Manu!

The individual, the one, has duties to the many, the whole species, in the aim toward the sapient goal of correct thinking and upright feeling. The individual is equivalent in value with the collective or species. Balance between the individual acting in, with, and through the collective is possible only when the truths *fem with man*, each as individuals, make up society/the species. Moral fem with moral man make moral societies. Rational fem and rational man make a rational society more likely to lead to moral societies.

Make one logic-affirming agent voiceless, worthless, and powerless "in" man, and H/he makes irrational and immoral society—by himself. He, Adam and God, named her w-o-man, showing that he is no more rational than w-o-man. He made two irrational men of opposite genders = mankind, where being man in reality entails only being male. This irrationality creates the immoral as model for behavior.

Chapter 11

THE ISSUES IN DIFFERENCES AND SIMILARITIES

In 2 = 1 man, gender difference divides and separates mind from body. In reality-as-it-is, gender differences in body act in, with, and through the similarities of mind in both fem and man.

Consciousness is not a mystery. Nor is it a "gift," a soul gifted from an outside mind. All the sensual data and experiences coming into the brain create streams of thoughts running back and forth from object (me) to subject (I) on neurons and synapses to make the awareness of self in the mind, consciousness. We are *self-reflective* by the fact of being self-aware. Our *self-reflective* nature makes us identify our self-aware self in name. It is what sapiens do; identify the self. Like bees make honey, sheep make wool, and beavers make dams.

When fem has no choice but to identify herself as a man named by man, her rights in natural law are wiped out. She is made insignificant as to what constitutes mind. There is no mystery here. Sapiens can name good aims and goals in truths to create moral societies, or they can embed lies, creating the chaos of irrationality in the species.

Thinking changes and enhances our species. It is a qualitative difference from all other animals. Our similarity is our quantitative animal similarity in relation to all other animals. We *are* animals that make and use symbols to articulate our self-reflective natures, consciousness. Making and using symbols is central to being conscious. A child who does not learn the symbol system can hardly *reflect* upon utself. Symbols as names are the tools to build self-reflective talents, aims, identity, consciousness, and self-esteem.

To *be* sapiens is to relate experience, memory, and reality in the mind. This does not make us superior to or above other animals, just different from them. The mind cannot make us supernatural entities; it does not allow us to transcend our animal nature to walk on water, fly in the sky, or zap-in solve-all prophets. We have to *do* thinking to *be* sapiens, relate experiences, name existing entities, and state facts using the symbols we ourselves make to be used.

Objectivity in mind activity, then, is to external life what subjectivity in mind activity is to internal life. Who is going to say that internal life is lower or of less value than external life? Is public life higher than private life? How does one live external without the internal life? If one does not think correctly in ut's internal life, how is ut to think correctly in ut's external life? Splitting external/public from internal/private cannot achieve consonance-in-self, because this is the same old 2 = 1 splitting of creature-mind from creature-body. Life is seamless, not split and filed in separate *opposing* compartments.

Symbol making, the public/social act of naming ideas, is a sapient talent in both fem and man. Symbol using is both public and private. Fem were not allowed the public sphere of speech for forty centuries, so her symbols were banned. Since public man hardly ever divulged his private opinions, and fem as woman hardly ever experienced the public realm of speech, neither would achieve consonance-in-self to achieve an integrated self. Two dissonant men of "opposite" genders made one illogical, irrational, and immoral mankind.

The commonality/*similarity* of mind in fem and man exists. Both have minds that can enhance their lives by the thinking they do. The similarity of mind distinguishes both-as-each-of-two thinking animals within the same species. Mind is similarity; body is difference. Gender difference in body impacts on mind similarity; it makes two gender-differentiated beings, two sapiens; they cannot both be man in forced-together opposites. ***Both must respect the laws of logic to be logic-affirming beings.***

Mind *has* the talent to categorize correctly, to discern differences in similarities. Darwin certainly knew how to read differences in similarities. There is no escape from the limits set in differences and similarities. It is when difference is embezzled in gender-as-division of mind and body that lies in false names flow. In sapienity, mind is mind in both fem and man, a category in science. Just as every tree, pearl, and giraffe is valued for itself, every fem and man is valued for utself; mind is respected as mind in every sapien *by definition*. The differences and similarities in reality are welcome.

I realize debunking the traditional hierarchy of men will be viewed as creating a *lack of order* in man's world; I may even be labeled anarchist. But who or what has the most value? Without air or water there is no life. How can creature-mind be more important than the planet we walk on to exist? In fact, the hierarchy man made destroys the natural order in chaos. Wouldn't it be boring—and weird—if all tall trees (good) grew behind all shorter trees (bad)? Wouldn't it be confusing if all marsupials were named kangaroos? Creature-minds stand above all creature-bodies—then invent "the *soul*" for salvation! Using body, size, color, shape, and genitals, the species are "ordered" according to + or – male. There is a place for hierarchy, but gender is not its Creator! This is to use gender destructively.

Some determinants are set in differences, others in similarities. Determinants limit. Sapiens cannot fly; they have no wings. No fem or man can kill for food; they do not have claws. They cannot see in the dark. We are determined by our mind-and-body makeup, its upright configuration, highly flexible hands, eyes that see in color, and brain that evolves self in the mind through symbols. *Differences* distinguish us from giraffe, monkey, and titmouse. Differences distinguish entities one from the other.

Mind, fem and man's similarity, has limits because the brain, physical, limits mind. Limits are what give us the much-sought-after freedom, the will to act and create as sapiens. We do not have the free will to be a "flock of sheep"—needing a Shepherd imposing woolly, free-will ideas in false-to-reality symbols, finking lies. The limits of difference between fem and man are mostly physical; estrogens and testosterones influence how we *see*, affecting emotional life. Semen does not possess limitless magic giving H/him divinity as mind. Like it or not, both must use logic to do thinking.

We have the will to use the limits of the brain in order to develop the self as sapient, thinking entity. If rivers had no limits, all would be flood; the water could not be harnessed for use. When mind in Lords has no limits/free will, H/he "speaks" nonsense into being. What good is a limitless finking manmass poisoning rationality with irrationality? Differences and similarities are determinants that must be respected for learning how to reason logically. For the following reasons, both kinds of determinants must be respected:

a. ***Both feme and male mind have the same cerebral determinants.*** The brain is a physical organ in both; therefore, neither male nor feme mind is limitless. Limitlessness vomits conjectures of every size, shape, color, and race using gender as axe to divide valued from non-valued members. Thousands of religions, each with their own racist-sexist-classist God/Lord, seminate the world with the purity of their holy conjecture; "The Truth" is far easier to believe than seeking out the facts to find finite multiple truths.

b. ***Both fem and man have memory.*** Historicism makes memory problematic; under "the doctrine of man," the story out of parish theocracies and secular patriarchies is not about what is true to reality. It is about *man* (as man and woman), mind and memory so altered by patent lies; the need is for a Holy Father to soften the blow of built-in inequity and injustice to make you *accept your lot* in life. Born in the violence of original sin, the Father-Subject-and-Mother-Object paradigm in man institutionalizes inequity-with-suffering. Lies about ourselves are memory; the only justice is in the Lord's heaven, for it certainly is not to be found in hell on earth.

Memory serves us best when we accumulate truths named in true-to-reality symbols. When fem is fem with man as man is put in our memory, these ratiogenic truths make thinking easier. We *can* use facts to make a society committed to doing good reasoning to act for the common good. From the accumulation of facts and truths, *sufficiency of mind* is realized. Then we have no need for moneyed props, Lord gods, airy-fairy whips of religions, cults, magic tricks, false sciences, and parasitic systems ensuring that the common evil of mutual enslavement to a big lie be upheld—as God's *providence.*

Truths and facts in our memory are efficacious in defining sapiens as sapiens, since the indivi/duality of the self is respected in every member. Ut is valued for utself from birth *by definition*, and this makes self-respect more efficient, a firm foundation for self-esteem.

c. ***Both fem and man have to learn what it is to be sapiens from birth.*** The young of almost all species must pass through a learning stage to be a competent member of their species. In sapienity, learning is complex. Ut learns *similarities* and *differences* to categorize, the method of duality, which needs more time. Learning how to think is a long process of purposeful experience, method, memory, and knowledge, taking twenty to twenty-two years to reach the competency, independence, and maturity necessary for good relationships among inter-independent individuals in ut's species. Ut learns to be an honest self, not needing special props or false comforts, since ut sees others affirming that what is fact is indeed correct and moral. In the process, wants and needs are redefined and realigned for coherence.

To learn the symbolic system at all, no being with the potential and capability to use symbols can live in isolation of others. No one can learn alone. Self-interest without interest-in-other-self leads to the selfish big #1 "I" in *MeMyselfandI Inc.*, arrogantly dependent on an outside mind, God, watching over big #1 me, *special* in His eyes, as man's big, fragile, selfish ego dictates lies to the selfless muted "id" w-o + man. From its very beginning *in Manu*, children memorize the "me superior, you inferior" axiom in sexism, racism, class, and irrationality.

There is little in sapienity that is not influenced by the symbols we make and use. For the common good of all, ut learns to reflect on reality-as-it-is in symbol, to be as correct a thinker as possible by learning/being taught true-to-reality symbols. With selfual development entailing other self *by definition*, ut can arrive at a level of maturity not afraid of facts. No child learns by H/himself; many others of both genders teach the child. *Selfual* learning is learning with the reality of what other selves see in order to see that ut is upholding the same rational level of consistency in ut's sight and thought processes expressed in symbol, the major tool of communication. This means that selfual development in sapience has checks and balances—and this is clearly due to limits set in reality's determinants in differences and similarities impacting on the brains and minds of both fem and man.

d. ***Both fem and man have self-awareness, consciousness.*** Learning the symbol system as a child, ut develops consciousness of utself by seeing "the other self" from which *identity of self* starts to evolve. "I" subject/"me" object are clearer in view of other self, *you* subject and *I* object and vice versa. Mind integrating with body identifies a self where being object and subject is a dual process in the indivi-dual.

When "The Word" dictates a third "man," a *soul*, is it selfish? To deal with facts that aim at neither selfish nor selfless, ut aims at the dual basis in developing *selfually*. Ut is educated to integrate other self in the definition of utself, preventing ut from becoming selfish or selfless with a *soul* to save. Selfual self-awareness gains the strength to uphold the truths in reality, including mortality. Ut deals competently and fearlessly with truths because it has correct information about mind, body, self, society, nature—and death. Ut acquires the skills to discern and evaluate similarities in differences and differences in similarities. Sapiens define selves for life and living, not as souls for salvation in death for God-man's glory. Ut has no fear of death, ut does not live for heaven, ut lives for life. Ut knows that when ut dies ut's consciousness stops, that ut's life has been lived.

e. ***Both fem and man have the responsibility to make correct symbols.*** Language is not a gift; it is twenty million years of hard trial and error learning to acquire sound-with-meaning skills. Imposing belief in "resurrection after death" carries no responsibility to be rational, mature, or moral. Creating knowledge in the very act of making correct and reason-based true-to-reality symbols useable to live life as a logic-affirming being defines maturity. The most important inalienable/natural birthright sapiens have, then—since the aim is rationality and truths—is the *right to correct information.* **This right does not exist in any 2 = 1 constitution on planet earth!** When have you ever gotten the real truth from your state, institution, corporation, community—or church? In God-fearing *hu*manity, there is little responsibility to give out correct information. Proofs: (1) w-o/man, (2) *in*, (3) man, three lies that make a big lie.

In the so-called modern world, reporting on the state of the nation is common, reporting on the state of the citizens, seldom, reporting on the state of the mind, never. This is clearly because large amounts of correct information are missing in 2 = 1 man.

The single most important and most basic right in sapiency is *the right to correct information.* The category of gender is the category of gender, not a division of mind and body splitting two into men of valued and non-valued men. Fem, feme, and being sapiens are facts acquired from doing correct categorization. Consistency in thought for consonance between symbol and reality is necessary to obtain and assert facts.

This *right* by its very nature entails *the irrevocable responsibility* to pass *correct information* to the young. In critical and moral thinking, ut cannot speak of rights without responsibilities. All legislative bills to this effect should be Bills of Responsibilities and Rights, since rights mostly issue from responsibilities, not the other way around.

The reason for this is that rights in, with, and through responsibilities have checks and balances. Ut learns to respect reality's determinants and limits rationally and creatively. I do not see facts as "cold and hard," but as full of potential to create. Nor does using facts turn one into a robot. I see 2 = 2 and Q is Q as bases for creating the *common good*, a firm foundation for self-esteem, self-motivation, and creative innovation. Morality cannot be honestly defined devoid of selfual responsibilities. Rights only make the slemotional "I want!" explode, all too obvious in "mankind." Man's sex "rights" attest to this!

Responsibilities in consonance with rights are what maturity is about. Sapien responsibilities with rights are communicated in true-to-reality symbols.

g. ***Both fem and man are in society/the collective, each as individuals.*** Despite many animals having complex social systems, none name their social systems, only sapiens do. Few animals enhance their social arrangements. They are not conscious and self-aware like sapiens. An infant sapien needs up to twenty-two years to learn the symbolic communication in ut's association with others that leads to the integration/identity of a consonant self, a self at home in the cosmos, a self ready to live an inclusive, rational, thinking life with others as sapiens.

Dichotomizing two as opposites to meld them into one, only to split them into higher and lower men is irrational. Creature-mind and creature-body make smut and *the common evil* that drips into individual and social consciousness. The process of its percolation suffers hundreds of prejustified *in semino* fantasies as Absolute Truth. The young cannot see indivi*dual* responsibility in splits; dumbed down by facile falsehoods, they react—dumbly—and become narcissist individualists on the defensive, selfish or selfless.

In sapienity, both fem and man, each as utself, are both subject and object in self-awareness. There is no mystery in this. Seeing utself as animal and thinker does not make ut boring, banal, ultra fashionable—or above all other animals. Fear is not a mind-controlling device in logic-affirming individuals. In reality, ut is both subject and object.

The $2 = 1$ ideology/theology/manuology uses fear to stop ut from examining what H/he imposes as Truth. Fear mongering is big business. Bullying everyone into the "human condition"—violent, obscene, and sex crazed—is immoral, tragic, and joyless. Male divinity is smuggled in as the "mysterious more" of man—semen being the first principle of everything—fabulous and awe striking. Mystery is the best way to dupe. Such lies take the joy out of doing good reasoning and the pleasure out of living a thinking life in the beauty that is (was) planet earth.

Where two minded selves are not in consonance with nature, reality, and society, all lose. The Truth in man is higher than the many truths seen in reality. Is Nature higher than nature? Is Man higher than man? It may be apt to say that *confusion* comes from the conned fusion of melding two into one. Etymological dictionaries do not explain symbols in relation to other symbols. *Why* is Truth higher than the many truths?

In sapienity, every individual is an inter-independent self not afraid of facts in the face of brick-wall resistance to the 4,000-year-long $2 = 1$ man who wants to get away with self-flattering lies and false comforts. Facts give ut strength and equanimity. Fact: Self and other selves make up society. This does not make things easy, but it is the difference that tells between selfual creative individuality and conforming $2 = 1$ selfish and selfless individual*isms*. Zig—power, money, and sex work wonders in humanity; zag—to be God fearing bestows morality! Man does not a species make; H/he makes a manmass.

The many is everyone as individuals each responsible for ut's own thought behavior in the collective; where ut receives correct information, ut will be a better citizen in ut's society. The *correct item of information* that is/ought to be in knowledge is the fact-based symbol. Where two "men" accept irrational self-identities, society is a bogus entity. A believing, glued-together-by-lies society is not a society; it is a manmass walking robotically in lockstep behind an *a priori* Solve-All Holy Alpha Male God.

Too few see themselves responsible for their thought behavior. Hundreds of Prisons, International Prostitution Inc., Global Porn Ltd., WMD, and such make big bucks for higher men. *Wor*ship Him: all OK. If you are not a ruler follower, you will be punished, shunned, imprisoned, or receive some form of revenge for not locking in step.

The absence of mutual trust leads to a proliferation of lies, each party trying to deceive the other, so that the "presence of trust" in a lie-based species does not necessarily lead to truth.

In social relationships, the shared expectation of "mutual trust" leads to collaboration and connivance between the liars and the lied to, to maintain the plausibility of the lie, as well as the "plausibility" of trust. That is, we no longer know who is deceiving whom. (Barnes 1994)

Naming reality-as-it-is names truths necessary for creativity. From the little acorn grows the giant oak. From the apple seed, no apfig. Names are not just names. Names that carry truths respect the intimate relationship between logic and naming according to evidence seen in reality. A not-male man does not exist in reality. Names in language inform us of logic, or its lack of logic. What is a Be-All, Solve-All, Supernatural Father in the Sky?

From the thesis of rational fem *with* the thesis of rational man is built the foundation upon which rationality stands and evolves. This means *language reform of the most radical kind*. Not political correctness, purism, feminism, or objectivism: simply that *the symbol reflect reality-as-it-is*, correct information, because reality determines and limits symbol making for rational speech.

Symbols communicate almost everything we do. We name what there is to be named. The symbols *sapiens, self, selfual, ut,* and *ratiogenic* are tools that hold truths good for further reasoning. *Siology* invites ut to report correctly what ut actually *sees*. We cannot see souls or spirits; we can see only *the self*, the integral unit of body and mind identified as a self. Symbols furthering good reasoning are necessary to rationality; this is what life lived as thinking life, life-affirming reason, means. Oppositely, one spouts illogic.

Everyone born into the species is born with a mind that can make and use symbols to *identify* the self. In my view, almost everyone has sufficient intelligence to do symbolic activity. But as with math and science, ut must be taught linguistics from the age of six up. The trap of predeterminism, a.k.a. *Providence* a.k.a. God's Plan a.k.a His gift of free will a.k.a. God giving language to Adam, destroys acquiring the skills of discernment to do the steps required in identifying the self to become a mature right-feeling and critical-thinking being.

Being predetermined (as sinners) is snaky. It zigzags in every direction in the Truth Q is and is not Q revealed *a priori*. Men can collude to keep fem out of high-paying jobs and board rooms, pay her pittance for jobs deemed *feminine*, and keep her out of the loop of experience. Fashion is her *alma mater*, beauty her obsession, and babies her destiny, it is *pre*determined that it is her role to wash his shorts, make his dinner, and be accessible when his desire pops up. Unaccountable virility for control appears so natural!

When providence becomes Providence, the snake bites. God provides, *wor*ship God. Few see that Providence predetermines God's plan, H/his gift of free will, the Father's gift of the One Man. A moral imperative in Colossians 3:18, "Wives, submit yourselves unto your own husbands, as it is fit in the Lord." The husband is valued higher than wife who has value only for procreation and obeying, *maintaining the plausibility of the lie*.

Getting out of this rigid, inflexible, pornographic box is not as hard as it seems. Rational*ism* is not rationality, individual*ism* is not individuality, predetermin*ism* is not what being determined by limits in reality is, including one's own reality.

Determin*ism*, gender-as-division of mind and body doled out by God-man, is the human belief that everything we do has One True cause. So if you pull out "a cause" for your bad behavior, then you are not really responsible for it. You could not help doing what you did, implied in the patent slogans "He's only human," that is, a sinner, or "it's a human error," where the very *wor*d human is an error, or that God made you the way you are, a sinner—the body (feminine flesh) makes man sin. Determinism derogates determinants in reality and reason that set rational limits. All "causes" are in one immaterial Holy Cause-All Alpha Male, God: the Truth. Therefore, giraffes must make chili for orangutans!

Symbol making has rules to discern and name differences in similarities. Ut is determined by the limits of ut's reality. Ut does not have wings to fly, a beak, or a trunk. What ut does have is a mind that can *see* ut's *self* as an independent body-and-mind unit. No umbilical or phallic cord attaches ut to man via Holy Alpha Male Cause. Ut is determined by the limits of ut's *own* finite physical brain: This difference-in-similarity in both fem and man as speech-using animals makes all the difference in the cosmos.

Ut cannot pretend to be a doe or a boar for long. This, however, did not stop Lords from identifying with bulls, rams, cocks, and bucks. Why would ut tether utself to a manmass that makes ut a dittoing robot? In 2 = 1 man, differences are leveled into One man similarity: His gender = power over opposites. Reality is nowhere in sight; rule following does not concern him.

It is unfortunate that responsibility for our actions is not a state for which there is a definite criterion, at least not yet. We can only ask whether one is responsible for an action or belief when we rule out falsity, a certain negative condition, a harmful method of thinking, such as ignoring a fact or acting under a compulsion, stopping a critical criterion to be mobilized. But no one saw the evil intent in information withheld making lies = Truth that ambushed our species and sabotaged the mind following Manu's legalization of feme slavery 4,000 years ago.

For once, "all actions have One cause"—and "God knows the least sparrow that falls"—this cause outside the mind is a ready-made excuse for all behavior, good and bad. This has two unfortunate consequences. First, it treats cause as *excuses*. Wishing belief to be reality, abracadabra, God created *man* "born in sin" excuses all evil. It is easy to believe that individuals cannot help doing what they do because of their class, race, gender, upbringing, or conditioning—all are born in sin! When things go wrong, protests and demands for rights are loud! Where the cause of actions is "sin" against God, belief arrogantly calls forth faith-based "wisdom." Reason-based wisdom is for all practical purposes aborted.

Is it not better to be determined by the limits of our bodies, our minds, reality, nature, and logic than it is to be blessed, that is, wounded by Providence that makes us sustain massive deception and self-delusion at all costs? *The common evil* in methodological solipsism is the magnitude of missing information—*institutionalized ignorance*—legitimating finking, false thinking causing behavioral chaos, individualisms, and freakish behavior of every imaginable kind, including justifying sex slavery (*blesser*, Fr., v., to wound).

Let's look at sex slavery, euphemized as the sex trade, excusing Lord Pimps and madams. Blame is blown away: The girls "choose" this kind of life—like boys "choose" the sex-powered privileges in the faith-based manmass. An estimated 27,000,000 "virgins" (many too young to have sex) worldwide are made to serve in Lord Pimp's brothels. Two million serve as high-class "escorts" in Lord Pimp's posh bedrooms. Two million "choose" to sell their body at large for drugs or lack of employment. All are low estimates and do not include rape, incest, and child abuse. Are we to believe that 2 = 1 man does not have an impact on the species and on mind? How blind are we? In 2 = 1 manuology, we are our genitals: Girls have virgin vaginas to serve virile penises. The selfish vs. the selfless! Divinity vs. givinity! Mind vs. body! Assume the *enemy*! Arm yourselves!

Pimps make money by making the vaginas they own do ten to twenty penises a day. The penis as weapon of sex power! I call these Weapons of Vaginal Destruction (WVD). Thirty-one million vaginas serving an average of fifteen penises every day = 465,000,000 penises. Half a billion penises out of 3,000,000,000! Out of the 3,000,000,000 roughly 2,850,000,000, or ninety-three percent, support religions financially. In *in manu*, genitals have primacy over mind: Virility is holy. In the Doctrine-Theory of Special Man, *we are our genitals*. No "pro-lifer" has ever spoken against this aspect of the esoteric feudal system, the filthy sex slavery of children in man!

Moreover, in cannon fodder for higher men, too many lesser men are "sacrificed"—killed—in the name of higher men, we may never know the numbers. Lesser men are Abraham's sons born to be sacrificed! The Holy Sacrifice of the Mass, Jesus, son, born to be sacrificed on the cross for the Father who created humanity born in sin! Methodological solipsism gathers sex-obsessed depravity as we all man it up to heaven.

Yet it is only through limits that we control how we as individuals in our species behave because limits define rules. Developing selfuality means learning to be a rule-following being. To act *in consonance* with facts and truths is to follow the rules to become mature. There is no other way to behave maturely and act morally.

To act by the lie and illogic is to never grow up, and, in fact, to regress into an adult childishness. For when the adult *needs* make-believe,

Solve-All God-man to live by, this is not moral behavior. It is insanity. The child, on the other hand, merely uses make believe to develop imagination. The sufficient mind uses truths in accumulated facts existing in the real cosmos for creative purposes and moral behavior.

The harm done in withholding information should now be fairly obvious to anyone who *sees* Q is and is not Q imposed on the species by the religious-secular belief in 2 = 1 man. WMD, WVD, unfair welfare systems, wife beating, Lord-made global capital*ism*, world wars, universal brothel institutions, out-of-control porn, global whore mongering, faith-based wisdom in saviors, and prophets of every shade need lies as solutions. Our cities are joyless, sky-scraping city hubs having rich suburbs and poor, lonely slums, disparate ghettos in tin huts among megahouses and never the quads do meet. Pollution is thorough and universal. Seminal megabucks are FIRST. Animal species are disappearing, the trees of the planet are at an all-time low, and almost all waters are poisoned. The food chain is threatened. But still, Power-$$$-'n'-sex are the criteria for status, power, and prestige in man. Big-Time frauds and embezzlement are the new crimes, crisis and failure management the new businesses. A deep global malaise sits on the species. Humanity's know-all rulers bombed the species with lies, and the slice-you-to-pieces shrapnel of Patriarchal Language made ruler followers and mind insufficient.

All the while, *in sapien reality, gender is simply a classification used for categorizing to better discern differences in similarities.* The *similarity of mind* in fem and man develops, distinguishes, and affirms good skills of discernment by *seeing* the *differences* in order to be two logic-affirming agents, thinkers, as the foundation of rationality, simple, forthright, and true. The aim in the Rofemtic Movement is to reestablish rule following.

Chapter 12

RELEVANT ISSUES IN

A TRUER THEORY

OF OUR SPECIES

What do sapiens do? They invent sounds to name objects. They invent visual characters, letters, to write them. After millions of years, they identify themselves as speech users, naming the relationship between mind and body—the self—wisely by the symbols and names they make. This knowledge of self leads to an authentic identity of self. Sapiens see to differentiate, see similarity and name all acts, behavior. To be sapiens is to do the thinking in the mind that creates an authentic identity of self as thinking animal. Both fem and man can do this thinking entailing logic to identify the self. Fem and man are first and foremost *the foundation of rationality*. Sapiens live a thinking life. They cannot live any other kind if life. They cannot live a wool-making or honey-making life, less so a lie-making life.

Belief in 2 men = 1 man stamping the Cause-All Alpha Male on the mind tends to make adults less responsible for their actions and behavior. Q is and is not Q makes pathogenic *resistors to evidence*. Believing in souls, they grow either selfless or selfish in the race for salvation. Souls, separate from the self, are to be saved. "Sin" flourishes!

Where the aim is respect for reality in naming as it clearly is in being sapiens, 2 = 2 is the rule and selfual is the aim. How is self-knowledge acquired without having the choice of creating a *selfual* identity? The aim to create an authentic identity is another concept not named in

Patriarchal English. No empathy for other self is in the human aim, the appeal is to special man and his brotherhood, the idea of "man's *soul*" rules the species.

Soul does not give itself to usage in language. One cannot say, "She hurt hersoul" like, "She hurt herself." Soul does not work as body-mind consonance. Neither does spirit. So "the normative use" of soul and spirit do not support rules relating to reality nor reality-based language. There are no rules where souls, spirits, and ghosts abide. Astrologists, tarot card readers, and priests can make any claim they make about them Truth.

In the inter-independent self, each thinker is *alone*, *individuated* in selfuality. "Alone" means separate and distinct as a strong self. The one (alone) in the many/society makes a collective of inter-independent mature selves, flexible-minded citizens. The moral fiber of societies in sapienity stands on the fact that no symbol-making self, although alone and independent, lives in isolation of other selves. Thus, the term inter-independent is applicable in reality's law $2 = 2$, strengthening the inclusive-denoting aim in selfual.

Ut *is* alone in, with, and through ut's own mind, ut's own self-awareness *with* other selves in sapient identity. In view of the inclusiveness in isonomic naming and selfuality, aloneness is not fearful. It is reality. Reality does not do fear mongering like $2 = 1$ man of opposite genders in realism. Gender-as-category uses differences and similarities to balance and integrate duality-in-self in order to achieve self-integrity and strength to see the relationship between intellectual intelligence and emotional intelligence, knowing that the other self counts as much and is as valuable as ut's self in ut's identity.

To respect other mind is to respect ut's (own) mind, so it is in ut's own best self-interest to see the limits in other minds, the similar determinants. This lets ut better see the truths in duality and how they work. This is not taught in schools because of parents' singular *right* in humanity to indoctrinate their children with their beliefs without the responsibility to pass on correct information, facts, and truths. "The rights of man" stand in humanity, reiterated by many leaders around the globe, including President Obama. The responsibilities and rights of thinking beings as fem and man are nowhere in sight.

Learning the skills to balance dual elements is like learning the art of bicycle riding. Ut not only needs truths and facts, ut needs the experience and evidence of correct relationships in cause and effect as well. Ut needs this to learn how to create a self. The correct relating of ut's mind with ut's body goes to make a sapient and selfual identity in which values, intellect, and emotions are equally engaged. This helps ut to reach a level of maturity leading to a level of happiness not easily bribed by the promise of heavenly reward.

In view of the "golden rule" between rival True Gods, I call *the rule of finite multiple causes* the *forthright rule*. There is no promise of heaven in it. The fact of multiple causes is in full view for all to see. Mature selves act alone in accepting the evidence of multiple causes, which respect all minds. Inclusion by definition names multiple causes. What is to fear in facts? The beauty in the *forthright rule*: Life, finite, is life. There are no ad hoc enemies in the forthright rule, no reason for warmongers and warriors to exist.

Aloneness is a desirable state for learning, creating, imagining, inventing—*with* others in society. No one is "above" in the sky judging ut with an all-seeing eye; all are on the same level playing field with everyone else. This does not level beings to being same and identical. It motivates ut to distinguish/identify ut*self* in ut's society as an individual.

The brain is a physical organ in the body, physical, finite mortal determined by its physical properties as part of the body. Although the brain contains millions of neurons, the mind cannot tap into an *infinite intelligence* having *supernatural powers* outside of all minds to zap him privileges because he's special. No God informs the finite brain. With correct information the sufficient mind can do wonders, but it cannot "transcend as a soul" to talk to a bodiless God; this is a form of insanity. The finite qualities of brain and mind exist in finite quantities of neurons to learn to balance body and mind in reality. This is scientifically showable and has practical value for living and learning.

Reason, science, experience, probabilities, and more are necessary in creating rationality through language. Science is not reason and reason is not science, but the achievements of language in both are evident. The necessary involvement of language in all disciplines is obvious. No correct design thinking or hypothesis can be made in science without correct information communicated in symbols showing correct reasoning. You cannot hypothesize balance or truths in science or reason using Q is and is not Q. A hypothesis about learning and achieving balance can be made only when nature's and reality's laws are respected. Design thinking starts when ut sees all the evidence and relationships that science, reason, and reality provide, and the particular circumstances at issue in time.

Logic, then, is very much involved in design thinking. Symbols and names based on correct premises fulfill a specific purpose. The relationship between these premises must correspond to the cause-and-effect order; being true to reality and trial and error in experience is to come to a conclusion to create fact, a truth. Logic is intimately related and involved in conceptualizing and naming. Science cannot use an apfig. Or a w-o-man!

Creative thinking about our species is mediocre in finking; gender-as-division pits the One against the not-one, wasting energy, time, resources, and talents. No educational design can be the goal to guide thinkers to a true and authentic identity of self as a strong, mature individual where false ideas abide. Moreover, critical thinking is quashed at the start, since false theses are protected at all costs. In the lie, logical and judgment thinking do not stand much of a chance! The voices of dissent are quickly quashed. And if a voice of dissent cannot be quashed, assassination solves the problem. Back to life = death.

It is clear that $2 = 1$ ideology put scientists in a box of *a priori* scholarship, and thinkers in a box of man-serving traditions and conventions. They *look back to Manu* to see the future. It is not a good way to walk forward, but it explains why there is always a nasty backlash to every small step forward society tries to take. The ideology held science, reason, psychology, social cohesion, and critical thinking back for several thousand years. It also held up moral and emotional growth and hung them on a God-peg, only to slime them up with start-up semen from unaccountable virility.

When reason involves past, present, and future time in science, they have proportional weight in the minds of feme and male scientists. Hierarchy of valued beings (special men) is not in real time. Rationally determined categories in science do not force hierarchical planes, whereas gender-as-division, man-centered scientists, often do. It is not science, but believing scientists that ditto *a priori* biases in their work. Many scientists are as afflicted with manusclerosis as God's "flock of sheep."

Correct categorization helps to learn the skills of discernment. Emotional intelligence is built on consistent facts, truths, and seeing the relationships in reality-as-it-is that show in plain view to everyone what being consistent is. Symbols that show consistence in thought and reality help to build emotional intelligence *with* intellectual intelligence. The more facts ut possesses, the more intelligent ut will be, and the more ut will commit to using reason.

Patriarchal Language warps emotional intelligence. When fem as fem is posited in knowledge, the fact brings insight in line with sight, changing attitudes. Seeing femity and accepting it as fact, ut sees $2 = 2$ with both sight and insight, since ut sees manity as included other. Achieving balance/proportion, a correct ratio between self and other self, is a delicate, dual-based, complex task, but it is not hard to do. In the process, empathy, respect, and trust evolve all good necessary in an emotionally intelligent being.

Seeing $2 = 2$ stops the old false $2 = 1$ from becoming new again, achieving "more of the same" destructive habits in false belief. Learning the skills of discernment changes attitudes; changing attitudes changes behavior. We *want* and *need* knowledge, facts, and truths leading to moral behavior. It is often hard to discern whether a small detail is a difference or a similarity, but it is important to do so.

Differences and similarities make *sub*categories in larger categories. Reds are a subcategory in the category of color. But a group of not-red is not a subcategory of red. W-o-men, not men in $2 = 1$ man, make a category of not-men *opposite* and are a subcategory in man, the not-male antithesis.

Gender-as-division/concepts-in-opposition induces conflicts, mind conflicting with body. Induced by the *law of the excluded middle*, the antithesis, the one is too high and the opposite too low to be of any use in any conflict resolution; warring is the natural solution. Ut is not to *see* that the genders as both men are predetermined on separate hierarchical planes of value in hu-manity. When was w-o-man ever on equal footing with man? She is below in name, identity, value, and mind, immobile on her small high pedestal, prettified as wife and mother, or "fallen," and thus a slut, far below special man on his altar.

Gender as category in science puts feme and male closer to the center of the same playing field *on the same plane*, so that the possibility of *balance in value* can be deduced in the probabilities that are in their similarities and differences. By implication, *the skills necessary for balancing* dual elements are seen as possible, and thus an educational focus. Skills of discernment ought to be in the curriculum, but they are not. Our schools fail here too. But again, "parental rights" in patriarchy are *a priori* before the responsibility to pass good thinking skills and correct information to the young.

Ut being both subject and object, how does ut balance objectivity and subjectivity? How does ut proportion the roles of being object and subject? Ut has both the capital of mind and the capital of body to identify as an independent self and the social need for others at once, but how do you balance this dependence with independence of self? Ut has the talent to both generalize and specify, but how does ut balance these? Present education does not teach skills for doing balance because it is still in the $2 = 1$ ideology. The One romantic past of dual*ism* is that parents have the God-given right to indoctrinate their children with their beliefs; secondary knowledge is salt and peppered with their beliefs.

In talk about initiative and motivation to learn skills of discernment to do balance in $2 = 2$, ut will not see off-track thinking, capitalism vs. socialism, objectivism vs. subjectivism, individualism vs. collectivism defended. Relics of "concepts-in-opposition" are extremes on separate planes of value, the One hierarchical, the opposite loerarchical. Just looking at the opposites/negatives, ut can tell which ones are the special and positive ones on the higher plane! Learning how to discern using correct symbols makes achieving the act of balance easier.

The *ism* is not thinking. *Ismitus, the virus of isms*, is a result of gender-as-division ideology, *manusclerosis*. Mere Words zap reality into being. (The name) God exists, zap, God exists. For instance, in Q is and is not Q, national*ism* hides protection*ism* in nation building. Eat*ism* is living to eat. Balance is not in *isms* because they are rationalized on hair-thin bases like those in the $2 = 1$ scaffold of the lie that is mankind.

Skills acquired to do balance in self-identity develop maturity. When fem and man are closer to center on the same plane, man is not valued more than fem. Sapienity includes both fem and man by definition. Both fem and man have both mind and body, and the attitude in seeing both in the species are in the symbols *by definition*. **By definition** *holds the full intention of inclusion on the same plane in the symbol that is consonant with reality in name.* This is better economics in speech than is seen in any issue you choose to discuss in the $2 = 1$ ideology that is mankind.

Feeling right about an issue is not necessarily being right. More often fueled by false information, feely emotions are conscripted. Many a "gut feeling" has gone tragically wrong. Hitler had a dead-right feeling that Jews were superfluous—invoking the name of "Gott" all the way. Split valuation trained him to go by his slemotions, so obvious in his hatred of Jews. It is easy to restrict seeing to "deep" (mystical) feelings, defending at all costs any point of view favoring such feelings. Feeling right is not necessarily to know the facts and truths that influence the cultivation of balanced and upright emotions. Warped or hu-Man emotions make common evil blast off like fireworks.

In knowledge, truths, and facts, there is nothing to defend. You do not need the loophole of tolerance, free speech, or gut feeling to do or defend critical, creative, or judgment thinking when done with forthright information and upright emotions. Where there is no missing information, the facts allow ut to go forward and create to enhance ut's own life and all of life. Correct knowledge makes thinking so much more effective as well as so much easier. Commitment to facts and truths is more pleasant and easier.

Ratiogenics, true-to-reality symbols, *by definition* make commitment more pleasant and easier. So it is not a case of new symbols for the sake of new. The accusation of "neologism" is a red herring, as are purism and feminism. Where information is missing, it must be made known by name, if it looks new, then so be it. But derogation of a truth by name calling or throwing a put-down missile is to stop a fact from being named precisely, because truths expose lies. This is why reason was/is derogated as whore!

Rediscovering, restoring, and/or making true-to-reality symbols true by definition are necessary to reinstate the *possibility* of doing balance in the sapien species. It is necessary to reestablish the *probabilities* of *fem with* man destroyed in 2 = 1 ideology. Facts help to design true hypotheses. The facts as such are not the design, but the items in the design. A supernatural Intelligent Designer like the One Holy Alpha Male Cause-All God zaps in mantasy-fantasy to make a huge scaffold of lies work to His advantage.

My design/hypothesis is that *sapiens are a species consisting of two gender-different animals, fem and man, having the similarity of mind to make and use true-to-reality symbols to enhance thinking life and all life forms in the cosmos, and* **both must use logic, concrete evidence, and cause-and-effect relationships to make symbols that name truths**. This hypothesis *by definition* names two in a partnership of *necessary thinkers* who act in the civilizing process of our species as **the foundation of rationality** to become wise, mature, rational stewards of our species as sapiens and of planet earth.

Manu sabotaged all wise stewardship 4,000 years ago. So it is necessary to name what was not named. It is necessary to restore Q is Q and 2 = 2 to establish authentic identities of two contributing minds to reestablish the foundation of rationality.

The preponderance of negatives in 2 = 1 ideology overwhelms the positives obstructing the achievement of balance in self to do creative thinking. Being not male, not Jew/Catholic/Muslim, not white, not rich, not educated, not employed, not on a higher plane, not on the value scale go into 2 = 1 finking, sliding to first base on slemotions.

Correct symbols are needed to show possibilities in probabilities. Ut must reduce contradiction, confrontation, and conflict. If correct symbols are derogated as neologisms, purism, or even as "new doctrine," then ut should look closely at who is trying to control language to control body, mind, and society.

To give an example of the attitude when reality is respected, I wrote lyrics to the well-loved melody to "Silent Night," imposing in song that the virgin birth is Truth, sung on December 25, the birthday of saviors since 6000 BCE. December 21 has been the Solstice since the cosmos came into being and has been celebrated by many for centuries.

Solstice Night (sung to the melody of "Silent Night")
Lyrics © Louise Gouëffic

Solstice night, awesome night
Deep in sleep, in its might
Nature's cycle brave and bold
Nature's brilliance here to unfold,
Brings the sun back tomorrow,
Brings back the sunlight again.

Solstice night, very long night,
All is bright, all is right
Trees stand tall in sparkling snow
Stars above are all aglow,
Brings the sun back tomorrow,
Brings back the sunlight again.

Sparkling snow, stars all aglow,
All is right in the night,
Delicate like thin lacy ice
Giving hope like love's old device
Needs wise stewardship now,
Needs wise stewardship now.

Chapter 13

TOWARD A REASON-BASED
TRUE-TO-REALITY APPROACH

Changing two minded beings into two men of opposite genders, which I call the Greatest Social Engineering Project, was bound to fail. The patriarchal act of naming fem w-o-man who is not a man would not sustain rationality. Sooner or later someone was bound to try the premises in mankind and find them false.

Raising the One in value to lower the value of the not-one shows higher man's "rational detachment" from the feme constituencies of birthing, body, and mind as procreating vessel, muddling with it the distinctions for categorizing in knowledge and getting consensus in society for law and good governance. Making two into one man is the slemotional attachment to *de manu in manu*, patriarchy.

Why should the social structure of our species as provided by Fathers have special priority over the natural structure as provided by evolution in reality? Why the incredible assumption that the *world* must conform to H/his specifications?

It is not so much that the project imploded on itself as it is that it got too big and too hard to enforce, even by Lords. Confused lesser men today are punished in thousands of costly jails "and keep humanity lookin' good." Lesser men, the most confused men on the planet, cut off from the privileges of Higher-Man Culture, do not understand why they cannot also "know" many beautiful broads and have big cars, exotic vacations in exclusive places, mansions around the globe, and bucks galore. They see that they do not systematically partake in H/his special privileges granted by the Lord in H/his system. Not all men are created equal; many are born to serve higher men.

Lesser men are left with little choice but to meet frustration head on with violence, like "girls" have little choice but to meet lack of opportunity and jobless survival with prostitution. Imprisoning lesser men makes the Big Guys look good, while *their much bigger crime against the mind goes unpunished.* As long as lesser men fail to see the 2 = 1 system, they allow Higher-Man Culture to exist. Cultured ignorance through missing information—it programs and guarantees failure in lesser men as it does in fem.

Lies are messy, always needing more lies. The thousands of books on mankind are proof of failure. Lies build castles of inconsistencies, a house of cards needing zillions of hair-thin explanations, causing massive confusion. So *obedience to the Lord* covers and hides the massive confusion; ninety percent of the six billion on earth believe in a Lord-ruled world. *Lies train the masses to be ruler followers, believers in the Lord.*

So drugs and drug lords, sex slavery, abject poverty, AIDs, gangsters, divorce and broken families, megabucks, working poor, depression, alcoholism, violence, killer viruses, wife beaters, sexual abusers of children, defrauders, embezzlers, serial warring are procreating at an unstoppable speed. Why? Humanity does not work; even with its proliferation of Solve-All Divine Males in the Sky, the rulers we must obey! It is dysfunctional, made so by manusclerosis.

A critical mass of responsible thinkers is needed. A critical mass wanting and having truths about our species to restore and uphold thinking as thinking is needed to reestablish sapienity. Sapiens as a name carries the aim of making ourselves wise by the logic we put in the symbols we make to use about ourselves, life, and the cosmos.

It has always been the case that about ten percent of the species did correct thinking, but, like wives, had to keep silent. What happened to Galileo shows us that to expose false beliefs is dangerous. The voice of a responsible mind is bad news to 2 = 1 *man.* Lords must make sure that consonance in the symbol/name of an entity does not match up *with* reality-as-it-is, for example, fem as fem. When consonance between name and reality is clear, the godfathered 2 = 1 man disintegrates before the eyes.

But ten percent is not enough. Just as a critical mass of firefighters is needed to fight a fire, a critical mass of responsible thinkers would bring about respect of mind, commitment to consonance between symbol and reality, and the habit of consistency in cause-and-effect relationships in symbols. We need at least thirty to forty percent, a tall order. But it is the basic ten percent that kept the species afloat in the first place. Knowledge and thinkers hold things together, not-believers who fink. A substantial increase in independent critical thinkers could and would turn things around. And like gays and lesbians, they would have to come out of the closet of silence, maybe a Rational Pride Day.

But Higher Men own so much wealth they proselytize *in manu* in millions of seminal ways in millions of seminal books. Today, global politics is obsessed with if you are not a capitalist believing in the forces of "the Market Place" regulating everything from soup to sex, you are a socialist doing social engineering—when (Hu)*manity is the Greatest Social Engineering Project ever attempted*! Man confidently assumes himself in every constitution, legal system, private and social institution, and ruling body. A critical mass of thinkers wanting truths will start to reduce this omnipresence. Perhaps we can even dare to dream of fifty percent rallying for reason in naming reality-as-it-is.

Doing correct thinking leads to doing better science about mind. First, a mind having true-to-reality ideas, correct information, gives ut a determined-by-truth *flexibility* that leads to creative thinking. It is not enough to do only critical thinking, situation thinking, or design thinking. Ut must get the skills to do creative thinking to enhance ut's own life, and in so doing enhance all life. The probabilities in fem and man as authentic sapient beings lead to creative possibilities not seen in 4,000 years.

Second, duality of mind is in the name sapiens *by definition*. Duality is now a standard of two in name, concept and truths, because $2 = 2$ is so in nature and reality. To resist this evidence is to be immature. Forthright real standards are conducive to creative thinking.

Let me say here that I have always been horrified at how quickly Higher Man acknowledges different minds in his ranks, Jesus, Mohammed, Napoleon, Stalin, God, Bismarck, Kafka, Rushton, Kierkegard,

Hitler—males of all stripes—while refusing to admit feme mind or fem as fem in H/his ranks.

Third, duality is the basis for plurality. The moment ut posits femity and manity, duality of self, ut posits *the probability of plurality* in societies. Q is Q holds 2 = 2, making plurality a probability. Destroying duality destroys plurality. Self-named Holy Alpha Male the One True Cause-All, Solve-All God is always only one.

Reality shows us that black skin is no more and no less significant than blue eyes, and that white penis is no less and no more significant than black uterus. Intelligence in any and all newborns depends on ut's geography, social situation, self-identity, educational opportunities, nature's quirks, family wisdom, accidents, intellectual milieu, attitudes of forebears, genetic inheritance—in short, the fact of multiple causes. Welcome to multiple causality. It exists everywhere in reality and cannot be escaped.

The massive confusion *in manu* overwhelms our powers to see what is good or bad in two "opposite" men born in original sin. Yet individuals, like trees, in and of themselves are neither good nor bad. He becomes *bad* by too many lies and false beliefs that he cannot use. Most criminals are made false item by false item in 2 = 1's unfair system, an unjust institution based *in manu*, like fem was changed into a prostituted woman false item by false item. No baby is born evil. One is first deeply hurt and made angry at a young age and then turns to crime for *his* justice. All done for lies. There are few "purely evil" individuals; most criminals and prostitutes are made by the false system through the man culture.

Fourth, correct information levels the playing field for all. We are and must see ourselves as finite fallible sapiens, neither good nor bad. Having sufficient mind to solve our problems, we make truth-carrying symbols useable to create a moral society. Plurality of selves and minds lead selfual beings to do creative thinking that leads to doing moral thinking and behaving morally more consistently. Choosing to act from correct information is the basis for better behavior and morality.

Plurality shows the fact that multiple causes exist, causes from which related effects occur in consistent ways, like acorn → oak. But like evolution does not cause technology, the body (brain) does not invent concepts, the mind does. *We* say acorn → oak. The mind does not build bridges, the body does. Nature's evolution of the dual-based sapient animal millions of years in the making is a duality that establishes facts and knowledge.

Relating effects to their logical causes is one of the elements in correct thinking. Correct information is finite and fallible because the finiteness of things is a determinant that limits. Limits determine outcome as well as causes such as insight, opportunity, and chance.

Intellectual development then has many causes. There is a difference of outcome for a baby boy born into abject poverty and a baby girl born into wealth. There is a difference in insight in a baby born in a hot, dry desert and one in a moist, warm, green country. The Inuit have some forty expressions for snow in their language. There is a difference of opportunity between a baby girl born of highly motivated self-educated forebears and a baby boy born of highly educated don't-give-a-damn ones. Intelligence, like most things on earth, has many causes.

Therefore, there is a big difference in conceptual skills between a boy born in the manmass believing "he is born in sin" and a child born in a society that teaches ut to reason consistently and has correct information to start life with. I rest my case once more.

The natural kinship between correct-thinking individuals, therefore, must be named. Blood lineage, worship, and personal autonomy in Holy Alpha Males do not cultivate kinship. In my lifetime I never heard an Aboriginal talk doe or a black fem talk bitch. But I have heard *special* white men talk ram, bull, stud, and big bucks.

The quantitative value in isonomic concepts, fem, man, black, white, or red, are named for each of their qualitative values in sapienity so that every symbol user sees utself as a contributing member of the sapien species, not as separated "race" or a One. With the possibilities in probabilities transparent in symbol and name, ut can then confidently start a creative program of being necessary to ut's species as an authentic self and good thinker. Being born in the sapien species is the first criterion, ut is included *by definition.*

The quality of thinking in balance with the quantity of thinking the species needs from each and every right-thinking self makes a moral collective. Society need no longer be feared as being "against" the individual or self like it is in 2 = 1 *man*. Society is a collective of thinking individuals *user friendly* to the thinking self.

Mysterious embedded bias always needs righteous-two-shoes *sle-motions*. Transparent reason-based language enhancing the kinship between ratiocinating beings does not need mutual pat-a-backs or the bomb. The kinship of fem and man as sapiens is self-unifying and self-developing. There are no longer lesser men and not-men being forcibly sanitized, that is, hu-*manized* to serve higher men. This reduces unfairness, injustice, confusion, frustration, and violence. In the kinship that is sapienity, all babies start out more equitably on the same level playing field, since all start with the same correct information leading to the development of and balance in self, the aim in selfual. Cocksure L/lords, H/holy Heads, dead-right K/kings, and knock-out S/saviors have no place in this.

Like bees, wolves, and whales, mature sapient individuals *create self-organizing systems*. Rational societies do not need Lords dictating false, unworkable schemes. Striving for selfual inter-independence, they understand consonance between mind and body in being consonant with reality. They use duality for balance and ut expresses this knowledge of balance in ut's society. In sapien kinship, then, the divine grounds of status—wealth, position, race, class, and split value by gender—crumble.

Real/scientific classifications taught in, with, and through correct knowledge concerning two thinking beings replace the false 2 = 1 divisions. Ut's individual and collective value in doing good thinking to be a good thinker is visible in society.

Creating an authentic identity is easier in sapienity. To create an authentic identity *interest in other self with self-interest in one's proper self* is the natural teacher of maturity. The aim in selfual entails considering other selves; it teaches the skills of balancing truths necessary to a code of ethics. Oppositely, self-interest goes selfish or selfless, the cultured selfless serving the privileged selfish.

We talk about our *selves* because our *selves* are the matter, concrete fem and man, that make symbols from our nature, sensations, experience, and mind, like the matter for making wool comes from the nature of being wool-making creatures as sheep. But (my) *self* does not live in isolation of other selves. Other selves are every other self, each as individuals whom "I" encounter and see in my life.

It is in symbol making that the responsibility to create an authentic identity rests. Names are the tools of talk, speech. The right and responsibility to use Q is Q and 2 = 2 in symbols goes hand in hand in correct speech. Basic to knowledge, facts accumulate to build intelligence and wisdom. Names are important in building an authentic self, a self who is not afraid to be one's self. Correct names are the intellectual capital of an authentic identity.

In 2 = 1 man, fem is not fem, she is an object named by man as a man who's not a man, as object she is also nature, churches, planes, ships, cars, factories, newspapers, buildings, universities, *alma maters*, sister plants, mother houses, daughter cells, grand old dames as buildings, objects made by, for, and used by man. As object, *she* is the mother of all wars until girls believe they are objects in mankind. Indoctrinated thus from infancy, this objectification process is "boyed" by seminal *slemotions* as "humans born in sin" before they are critical enough to analyze what is being done to their minds. The pronoun *it* to denote objects in Patriarchal English is dying fast. *Why* are objects "she's"? Men are subjects, being mind he controls "her." Gender divides mind from body, subjectivism writ large.

But *manucrats* make us believe that the subjective is *opposed* to the objective. That social element is *opposed* to ownership of capital. That rational life is *opposed* to emotional life. That *fem* is *opposed to*— enemy of—man. Enemy? She evolved estrus out of her nature so males could have sex year round. The axe of sex is *for control purposes*. In this, *H/he* is his own worst enemy, but control and supremacy are sweet, lonely, and violent in the confrontational entertainments in the scramble to the top.

In opposites, is procreation then "opposed" to creation? He creates, she procreates, the seminal paradigm. One is relegated to secondary role, and thus has less value! Creation *opposed* to procreation? What an absurd idea!

Sheep make wool, and procreate. Bees make honey, and procreate. Oysters make pearls, and procreate. Cows give milk, and procreate. Would it not be a boring, not to mention silly, planet if all species procreated primarily to become *same in Alpha Male One*? There would be no wool, pearls, milk, or honey—yet man would have fem become a man "regardless of gender." It is no wonder *self-motivation to achieve rationality* lost its emotional commitment. Stupid go-nowhere aims deserve cynical apathetic citizens.

Mind and body, 2, in fem and man, 2, make symbols and procreate, 2. Both roles have equal value. No wool maker, no sheep. OK, pro-lifers, go and have a good cry here. But balance implies a second element—mind—to learn the skills of balancing. It is interest in other selves and utself that ut best learns the lesson 2 = 2. The evidence is clear.

In restarting self-motivation, *wanting* truths is paramount. Like most animals the sapien is curious by nature. The motivation for advancing technological knowledge rests on the need to enhance physical life. Advancing intellectual life in self-knowledge is a whole other ball game. Resistors to evidence set back the self-motivation to find truths to enhance intellectual life and develop mind. Evidence resistors, such as pro-lifers, want to control other's lives. They don't want evidence, logical arguments, or premises based on reality showing their beliefs to be lies and their values false, unfair, and unjust. They don't want to know that lies destroy the self-motivation to look for facts and truths; they don't want information that goes in to build an authentic self-identity. They want *ruler-follower sheep* like themselves, not rule-following individuals. They want yesmen for the manmass.

The selfual method of opening and closing, looking outward and inward, and being objective and subjective is flexible, self-correcting, *by definition* creating a flexible mind not afraid of life, one's self, or others. Since ut can use only facts and true ideas, this gives ut a source for lifelong self-esteem and self-integrity that builds self-motivation to acquire the emotional intelligence not afraid to create ut's identity as an authentic fem or man.

The Rofemtic Movement, then, is like no other movement since 2400 BCE. It sources the self-esteem that propels natural self-motivation to seek out emotional intelligence not afraid of life. It runs on the serenity of knowing that ut is in consonance with reality, including the necessary feme and male distinctions in thinking *self*. Eliminate one thinker, and balance, outcome, and direction are changed for the worse, evident in historicism. They are the only two who can be the foundation of rationality and thinking.

When *femble*, the strongest hemp plant on earth, was renamed *carl* (male) hemp, it helped to set the belief that only males had strength. Philosophers deduce from this that the male also has special mental attributes that the not-male does not have. We see how language was abused in inventing *carl* hemp to replace *femble*. Naming was abused to make people believe that only males have mind and strength. Most beliefs are created this way by lies embedded in language that we are to share and use every day.

So what goes into establishing truths? Truths are made by naming the cause and effect seen in reality in symbols that reflect this relationship. Truths can be tried in the court of reality. Lies cannot; this is why they are not seen as the cause of common evil.

The more I read philosophy in university, the more I lost the good common sense and practical rationality that my mother and father had instilled in me. Having embedded falsehoods written in books prescribed by professors for reading had a harmful effect on my mind. All written in the H/he-gear, they made me lose the self-esteem my forebears had so painstakingly instilled in me. It took me years to see my own value as a minded being.

Not until I saw the sacred 2 = 1 man secret did I see that any old thing could be Truth in H/his philosophy. Saint Thomas Aquinas said the "female" was a misbegotten male and put divinity in the real male in *Summa Theologica*. Kierkegard said it was only right that women should suffer in childbirth for having brought sin into the world. Hitler disseminated an Aryan male theology claiming *Gott* to be a white, blue-eyed, blonde-haired male, dittoed today by Mormons. English imperialism serves man well with The Word woman; fem is not registered in dictionaries. Philosophy ought to deal with truths, but philosophers seldom do believing; they are born in sin—and as men they have a vested interest in humanity.

Scientifically, the Doctrine-Theory of Man is false. Science deals with facts. That fem exist as fem is fact. Rationally too, the theory of man is false; it is inconsistent with what exists in reality. Yet scientists and philosophers went with 2 = 1 man. Who are we to trust? How was the "unread" manmass to see the *de manu in manu* deception being imposed?

There are many things not popular in 2 = 1 man. The symbol *popular* comes from pope/papa, F/Father as Creator/Cause of the *pop*ulation, the species created by Creator Manu/birth giver. Trees are not popular; eighty percent of earth's trees have been cut down. Many animals are not popular; like fem, they are cleansed from the planet.

Rationality is certainly not popular among individualists dependent on L/lords. The manmass fears truths, correct information, and hates facts; masses are popular, Yesmen, too, are popular: I love you to the extent that you "yes" my lies.

Six and a half billion saying that from the acorn a maple grows does not make it so. As popular as they might become with the kept-ignorant manmass, favorite lies and biases have nothing to do with truths, facts, and rationality. Whatever the role myth played among our earliest forebears has been twisted out of purpose and proportion. Myth served to start making the first sounds when thousands of "gods" explained unexplainable phenomena. Ceres → cereal. Today myth is life, God-man and H/his virgin is reality.

In most groups, leaders emerge. In sapienity leadership comes from individuals most in consonance with knowledge that critical thinkers agree on and act upon. This creates both centering and diffusing forces—impossible with far-apart 2 = 1 split beings on separate levels. Reality, nature, mind, experience, and scientific and creative thinking are all resources from which truths are extracted and named by clear and critical thinkers in the collective. The concept of *leadership* changes when both centering and diffusing of truths are in balance, also helping to develop emotional intelligence. Leaders have the moral responsibility to see to it that correct information is passed on to the young and used in the collective. This is not what Holy Alpha Male Lords want! They want followers. Followers are good believers. Lords are not *leaders; they are rulers*. They command.

Leaders having good emotional intelligence know that in reality probabilities provide *continuity* for the possibilities in them in spite of the fluctuating/changing conditions in probabilities. Fallibility is a constant factor that is *the best source of self-motivation to acquire knowledge we can have,* acquiring knowledge being mind's most interesting activity. Flexibility, being open to new evidence when the fallibility factor kicks in, makes it easier for leaders and citizens to put theory and practice in consonance with one another to reach reason-based wisdom *with* emotional intelligence, a model for trust and justice in policy making working for the equality of value of each and every sapien.

Equality in value is the best equality we can achieve. To have a kinder and gentler species, respect of mind in all for justice from *other selves* must stand true. Oppositely, equality is a bogus ideal. W-o/men are almost always paid less than men in "free-will" man, where money, sex, and power rule in the greed and lust for control.

The *continuity* of truths is necessary and see-able. Evolution brings about differences while keeping similarities constant, the basis for continuity. Millions of years ago the giraffe did not look like the giraffe we know today. Yet one can see today's giraffe in the primitive giraffe. Laws in nature sustain *continuity* between differences and similarities in evolution, the reason why fem did not evolve mind-less during the 4,000-year-long 2 = 1 man project. Fem is on the same track of continuity-in-evolution with man, but scientists, rationalists, historians, and philosophers ignore this fact.

Continuity is blown to hell in 2 = 1 man. So conflicts are rampant. Massive con/fusion reigns. Creationism is Truth. Evolution is a lie. And science is turned on its ear and like reason devalued. Wars are the simple answer when His Truth is challenged!

Continuity in ut's self-identity as a consistent thinker is the best architectural strategy for ut's self-esteem. The shared value in having/owning correct information, facts, and truths takes place at the level of one's identity in consonance with other self/ves. Continuity of consonance between body and mind, male and feme, subject and object arrived at by observation, logic, experience, nature, reality, observing the laws in these, sees and respects the hard evidence in them. *Consonance in symbols giving correct information is the basis for continuity, the stability that gives ut the moral self-esteem to stay honest in the face of change.* Authenticity, dignity, and serenity in stability feed self-esteem, making ut strong enough to face change when the fallibility factor kicks in.

The rofemtic attitude, then, dissolves the toxic $2 = 1$ lie, inviting true-to-reality concepts by making known the many concepts and truths hidden and/or missing for the past four millennia. It does not "feminize" marginal/lesser men or make women glorious victims while "romancing" the God-planned struggle and strife in $2 = 1$ man as a badge of honor for the Lordly aim of making "sheep" needing to feed at the manger of "original sin." The selfual individual is able to stand on ut's own and act morally in an individual-friendly milieu/collective. Individual and society act as a team once rationality and correct information are common to all in the species. Moral individuals create moral society. A critical mass of correct/moral thinkers is the basis for a moral collective.

This is not like the "moral majority" where patent patriarchal $2 = 1$ Lie is *Self-Righteous Conservative* Truth. Studflated heroes, propheteering messiahs, and profiteering saviors are too obsessed with power to see the self-righteous selfishness of rich evangelical Lords wanting to control. It may be that planet earth has had enough of this; there is nothing left to pollute. Seeing the shaky-flaky dance of the *in manu* "New Age," it is not hard to see manmass fatigue: Astrology, miracleology, iridology, reflexology, pornographology, religionology, playboy sexcapology, drugology, defensology, wealthology, whorelogy, gunology, jailology, dropoutology, dietology, trinitarian egoology, theology, and sheology abound in the manutopias of *de manu in manu*, violating mind as it goes from one "neutral" male hand of control to another.

We need truths, facts, and good reasoning to show respect of mind. Maybe the time has come to obey the laws in reality. Maybe we can rid the mind of *Q is and is not Q*. Maybe radical language reform can be implemented and true-to-reality concepts established. Maybe we can change the in-sight of our species as gender-hinged creatures clinging to heaven's sky-ropes to having the insight to view mind and gender in natural light. Maybe we can create sustainable rationality, morality, and honest emotions and be the actual species we were evolving ourselves to become before Manu changed it with unjust malicious law. Maybe we can be the thinking animals that our ancient forebears started to evolve us with their *primitive* intelligence.

Maybe the will to need and want facts to do constructive and destructive creating are the first steps. Correct information is necessary. But we also want and need a critical mass of correct/moral thinkers.

How mature do we want to be? In reality, every life form is on the same concrete plane. Valuation cannot be done when thinkers are on separate planes, snowed on with ad hoc values willy-nilly, on a planet where one is not even a thinker in H/his *wor*ld.

Values are values. Murder is murder for everyone everywhere in every instance. Everyone needs pure air. To believe that values can be put on nationalist or sectarian or idealistic planes that split values according to an ad hoc criterion such as gender, race, or being special, where my values are higher/better/more worthy than yours is a non-starter. And dangerously divisive, for whom is murder not murder? How is it that males have divinity and not-males givinity? Only in mind pollution(!) as we ride the run-away sludge train to an all-out war between religio-political theocratic fundamentalisms fueled by the huge American military-industrial complex selling high-tech killing machines internationally to make billions of $$$ for Modern War Lords where American Imperialism aims to become the Christian Super Power of the world. When will we say enough is enough?

The Grand Identity Theft of fem, half the species, as a man who's not a man has no match in scale. Mankind having no checks and balances created terrorizing effects and consequences far beyond even H/his understanding. He flooded the species with so many hair-thin lies that brought about behavioral chaos, individualism run amok.

Having the shared value of Q is Q, fem is fem, leading to $2 = 2$, fem with man, is an important part of correct information that will heal the mind, and I hope change minded beings into being rational and honest individuals, a condition necessary to make moral society. There is nothing hard in seeing this and instituting it one committed thinker at a time.

Chapter 14

CONSONANCE NECESSARY
BETWEEN RESPONSIBILITIES
AND RIGHTS

Rights without responsibilities are like life without water. Rights are assumed to be a property of man, like his arm, above all, the *right to believe*. That belief impacts on behavior is not addressed. So today we have a hard time with responsibilities. The demand for rights is the ruler followers' *amazing grace*. Giving the young the example of good reasoning and correct information and showing how these compute to contribute to peace and happiness is not important in 2 = 1. Negative commands "Thou shalt not do (this or that)" with "Thou shalt worship only me," who is God, the One True Lord.

Priests, clergy, and Lorded men do not preach the responsibility to look at reality closely to see if belief in God and obedience to Him is grounded in reality. They do not want to lose parishioners and believers. They want numbers of souls paying tithes; souls count for Ecclesiastic Lords like obscene sums of money count for Capitalist Lords.

One birthright in sapienity is the right-with-the-responsibility to act and behave as the real thinking animal ut evolved to be and was born as. In sapienity there are *no rights without consonant responsibilities*. To acquire a *consonality, a sound consonant with reality*, ut's character must be shaped by a language made of true-to-reality symbols. The right of forebears, then, entails the inexorable responsibility to do correct naming to show and give the example of the relationship in ratiogenic symbols at work in good reasoning, good emotions, peace, and happiness.

"The rights of man" are above responsibilities; "he" is above as collective mind. Man in whom "the seat of reason resides" has rights, and w-o-man has subservient-to-man rights with many, if not most, of the menial, low-valued work and responsibilities.

In sapienity, consonance between two necessary beings lets them see that they act as a *team to achieve harmony in direction* in the development of mind, reached by non-coercive means to do so. Body and mind, male and feme act as a team, like protons and electrons act together. No one defines the proton as a not-electron. No proton, no electricity. No feme, no rationality. No fem, no moral society; rights and responsibilities are as indivisible as mind and body. Although one can speak about each separately like one speaks of leg and arm separately, rights are not separate from responsibilities in society.

Hu-man rights, false *goods*, are not "goods" at all; they contain the right to believe, needing yesmen and masses of obedient lesser men. Responsibility is obedience to a higher L/lord; $2 = 1$ man "born in sin" must worship God. Men of both genders become ruler followers. A more irrationality-causing system of thought could not have been invented.

When I was thirteen, a two-story wooden building caught fire in the small town in which I grew up. An identical one two feet away was threatened. Nuns threw pails of *miraculous medals* in the "space of Grace." Then the local priest in full dress, carrying a gold-trimmed, satin-covered vessel of "holy" water, blessed the second building with pompous gestures and cocky bravado. It burst into flames. What seeing this did to my thirteen-year-old mind is indescribable. How much power did medals, holy water, nuns, priest, and God have here? Exactly zero. Myth and magic do not solve problems.

The *right to believe* sky-hooked myths does not entail the *responsibility to know* the facts and what they mean to cause-and-effect relationships to establish and report correct information. An unwritten tacit imperative in belief is that religions must not be criticized. So beliefs and their consequences are never tried. Tolerance is the white hole giving beliefs such as man = species "the right" to exist. Not only is the path to wisdom lost, we are, as a species, also bullied and pushed onto a fatal track.

The belief that "blessing with holy water" stops a raging fire—abra-cadabra—is not based on fact, scientific, empirical, or logical. Knowledge of how fire spreads, amounts of water needed, putting many hands on a water brigade, and appealing to individuals wanting to help is more rational. Praying at the bottom of a volcano ready to erupt cannot stop a volcano from erupting. Praying for a dying Lord who preyed on mind—to get into his rich heaven on earth—does not excuse nor undo His predatory life. It gives tons of false comforts to the manmass, confuses them and renders them cynically apathetic, but it does noth-ing at all for any problems at hand. Lourdes does not cure people, it plunges them deeper into the entrancing white hole of belief-without-knowledge covered with a satin duvet of false comforting promises, letting Ecclesiastic Lords off the hook.

A believing mass is pushed onto the track of *needing* a supra-natu-ral ruler-hero, a Holy Alpha Male delivering a magic fix-all pill precisely because it does not grasp the concept of individual *right with its con-sonant responsibility*. Just believe: All OK—God takes care of "the least sparrow that falls." When was man-as-species or group ever indicted for a crime against mind? Has religion ever been seen as a fraud? Law books do not mention "crimes against mind." To this day, law books do not state that *the abortion of reason-based, true-to-reality language* and *withheld knowledge* are crimes against mind. To believe, then, also includes the belief that people don't need knowledge! That belief *is* knowledge!

The very *right* to think correctly is taken away from individuals when *the responsibility to do correct thinking* is not in the formula. An authentic identity becomes impossible. Corruption, systemic $2 = 1$, has no checks and balances. Reinhold Niebuhr titled one of his books *Moral Man* [he] *and Immoral Society* [she-mass], reinforcing the indi-vidual and the collective as *enemies*. Opposites by gender are enemies!

Responsibilities without rights are like water without life. It is odd for me to discuss responsibilities when subservient rights were all w-o/man had for 4,000 years. But the responsibility to make correct symbols goes with the right to name reality like hand goes with arm.

In "duty to Lord," the *right to correct information for moral choice* is absent, not anywhere. Subservient rights, the right to obey and serve the Lord and follow the ruler, transform "souls" into obedient, servile, ditto "men" in man. Myth is wed to language.

It is a bad time to be speaking of responsibilities. Blame is the Self-Righteous Game in 2 = 1 man. Woman brought sin into the world. Yet the right to correct information for life and education, public and private, remains the same, always necessary, and it entails having correct information that broadcasts respect for all minds. Minds must have symbols reflecting reality-as-it-is to develop rationally, morally, and civilly.

All textbooks, reading material, media, songs, plays, fiction, and social assembly have the *responsibility* to use *fem, feme, gender as scientific category, differences and similarities as distinctions in category* to fulfill the right to make and have correct information in order to fulfill the responsibility to pass these facts and truths to the young and to one another. Where responsibility to transmit correct information is missing in common education, *learning critical thinking* is made almost useless. How can a child learn responsibilities consonant with ut's rights in a manmass that protects its religio-sectarian right to believe in *2 = 1 man* ruling on sky-hooked tracks at any cost? It is too hard to see Q is and is not Q riding on such high celestial tracking.

What is the big problem in gender-as-division of mind and body? "Opposite" (genders)! *Opposite* is not *other*. In man, there is + man and − man *opposite* Q is not Q. Man as a party of One-for-the-two makes a negative, an *opposite*, not-man, makes *not-Q* valid. In this kind of talk, there are only *special* rights for special men and responsibilities for lesser men and not-men. Responsibilities and rights are split on different levels in different playing fields. This splitting and putting concepts on separate levels is the eternal *soul* of the *enemy*-making machinery in man.

The concept of *other* considers and names "the other one" in a team. Fem is + 1 and man is + 1 = 2. *Opposite* excludes the opposing "not-one." Two opposite men make one because one "man" is not "a" man; 1 (man) − 1 (not-man) = 1 man; 2 = 1 because 1 − 1 = 1. Mathematics is miraculously jinxed by fraud and embezzlement built in.

In sapienity, the selfually developed individual is *other*, included by definition. True-to-reality symbols made in language state the existence of two thinkers, two minds, man and fem, in symbols that reflect this to be the case in reality.

Both fem and man have rights with responsibilities. All babies are born on the same level playing field where *rights* entail *responsibilities* to achieve *consonance* in all that concerns thinking beings. In the Rofemtic Movement, then, there are no freehold sky-hooked rights divined on seminal ruminations. There are only rights-with-responsibilities or responsibilities-with-rights based in reality.

Consonance is necessary in symbols to express justice for all, including those with disabilities, sexual differences, a lack in opportunities, brain damage, abuse traumas, and misfortunes. In serfdom (*serf* → to *serve*), the Capitalist Lord's wealthy abode is *opposite* the poor lesser man's mud hut who serves Him. The Cape Town Black Townships are glaring witness to lack of consonance. The whites in South Africa were true believers in God. If you are *not* rich, powerful, white, and male, you are lazy, stupid, fe/male, or lesser male, disabled—*poor by nature*.

Believers in Humanism do not want linguistic change either because their beliefs, like religions, are based in man and the belief that "human nature cannot be changed." The brick wall is ten *meters/mothers* tall. Methodological solipsism is thick, high, and complex.

The responsibility to put forth a true and simpler theory is necessary. The manmass believes $2 = 1$ to be a simple theory, but how do you explain "a man who's not a man"? It is done with millions of hair-thin propositions in thesis, antithesis, and synthesis—without ever mentioning the *opposite* man. Simply read books on Man published before 1970. The doctrine of Man10^{100} fills whole libraries assuming man species with cocksure certitude.

Lesser men and not-men do not examine the magnitude of the Convenient Man Lie. Trained to be ruler followers, they obey and *serve*. So Maori, Cree, black, and lesser men make up the majority in jail populations in the countries of *their beloved forefathers*, Lords. Few have much historical or intellectual inheritance from foremothers, and even less correct information. Men of two genders internalize the great *white* father image, regardless of color, creed, or geography. Many African-Americans convert to Islam, which says, "Allah made men superior to wo*men*." Many criminals find Jesus in jail! How good it feels to believe in false information! The race-gender-class splits riding on irrationality are so intertwined and complex the masses believe the package to be above their deficient heads, they memorize absurdities, banalities, and irrationality and believe. *Serfs ditto, believe, and obey irrational L/lords, the rulers* because the magnitude of confusion, cosmic in scope, is overwhelming. Four thousand years used (and wasted) to impose belief firmed up the lies in the Convenient Lie = Truth.

The constant forthright use of consistence in reasoning used in premises grounded in reality allows young children to grasp the truth of consonance in truths and facts. Children are much more intelligent than what society grants them. But no child reaching the age of reason believing in "w-o/man" asks, if not ap*fig*, then why woman. They have already been whiteballed by 2 = 1 man. Yet ut can *see* at six years of age that the apple is not a fig.

The responsibility of forebears in sapient education is the basis for moral societies.

Mind-respecting forebears involve their young as soon as possible in the acts of seeing, distinguishing, thinking, examining evidence, having experiences, relating cause and effect, and doing appropriate experimenting. Like the giraffe teaches its young to be giraffes, sapiens teach their young to *vise/see* well, to aim ut's *see*ing at the relevant details in order to become wise. From *vise*, seeing well, good *vis*ion, *sight, and insight* evolves the ability to be wise. Seeing correctly leads to thinking correctly, which leads to wisdom. (*Viser*, Fr., to focus the sight, *vise* → wise, like vine → wine; sapiens, to be wise, sight, taste, and hearing, sound → sanity, the senses lead to wisdom, *savourer*, Fr., to taste → savvy, from *sapere*, L.)

I am not talking here about becoming doctors or astronauts. It is about teaching the young to be rational and thinking members in their species. This starts in the first years of life. Everyone is born sapien, like baby giraffes are born giraffes. One is made human by cultural indoctrination, belief in false symbols imposed in the relentless repetitiousness of lies embedded in words; no one is born hu (man.) Girls are not born to become men in reality. Only in the sense that "man" means slave, being *in manu*, can fem be called w-o-man, wife-of-slave. As a separate and distinct minded being, she is fem.

So like the forebears of baby giraffe do not teach it to be elephant, the forebears of sapiens do not teach their young to be human, serfs *in manu*, obeying ruler Lords. *Every child participates in sapient life by doing ut's own thinking, using ut's own good mind with language consonant with reality.*

Teaching infants what each is as subject, object, male, feme, mind, body, and symbol maker and user is to develop character traits, physical factors, psychological capabilities, and geographic and time-place circumstances so that ut can achieve the best results in ut's development, an authentic self-identity. The knowledge of *being a thinker* by *doing acts of reasoned thinking* is to experience consonance. Where does irrational act fit in?

No giraffe can be a giraffe and not *do* what a giraffe does to *be* one. Being a thinker and doing thinking develops a self-esteeming identity. Bringing being and doing in consonance will keep ut out of false, quirky, attention-getting psychological problems. Every child born into the sapien species can learn to think, because every child, black-skinned male, red-haired feme, violet-eyed lesbian, and hairless gay— has a mind.

Where reason is used, ut also gets the skills to *balance ut's emoting with ut's thinking* to develop an authentic identity. Rationality does not rule out the pleasant sensations of emotions. In fact, rationality makes emotions so much more stable, intense, and pleasurable because they are forthright and honest. A rational being experiences reasoned-based emotions, emotions with a solid down-to-earth serenity, calming influence, and beauty, exhilarating in its exciting experience.

Human parasitic feelings, slemotions, create a dire need for dittomen and yesmen in a society always hungry for mantasy-fantasy ruling gods doling out magic pills, excusing "specials" from responsibility to satisfy their lust for control, pitting individual against society.

When facts are on the table for everyone to see and use, fem and man can develop a more rational society, more user friendly to ut as a forthright and selfual-developed being. Society is then *with* the individual and the individual *with* society. Moreover, ut does not need to fight for and demand that *access to information* rights be writ in law!

Sapien education then includes the *responsibility* of doing thinking to be sapiens. Ut is born with the right to be a thinking being by the very fact that ut is born with a mind, ut's senses, and ut's body configuration. Ut learns to be an efficient and effective citizen member, a *selfual being* in ut's species. The responsibilities of being consistent and constant in the respect of mind are the stuff of dignity, serenity, equanimity better than the ultimate goal so desperately chased after as "bliss in heaven" in $2 = 1$, life = death: sound-mind-in-sound-body happiness. There is no name in manity for this kind of happiness. *Consonality* and *selfuality* may be the closest symbols naming the serenity and honor that distinguish happiness in living sapien life as thinking life that most—unknowingly—seek.

Progress in $2 = 1$ man is about the studflation of man, wealth, power, and sex. Reason and science demand we look at all resources on earth as finite, including air, water, and thinking life. But progress in humanity defies life in all its forms by its sacred clause of limitlessness in Alpha Male, unjust and uneven all the way. How does one progress in limitlessness? Which direction does one choose? Today the gross imbalance of the supply and demand of material goods veils immeasurable intellectual dearth in truths and the pain in excessive confusion, runaway technology, WMD, warring, WVD, poverty, exploding sex slavery, out-of-control irrationality and myth, conspicuous acquisition and consumption, polluted air, poisoned waters, diminishing forests and lands, and deficient minds. Progress is the unaccountable seminal competition in the phallic activity to be Mr. #1 God. Jim Jones took 990 souls to heaven with Him, Hitler, six million, not to mention that the civil strife brought on by American Christians in Muslim Iraq.

Lords preoccupied with the rate of progress measure wealth and growth—by killing machines, destruction, and deaths. Correct thinking would change progress to allow better planning, make it fair, more even, and just, more attainable for citizens. But in $2 = 1$ man exploiting fertile lands, redirecting whole rivers, covering land with pavement, clear-cutting forests, and sending thousands of lesser men to the killing fields as cannon fodder are nobody's business but the Lord's. How fast H/he can get filthy rich is the goal in the twenty-first century. Greed once named a vice is now a virtue. The believing manmass is unaware that capital*ism* is achieved by special men by pitting man against man to keep the socialized w-o-*man* servile "in" man; the manmass do not see *esoteric slavery*.

Thinking life, in the meantime, is more practically livable, directed as it is toward being rational, it goes at its own—rational—pace. Just as you cannot rush pregnancy to six months, you cannot rush life by a delusion of grandeur in Holy Alpha Males who resurrect themselves as saviors who solve all problems, grievances, and injustices.

You see sapien progress by the critical number of selfual individuals aiming to keep their species and planet earth as natural as possible, more pleasant, less fearful, less riddled with violence, war, and whoring. The quality of good thinkers with the quantity of correct thinkers shows that thinking life goes at its own pace, since being *on the same playing field*, consensus, discussion, and integrated theses are more likely to take place to create rationality on earth.

So the issue of measurability in sapien progress is not wealth, possessions, length of penis, takeover bids, nor the number of phallic highs a nation can call up, all manumeters. It is the number of selfual beings skilled at balancing what in duality goes to make a society user friendly to all selfual beings. Ut learns facts, correct information, and the skills to think based on Q is Q and 2 = 2, moral bases for ut's honest emotions and desires. Making rational choices based on correct information in, with, and through honest emotions is what moral behavior is. The more individuals exercise choice based on symbols and language true to reality, the more moral and user friendly society is going to be.

Where progress is what the infinite One can do, gender, race, and class stand on divisions of male, not male, clean, not clean, white, not white, rich, not rich, minded, and not minded. Ninety percent get their identity from *negatives*. The elite ten percent, the *positives* of male, rich, white, virile, clean (non-menstruating)—hard, studflated, narcissist slemotions invade the scene, disseminating common evil, the peacockery rampant, varied, and individualistic. Few achieve an authentic self-identity in splits and extremes.

Where critical thinkers and right-minded scientists commit to finite resources, which is all we have, to define, describe, and explain finite earth and its natural existents, which is all we have, thinking progresses at a slower pace with truths in the finite mind, which is all we have. But what we have is more than adequate for our species.

The responsible individual is what is wanted and needed. The zenith of individual*ism* in doctrinal man is that the male is individuated. W-o-man-attached-to-man becomes Mrs. His Name, naming her phallic attachment. Possessed, it stops *fem* from individuating herself in her inalienable right and responsibility to be a logic-affirming being, fem in her own right and in her own name; fem's sense of individuation as her own name giver is canceled. Jane Norfem cannot name an authentic self: She must be a caricature man. Lions do not kill for the hell of it, yet man destroys fem and her mind for the heaven of it. Destroying the individuality in half the species destroys individuality, and the cesspool of individualisms floods the earth. Chaotic behavior is the consequence.

What is individual*ism*? Individualism is the "personal" autonomy to be excessively needy, needing ritual, prayers, mantras, magic, force, war, fashions, drugs, marks on the wall, public strokes, gifts, corporate perks, repetitious dogma, and a prepackaged fear of God in a reward-him-punish-her system. God allows a whip "the size of his thumb" to be used on recalcitrant wives! The *veneration gap* between the Lord in His refinements of wealth, status, sex, and power; the superman in control ruling the massed; and socialized woman and lesser man is obvious. Nietzsche's *superman* celebrates the irrationality (cultured ignorance in individuals) of the masses! Lies and false power create individualism. Today whole nations are infected.

Individuality is best expressed when fem and man identify themselves with the truths of being fem and/or man. Both have more than enough brains to do this simple task. Both can respect the evidence that goes to make an authentic identity. Nature evolved fem and man, so nature is neither for nor against them. Nature just is. Fem and man are animals by fact of evolution. These facts make them neither good nor bad. They are part-as-wholes in reality, simple facts make many truths! To resist evidence is to be immature, whence individualisms.

So if we did not achieve consonance with nature, then it is because it is imposed upon us that "Nature (too) is *against* us"—*enemy*—again done in "The Word": Nature (body/object—*she*) opposes man (limitless mind). Mother Nature is mean! This is deadly anti-rational bunk that develops individualisms with very harmful implications for all, including nature. But enemy making is 2 = 1 man's favorite pastime, dichotomy using sex as the axe to split potential thinkers into opposed camps of believing men.

Mind and body, animal and intellectual activity, symbol making and using, feelings and emotions, the facts of nature and the evidence in reality are all used in developing selfual individuality. Duality puts all issues closer *to the center on the same plane*, making it easier to learn the skills of discernment to find truths. The selfual individual, near this center with other self, can *vise* at/*see* vital truths, giving ut what is needed to learn the skills to go to real adult maturity. *Viser*, Fr., from L., to aim the sight, made visual and visibility. All reason and justice demands no less than that we see things correctly, reality-as-it-is. To see Q or not to see Q, that is the sapien test. All sapiens, be they black, disabled, feme, highly intelligent, male, and so on, must see the same evidence to have the basic truths necessary for selfual identity. Truths are tools to integrity and authenticity for living life as thinking beings.

The mind in its capacity to see/visualize the self as both object and subject is its self-reflectivity. How does consciousness start? Not by being a One. But by seeing other like selves, observing other minds in action. Selfual contains the truth that ut cannot learn the symbol system without mothers, fathers, and many others teaching ut at a young age. It is in this learning process that self-reflectivity, developing consciousness as a *moral process* starts in creating ut's identity to become a genuine individual. To be selfual, ut has to be as other-self-centered, as ut is self-centered to create an authentic self, able to stand up as a thinker in the face of clever head tricks like divinity in males.

There is no true or real individuality without considering other self in the equation in the making of an authentic identity for the self. Self minus "other" self = individualism. Soul + the "opposite" not-one = individualism. Man + not-man = individualism.

Truths that develop selfual being undo the privileges of money, sex, and power grabbed by Holy Alpha Males. Doing good reasoning and thinking critically, doing constructive-destructive creativity, being a wise individual as role model, living as a good moral thinker give *value* to the sapien as sapien. Valued thinking life values air, water, forests, other animals, food, sex, self-power, and living life as thinking life. This is what it means to live by the multiplicity of truths.

When a house is no longer repairable, it is destroyed to create a new one. Creativity is a delicate balance between destruction and creation. Little constructive creativity exists in 2 = H/him. In balancing constructive with destructive, creating like matter *with* form, fem with man are a team. They are not enemies, opposites, like in 2 = 1 Truth.

One Holy Truth, 2 = 1 man, is belief in lies and fantasy. It is not about relating facts and truths. Many truths contribute to intelligence as facts to make knowledge, the more facts ut acquires, the more intelligent ut is, what sapiens need and want. Two truths, being feme and being male, two out of many forms of life have value both for creating the identity of being individuals living thinking life. Individuals respecting the truth of rights *with* the truth of responsibilities and all that this entails are more likely to be more mature individuals and more moral citizen members of the collective or society. To them, evidence is evidence.

Chapter 15

CALLING VALUES

Making value calls is intimately connected to making symbols consonant with reality; value is expressed in names that reflect reality. Although
value calls are not demonstrable, they must be rationally justifiable in
the sense that the most defensible calls be supported by the best reasons. The appeal is to reason, not arbitrary whim or 2 = 1 ideological
dogma. *We not only can reason about values, we must reason about
values if we're going to get agreement without manipulation or
coercion* (Hinderer 1997).

What should we value as good, or *bad*? Are values called by experiences sharing evidence and based on knowledge, or by ideology based
on belief without evidence?

In "the equality of persons in the eyes of God," Father Man-u fixed
a for-eternity *holy* inequality in 2 = 1 man of opposite genders. George
Orwell spoke of "evil is good" in *1984*, but did not talk about the highly
valued *equality of Lords, a.k.a. men lording it over low-valued men of
opposite genders*, a cross fitting covert inequality in most Holy Books.

It is important to see that equality of opportunity, condition, and
outcome in 2 = 1 are guaranteed-by-God inequalities of wealth, prestige,
and power by gender, race, and class. Those with the "chosen" *mentula*,
genitals, are the possessors, the rest possessed, powerless, cheap labor,
cheap sex, ready worshippers, and slaves. The blatant discordance
between what He named us, man and woman as human, and what we
are in reality, fem and man as sapiens, forces existence to be lived by
the one-size-fits-all value in the standard fixed in illogical, irrational,
and dishonest name, prescribing all to be man.

Three valuations, categorical, lexical, and index, of fem as *fem* are absent in 2 = 1 valuation. Everything is in H/his Name. Most citations are men's, and patronymics are almost all we have, skewing equality of opportunity, condition, and outcome. A job needs the best man!

It is to be noted that equality based on fair valuations impacts on knowledge and, in turn, on behavior—moral, social, and individual. Yet inequality/God's plan in Torah, Bible, Koran, Holy Book teaches man equality among males, the only basis of equality we have. "All men are created equal" is writ in the U.S. constitution. Where are all fem?

It is *behavior* that is either good or bad. Not air, trees, money, body, or sex. As goes the thinker or believer, so goes their behavior. We judge behavior, the good or evil of an act committed or omitted by the thinker or believer. A tree cannot consciously act. Moral behavior stands on both (1) *being* the minded animal ut is by birth, and (2) *doing* correct thinking for right choice in actions. Lies stop moral growth, the achievement of maturity and the development of an authentic self-identity.

Correct categorical valuation names fem and man as gender-different, logic-affirming agents in the general category, sapiens. In this, fem as fem is an independent individual to the same extent as man by symbol, definition, and name in society. Naming both fem and man both society and individual sees 2 = 2 and Q is Q in knowledge, leading to a more constant habit in making moral decisions, both now on the same solid criterion for valuation. Fem has value in *doing* good thinking and *being* a good thinker *with* man doing the same. Fem and man then have value as a team of logic-affirming agents.

Lexical valuation names fem as fem with man as man in the category sapiens, *registered* in dictionaries and books. The morpheme fem has value and is used to generate other symbols necessary to achieving rationality and maturity, for example, femhood and statesfem. Fem is a linguistic law, a registered name in the dictionary. *Fem* having lexical value, the need to indoctrinate the lie of both being man evaporates.

Index valuation acknowledges fem's contributions as a member of the team. Feme names such as Naaje Cosfem and Akia Femsal lets society know that she is an independent, creating, and civilizing agent with man, contributing to the species intellectually and physically. This builds practical self-confidence and self-esteem in fem *and man*, since it does not take away anything from him except his ESP (Extra-Seminal Power). In fact, it makes distinguishing himself easier. It is easier to highlight difference in diversity/duality (2) than in needing the fantasy of hard-drive virility to prove himself in monolithic 2 = 1 man.

These three aspects of valuation have an impact on the three factors of opportunity, condition, and outcome. Fem and man see that they stand on the same ground of probabilities seen in reality. Both see they have efficient minds as individuals and that the possibility of sufficient mind in the collective is real. So it is not facetious to say that the ground for *equality* of opportunity, condition, and outcome shifts with the mindquake that comes with the voice—*sonality*—of fem as fem. It should not be necessary to say that fem in tune with reality acting with man in tune with reality achieve more honest, more rational, and thus better results. Sky-hooks and seminal crooks disintegrate.

Undoing *pre*determined manu-spoken inequalities embedded in false identities is necessary. We must destroy false identities' predetermined inequalities fixed in stereotypes: of opposites, *moral man*, individual, in immoral society, collective, she, anti-man, enemy. Biblical "knowledge" of w-o-man is sin, even dividing priest from not-priest. Inter*pret*ation of "The *Word*" by priests, non-sinners, splits married and single men, sinners (pret → *prêtre*, Fr., → priest). Priest, male, inter*prets* God's Word to the (unread) masses is higher. Priests go to seminaries to stud/y God, semen → seminary, and *matri*culate in theology, the *body (feminine)* of "knowledge" about God, feather-bedding solipsism!

In predetermined false identities, girls suffer identity deprivation as be-ers/objects. Boys are gifted with identity inflation as do-ers/subjects. Man is subject of act, thought, and deed; she is weak, passive body, non-minded object. *Sorosis*, Gr., sister, fleshy heap or mass, is the attitude in global objectification, pornography, prostitution, and such. He is do-er (mind) and she is be-er (body). In reality-as-it-is, both fem and man are both be-ers and do-ers; both fem and man have both mind and body. *The holy balls in seminaries set up gender-as-division of mind and body entangling sex and gender in all issues affecting all facets of life.*

Social inequality between the fe + *male* and the male disadvantages the feme in man's system of value stratification. It makes her permanent victim in mankind, fit punishment for "the one who brought sin" into the *wor*ld, fulfilling biblical intent. Femes and lesser males below higher males strike valuation at its core, destroying it. Good and bad applies only to acts of behavior, not twisted identities imposed by sex-crazed, power-hungry weaklings who lust for power as they *stud*-y the *matri* in seminaries (cf. stallion → mare, stud → matri, as in matriculation).

Social, cultural, and individual identity deprivation for girls and identity studflation for boys are taught smack in the middle of the family, in home-sweet-home first, Mr. and Mrs. His Name. Girl learns her mother's identity is worth zero and boy sees that his is a special gift for a wife's deprivation, marriage, a holy vow blessed by God.

It will not be easy undoing the addiction to belief. Wealth, power, and prestige in higher men are big obstacles. But identity studflation harms males as much as identity deprivation harms femes. Sacred Socialism of femes collectively as serfs in Sacred Capitalism, man's machine of perpetual inequality to become possessors of wealth, power, and prestige creates big conflicts in the manmass. Conflicts keep H/his entitlement to be possessor hidden, needing the ongoing *dialectic of opposites— enemies*—making deficient mind believe that all the chicanery between the genders is normal and even natural. Divorce lawyers make good money on this philosophy, so too, sexual harassment lawyers.

Mostly social*ism in* capital*ism* and vice versa exist, eighty-five percent of the global wealth is in the ten percent of *neutral* hands of higher men. Balancing social elements with capital factors is not in God-man's politics. We cannot know what a society based on $2 = 2$ means, so we don't know what a team of logic-affirming agents can do. Those who dare to analyze "man as a party of One for the two" are called deviants, shunned and even punished, the dissenting voice threatened or quashed, sometimes assassinated. *Neutral* Control, through the lie, is a hundred times more addictive than cocaine.

It is in the act of each naming utself that everyone identifies utself as logic- affirming being, showing ut's thinking behavior in public/society. When girl is indoctrinated socially, psychologically, culturally, and financially as attached-to-male object from birth, boymen and girlwomen result. As harsh as this may sound, just look about you to see that this is truer than you dare admit. Mind is infantilized in believers; the manmass needs Him for solace and comfort. We fink all the brutal way to salvation to death = life in the arms of God, as life itself is bullet riddled with lies and confusions. *Resisting evidence is the hallmark of immaturity.*

Isonomic names communicate an *equality of value by definition* in practical and rational terms. Fem and man have value each as utself, like diamond and honey each has its own value. Iso, equal + nomy, name, entails the same consistent law of logic in naming that respects reality. The same arrangement of cause and effect, important to consistency in logic and to consonance with reality in both fem and man, shows probabilities. (1) Fem is the feme animal who makes and uses symbols to communicate (2) *with* (3) man, the male animal who makes and uses symbols to communicate = two distinct logic-affirming agents.

Both fem and man, *quantity*, have *quality by definition*, up front for everyone to see. No *mysterium tremendum* here to wool you over! Man and fem serve the truth function in sapienity as thinking beings by definition, so that *be*ing a thinker and *do*ing thinking are *in consonance* with reality as we *with* nature evolve mind and body to be.

What, then, is this autonomy so many desire? One is never without limits. Is autonomy the *right* "to do your own thing"? Is this not a Q is and is not Q in 2 = 1? In 2 = 1, H/he acts alone, *auto*, self, + *nomy*, naming; naming himself, H/he entitles himself to act alone as if the feme, *other self*, did not exist. Whence selfish Mr. #1!

The selfual fem or man is as independent in the collective as ut is dependent on truths and other selves. The fact of independence of self *with* dependence on truths and other selves is better named *inter-independence*. To behave as if no other self counts is to assume being #1 God. Knowledge of other selves makes the individual be-er as dependent on others and on truths as ut is independent as an individual do-er. Inter-independence is the best we can have, since we must do/act in consideration of others at all times.

It is an irrefutable fact that no one can discover utself in isolation of other selves. Observing and respecting other self/mind in ut's own growth to an integral and authentic mind-and-body self is as important as one's inner observations, IQ, and circumstances; a consonality has many causes. For in the social enterprise that is speech, everyone must have access to it in order to develop independence, maturity, and morality, since in symbols is where the self of myself and other self are communicated. Feral babies growing up in isolation suffer a great loss of intelligence and self-identity, barely able to learn to speak.

Just like you cannot make water without oxygen, you cannot achieve rationality and wisdom being the One. A moral society needs both thinkers affirming and distinguishing good logic-based thinking. Q is always Q in thinking that is thinking, whether creative, critical, analytical, scientific, or ordinary daily thinking.

Q that is and is not Q poisons thinking with so much irrationality it is daunting to do good thinking. Examining how ut is indoctrinated into humanity, what ut is given to believe, and then identifying the traits and appetites in ut's acquired emotional and valuation objectives has to be done item by item to undo the damage. But once done, the Social Engineering Project of transmuting two into one man, imposed coercion and internalized doctrinal Absolutes, become visible, exposing the 4,000-year-old grandiose hypocrisy passed off as Holy Truth.

Ut will find that being a product of human socialization is to have no true self or real independence: H/he commands; you obey. Even lesser men have to be alert that Lordly wealth, power, prestige, and sexual access do not erode for Lords, that w-o-man keeps serving H/his divine plan as "equal-but-different" serf. Providence does not "provide" hu/man serfs with the critical resources needed to assess the hundreds of hidden fiats in 2 = 1 man.

Independent thinkers disavow beliefs and belief systems that do not square with facts, truths, reality, nature, or laws of logic. Consistency, coherence, and consonance are seen in 2 = 2 where Q *is* Q. So I speak of selfual beings as having a *consonality*, an internalized sound, symbol system, a sonality *consonant with reality* to act upon. I do not speak of *per*sonality, the *mer*sonality, the mother-sonality banned long ago. But these are not the issues. The issue is having *consonalities, speech habits in consonance with truths, nature, and reality used to create an authentic identity of self as a fem or a man, sapiens, to create honest, trustful individuals for an honest, trustful species.*

The value in having a consonality is irrefutable. Consonance between symbol and reality, mind and body entails the agreement of cause and effect reflected in name. Since an apple is a fruit, it is dissonant to call it a fig, that is, *apfig*. Naming helps to call the value of the relationships between cause and effect for stable moral values; *the name must reflect reality*. No apple is a fig; no fem is a man. **No fem to affirm logic; no stable moral values**.

To acquire a consonality, ut has to develop consistency and logical coherence between thoughts, ideas, and sound. This entails accepting the evidence existing in reality. When ut uses consistence, ut posits probabilities from which the possibilities in these are affirmed and distinguished—or falsified—by other selves. A natural consensus takes place. Man's manipulation of mind by embedding lies and coercion by repetitious indoctrination is morally wrong. Knowledge does not need such tactics.

Feeling dead right about issues, for example, "homosexuality is sin," has no place in a consonality. Slemotions have no place in selfual beings. Probabilities are not about certitude. The quantity of existing examples showing the quality of evidence has a *fallibility quotient*. Ut can have no more certainty than what is shown in the probabilities seen in reality. Mind is stronger and more resilient where it does not have Absolute sacred certitude. Awareness stays high. But developing strength of mind or *psychephisis* is not desired when control by the neutral hands of L/lords is the aim.

Quantity in differences gives to probability what quality of similarity gives to possibility. Where one logic-affirming agent is absent, for example, fem, valuation goes awry. The more symbols-in-consonance ut acquires, the more intelligent and mature ut becomes, and thus the more self-directing and better citizen ut is in society. Ut becomes an authentic self not afraid of being utself *vis à vis* any characteristic historically used to discredit reason.

A consonality has a stable criterion in probabilities for the critical scrutiny of incoherent information, incompatible and false beliefs. Q is Q for everyone on planet earth, mars, and sky, so that $2 = 2$ always. As self-directed agent, ut will not be afraid to stand up to hold the God-fearing believer accountable for his thought behavior. Ut will see that tolerance of the lie to control the "masses" is not a charitable character trait. Dissonance is failed self-control, a form of insanity I call *manusclerosis*.

One who gets a consonality will want and expect the same basic rational and honest emotions in other selves. Ut will need strength of mind in others, encouraging strengths, since ut can never be free from social life and socialization. Social life, then, should be on the same rational plane as individual life. Where individual knowledge is in consonance with collective knowledge, ut is in a user-friendly, thinker-friendly society.

When fem and/or man formulate life plans, paying attention to ut's capabilities, inclinations, and honest feelings and elect these plans unencumbered by the coercion to conform to humanity's splits and stereotypes, their life plans are authentic. *Being* a thinker and *doing* thinking are consonant in their characters as bases for general behavior. Man and fem are then the natural thinking animals, sapiens, that evolution began.

Where a crucial number of symbols-in-consonance-with-reality is currency, *value* calling by "quantity with quality" is fair and easier. Ut internalizes cumulative value-in-consonance until ut becomes a selfual individual with a *consonality*. Ut does it by and for utself in, with, and through other selves, a dual track all the way. Good breeds good. Ut comes to know that *mind is sufficient for good action and moral self-direction* for the common good.

Naming is not "free will" to make any old name fit, for example, apfig and woman. The symbol fem builds *psychephisis* through true-to-reality symbols; consonance strengthens mind. Dissonance weakens mind, bifurcating it to accept Q is and is not Q.

Consonance then also has value for *skill training* to integrate two logic-affirming agents. Where quantity (of evidence) with quality (of evidence) is seen in integrating two beings, ut sees ut's social individual and collective participant roles for good citizenship. There are few real citizens in 2 = 1 man, believers being mostly cynical and hypocritical.

Competency in *integrating* duality, two logic-affirming agents, requires consistency and coherence to develop an integrated image of being a speech-using animal in the large spectrum of animal life on planet earth. A consonality leads ut to do what a thinking animal does by ut's nature: Think. Like the nature of bees makes honey and sheep make wool.

The value of consonance for self-motivation is high. Having symbols consonant with reality, ut respects the determinants that impact on thinking life, and thus all of life. Nature, reality, relationships between causes and effects determine and *limit* thinking life to the same extent good habits of thought in ut's mind do. Mind limited to knowledge of what is in reality trains ut to see probabilities to focus on possibilities. Ut needs what is necessary to do good thinking to acquire good habits of thought. Self-motivation is easier and more pleasant when ut's mind has the right things ut needs to be a sufficient mind. Knowing what ut needs to contribute to sapiens, ut is motivated to go after it with more passion.

Dissonance, concepts-in-opposition *a priori*, predetermines eternal conflict: "Every *man* for himself" confuses, warring and whoring the hallmarks. Belief's good 'nough. Life with drugs, booze, sex-as-sin, religion, porn, flakiness, poker, $$$, war, and God give comfort. The unspoken command: Resist evidence. Fear of truths sets in, a symptom of infantilism in manusclerosis. It's all about "God rest ye Merry Gentlemen" because "Long lay the world in sin and error pining—'til He appeared."

In consonance, more sapiens can participate more broadly in social life because thinking is based in stable, comprehensible probabilities, the same information accessible to all. Any child over nine can see the reality of probabilities and understand what it is; too much licorice (cause) = belly ache (effect). In respecting relationships between cause and effect, problems become solvable. Ut's participation in ut's social milieu is real; this is self-motivating. Ut can participate more broadly in ut's social milieu seeing that ut's contribution enhances the group/collective, reducing angry and vengeful reactions.

Where selfual beings have Q is Q and 2 = 2 as a frame of reference, it makes society more user friendly to ut as individual criminal mindedness shrinks. Mind is more efficient when ut can see utself as capable of doing thinking to build a strong, authentic sense of self-esteem.

The value of integrity in selfual being is multifaceted. Fem with man are sapiens is the fallible structural integrity existing in reality. The symbolic structure man with fem as sapiens reflects this structural integrity: Symbols and reality come together in consonance with one another because they have rational integrity.

Ecological integrity is called in being selfual. The duality of gender in the multiplicity of sexual life and procreation open to multiple causations, diversity, is a basic truth necessary to minded beings. Deny the evidence of duality, and diversity denied becomes a basis for conflict and war, for example, the means of grabbing *liebensraum* for Hitler's Germany.

Structural, ecological, and rational integrity are important for intellectual integrity to achieve a genuine selfual-based *integral society* of correct-thinking individuals who become a natural sponsor of its correct-thinking individuals. Ut can then be a *sapiential* contributor to ut's species, a wiser citizen, since thinking is now thinking. Such integrity builds sound and strong healthy mind in a sound and strong healthy body.

Emotional, sexual, cultural, organic, and moral integrity follow naturally from structural, ecological, and rational integrity. Consonance in fem and man affirm and distinguish the value of respecting logic in each and every member. Valuation is on the same playing field where Q is Q for all, since it puts the players on the same honest plane.

In a party of One-for-the-two, most live in ignorance, misinformation. Dissonant parts cannot be integrated. *Assimilation, the One swallowing the opposite* not-one, is imposed in H/his culture, built in by the giving-in weakness in not-men and lesser men cultivated by higher man to gain control, an imposed weakness I call *givinity.*

The integrity in $2 = 2$ destroys givinity and brings a serenity hardly experienced before. Ut, in a thinker-friendly society, has a deep sense of belonging to ut's species, since ut's contribution to ut's society is welcome, providing real psychological comfort. The politics in God's Plan does not provide such earthly pleasurable comfort.

One question in God's Plan is, is politics valid? Politics is the official *policy of exclusion,* the "is *not* Q" antithesis in Q is and is not Q. In the *Me-win*-you-lose game of $2 = 1$, pole opposites are played against each other. Either you are for me or against me, the enemy philosophy. Conflict methodology puts out lies, falsehoods; embezzles knowledge; conceals information; and uses big $$$ to win the megalomaniac endgame in the greed for *neutral* control. Citizens seldom get fully spelled-out policies with mode of implementation and costs. They almost always get nasty attack campaigns from both *opposing* sides.

Yet it is far easier, more pleasant, more economical, and more effective to use the knowledge of integrated fem and man, where coherence already exists by definition to be harnessed for policy making, planning, and implementation for setting fair and just laws and rules. Selfual individuals understand the centrality of duality in rule making and rule following in policies affecting the whole group, society, or species.

Democracy is where that cushy-pushy rule of God-fearing political $$$-men in their hierarchical garb gove*r*n by "we know what's good for you." No queendom dares challenge the kingdom of democratic man! Political man is L/lord in democracy. Yet there is no species where males collectively own and rule all femes collectively like in the hu*man* *king*dom, only in man, showing that politics is theological and theology is political man's dualism, the art of claiming in name that which you cannot claim in reality.

In sapienity, order rests as much on rule following as it does on a rule center in society. Rule-following citizenship issues from the selfual development of the individual. Other selves, as well as utself, need and want *life* is *life*, Q is Q, and 2 = 2.

The rule center in sapien society, then, is *biocracy*, rule by what all of life needs to live life at its best. *Biocracy* includes *by definition* the multiplicity of life forms containing many life plans. All life forms are respected to plan a good and honest integral rule center on earth. How else is the rational, ecological, wise stewardship of planet earth to be done?

Politics in 2 = 1 man does not address our responsibility as *life* stewards. The center is man. In his politics, false opposites/poles/politics need false names for political gain. In sapiens as sapiens, there is no need to hide lies, no need to defend secrets by sword politics.

Since no symbol user lives in isolation *of others* who use speech, so no life form lives in isolation of other life forms. All *life forms* make up the *ecological integrity* defining *life* created in evolution. Anything else is a lie. Politics divides to make enemies; it does not unite and create harmony. Biocracy unifies by including and valuing all forms of life.

Having said this, there can be no quick break from democracy to *biocracy*, the inclusive life-enhancing integrative process that sapienity with its dual-to-multiple causation implies. The first step is to stop the strife-full life that life = death to be in the Lord's arms that $2 = 1$ man conjured. As true-to-reality symbols take hold, individuals, institutions, leaders, learning centers, and social assemblies will bring people into a more reason-based society. Ut will act on truths and behave as inter-*in*dependent selfual being among the many, a society friendly to ut's emotional and rational capacity for truths and change. This is neither idealistic nor utopian, nor easy. But it is not the manutopian goal of Creator God-man engineering a limitless perfectible humanity born in sin, embedded in political language that set up the destructive system of *death* = eternal life and *common evil*.

Sapienity does construction with destruction creativity. Humanity does destruction creativity almost exclusively. Creativity is a dual process, allowing for flexibility in the intellectual and emotional commitment to create for the *common good*.

The value in *isonomic* names becomes evident. Since man is named as the male animal who makes and uses symbols to communicate, the same consistency in definition must be in fem's name: Fem is the feme animal who makes and uses symbols to communicate. Isonomy *values* consistence in causal relationships, giving value to correct relationships between cause and effect, correct information. *If both members of the species do not identify themselves as logic-affirming agents, critical thinking is of little help in many other disciplines because the foundation upon which critical thinking stands is the two members of the species*. Critical thinking cannot stand on a foundation of infallible mantasy-fantasy.

This does not do away with hierarchy, present in most categorization. It prevents sky-hooking *special* men on a skewed hierarchical valuation of men. Both thinkers must be on the same plane as thinkers, as logic-affirming agents, giving mind its value. Both closer to the center on the same plane makes it easier to integrate the thesis of fem *with* the thesis of man, discussed in the last chapter.

The value of a Rofemtic Movement, then, is true-to-reality language.

Necessary true-to-reality facts, multiple truths, correct information support the logic-affirming mind.

Believing revealed Truth is not knowledge. Lords do not take orders, they give them; obedience is law. The lie w-o/man can be dropped, like *fem* was dropped centuries ago. Using truths undoes the seminal evil that is the source of frustration, anger, and violence that lies beget. **The price of one lie is the loss of many truths.**™ No lie is worth the prices paid.

We can know moral ideas. When the foundation of education stands on fallible probabilities in reality, sufficient mind is a real possibility. Education has value to the extent that ut acquires the essential skills to see multiple causes and their effects correctly in the cosmos. Useable facts enhance life as life, furthering thinking/conscious life. The possibilities in probabilities derive from reality.

In the rigid neutral hands of Holy Alpha Males in the Sky, certitude in the Absolute needs many volumes of words to cover lies; learning is harder and takes longer. Sapienity needs fewer books, since limits bearing on facts and truths take far fewer written explanations than the zillions of hair-thin arguments needed to prop the 2 = 1 Lie called Truth; *falsity management* goes into full H/he-gear! It's called theology.

The ethics in two logic-affirming agents necessary for morality is see-able. Like the front wheels of a car go nowhere without the back wheels, no matter how perfect the motor, both sets of wheels are necessary for the car to run as a car. *Both man and fem are necessary to develop rationality, knowledge, and wisdom.* Every individual, group of two, three hundred, or six billion participates in thinking where Q is Q and 2 = 2. It gives ut the strength of mind to see that Q cannot be both Q *and not-Q.*

Knowing "fem with man are sapiens" puts all babies on an equal footing on the same plane in the same playing field. This does not level individuals to being identical. The fields of opportunity, condition, and outcome enable individuals in the species to get out of the rut of saw-toothed democracy built on 2 = 1 man, where capitalism and its kept socialized whore of fixed lesser men and inequities keep the status quo for higher men. Knowing dual causation opens to multiple causation opens the way for *biocracy, rule by the value in and respect for all life forms making life central to life profoundly ecological.* Since everything we do is communicated by symbols, using true-to-reality symbols makes the species wiser and the more moral basis for ethics. Individuality will distinguish itself in such a rich field of truths with their concomitant limits. Limits make creativity bloom.

The responsibility to demand the right to correct information, then to implement a Rofemtic Movement, will grow at an incremental pace until we reach a critical mass of thinkers committed to truths in knowledge. Not technocratic education, not cultural/patriarchal tradition, nor man-party/political rhetoric, nor higher men all peddling "Holy Truth" from Absolute-Man Authority, but probable facts, real truths, and correct information in knowledge, in short, multiple authorities. *Evidence,* seeing what exists, facts and truths in knowledge are some of the multiple authorities. Multiple causation—multiple authorities, so again, welcome to reality!

I realize this will bring down the ivied balls of academe on my head, but a Doctorate has value only within the criterion Q is Q and 2 = 2. One cannot just hold a Doctorate; ut must also do duality-based methodology to do balanced construction and destruction in order to do moral creating. But the blanket reverence accorded to the Doctorate in "the Humanities" allows their holders to get away with sophisticated embezzling of knowledge through technese, academese, and learnese without ever having to get on their knees to apologize. Their language is so "high" they read each other's *work.* The manmass believes it is too stupid to understand, so it does without "the knowledge," believing instead, and misses seeing any hoax. Thus, "immoral society" (she) serves "moral man" (He), all the while learned *fem* is absent. From *learned men,* this is intellectually reprehensible.

Truths do not need any *legitimizing mechanism or agency.* Correct information and knowledge stand on their own right. The cocksure assumption that man is two men flying brazenly as a legitimate concept needs millions of sophisticated hair-thin arguments hiding destructive-only creativity. *No pro-lifers, the most "moral" people on planet earth, make a plea for the millions of girls forced into sex slavery to be stopped. The eleven- to sixteen-year-olds are disposable! Yet the five-minute-old zygote is not! Is it God's Plan to have so many disposable vaginas for phallic pleasure on earth?* What is wrong with this picture?

The construction-destruction method is in most creativity. Creating is like a box of Lego pieces. It is a process of doing and undoing and redoing. In order to do correct and moral constructive-destructive creating in sapienity, it is necessary to have the following:

1. A critical mass of inter-independent individuals having correct knowledge, honest emotions, and skills of discernment sharpened in integrating dual elements.

2. Societies less fearful of facts and reality in which individuals learn to do critical thinking to develop rationality. Honest emotions from true-to-reality knowledge make commitment to good reasoning easier, motivating ut to do useful and moral creating.

3. A more open discursive order among sapiens whose thinking and feelings are aligned on the same plane of values in reason, nature, and reality to arrive at consensus *by definition* without using coercion, sophisticated lies, sword, and battle force.

4. An integral society of fem and man on the same level playing field to aid social planning to create a more real, open, and just social coherence of rational beings not needing to be massed-in-ignorance "to unite" them.

5. Societies of thinkers friendly to true-to-reality ideas, having interests and emotions communicated in these ideas, creating a user-friendly collective/society for the individual thinker.

6. A species in which obscene wealth and privilege for the lying few obtained by obscene low pay to the controlled lied-to masses is seen as **crimes against the mind**, nature, reality, and the planet. Eliminating the Power-Sex-$$$-Rape-Porno-Prostitution Co. Inc. to stop the excessive waste of intellectual energy that could be used for sapience and moral creativity.

7. Have a truer, more attractive rational definition of power as self-direction and self-discipline built on congruence, consistence, and consonance in self for citizenship. This respects ut's capability to

acquire natural self-control for self-direction in ut's selfuality and individual consonality and so act more morally in society/collective.

8. Have an international consonance between states where stable groups live, so that ideas and interests regarding sapiens and all life forms can be more easily diffused and exchanged. These states can institute education in correct information and in laws more efficiently, faster, and more economically, and by so doing open the field to *biocracy* so that the rule of law that respects what is necessary for all life, regardless of gender, race, class, origin, and species, can be implemented.

A Rofemtic Movement would abolish the immoral opposing paradigms of mother-object *in* Father-Subject. It would abolish Father Supernatural Higher Man and mother sub-natural inferior lower-man to affirm two real *thinking* animals on the same plane in nature with all other animals and life forms. This is as profoundly ethical as it is profoundly ecological. *Biocracy* will motivate societies to put up such institutions as *Sapience Centers* to support good reasoning as a constant basis for moral behavior, setting up a firm foundation of two logic-affirming agents. Almost everybody wins in this; very few, if any, would lose. It is possible to be morally creative in a milieu of good reasoning and honest emotions. It is mind boggling to think of what could be created using truths.

Chapter 16

A THEORY OF INTEGRATION

To impose 2 = 1 man requires a theory of assimilation. It swallows the opposite *in* man and excludes fem as fem by including her as w-o-man. In 2 = 1 man, inclusion *is and is not* inclusion. The con/fusion in two opposite-gendered men is not the answer to harmony in our species. So let us look at a theory that includes fem and man *by definition* in premises that suggest a theory of integration that is more rational and leads to better results.

How do exclusion = inclusion politics differ from integration? When yellow is mixed with blue, the blue acts as blue *with* the yellow acting as yellow. Both as each color integrate to make a third color, green. Assimilation would be if blue made the yellow turn blue—both the yellow-as-blue and blue = blue. Yellow *in* blue = *blue* as if yellow had no effect on blue, had a value of zero as its own color. In assimilation, yellow is not creating *with* blue to make green, yellow "in" blue is blue and creates to make blue dominant.

Fem as w-o-man in man = man. W-o-man has no effect on man = species like apfig has no effect on fig. W-o-man must think, say, and do as a man and give in to the beliefs of man. Like blue stays blue in assimilation in spite of the yellow, man stays male in spite of w-o-man. Fem is not *with* him as another creative agent in sapiens. Opposite, w-o-man is *in* the One, insignificant in dominant man. Her identity as a man-in-name but not in reality makes her carry illogic, destroying her right to identify herself as a logic-affirming agent. Assimilation where it concerns minds is destructive creativity.

The hypothesis "man, species" uses thesis, antithesis, and synthesis as method. Antithesis is *the law of the excluded middle*, what is *not Q* in Q is and is not Q. "Not-Q" is excluded only to be included as not-*man* in man, esoteric, having value only for man. Feminists called man's thinking subjectivism—only to be accused of being strident bitches.

In integration, the differences and similarities seen in two realities are respected as differences and similarities because they each exist as such. In integration, different-*with*-similar *parts* are "whole in *themselves*," each whole-in-itself having its own value. Each whole-in-utself, fem and/or man, has an equal membership in thinking life and participates to the same extent. One of the "whole-in-utself" parts participating is not assumed to be a non-influencing negative *part* or *not-Q*. Fem and man are whole-in-themselves as parts of the sapiens species having equal values. Being minded beings that make speech, fem has her thesis and man has his thesis. Life as feme and life as male are different, mind is similar. Two necessary theses need to integrate to arrive at sapiential wisdom.

Assimilation fuses 2 irrational men into 1 born-in-sin man. Assimilation destroys the foundation upon which critical thinking stands. In assimilation, w-o-man can never be true to herself as fem; she is not and never can be a man. Imposing lies, man also goes against a true-to-himself identity, but differently. Both lose.

Integration keeps 2 = 2 respecting the fact that two minds exist to develop critical thinking and create rationality, the basis upon which morality and good citizenship stand. In integration each existent identifies ut's self as true-to-utself. Both win.

Fem "whole-in-herself," feme-mind-and-body self, man "whole-in-himself," male-mind-and-body self are "parts-as-wholes" that are "wholes-in-themselves" in sapiens. Evolution produced two speech users simultaneously. Man and fem are denoted in isonomic names as sapiens, consonant with reality. As it is in reality, so it must be reflected in symbol.

The reality of two speakers implies two theses. These two theses will be different due to sexual life and similar due to mental life, both must affirm logic in speech. The theses are (1) the thesis of fem as feme, and (2) the thesis of man as male. Since in ***selfual*** development self-interest includes the *other's self-interest*, inclusion is *by definition*; this builds moral direction. The two theses, then, are *thesis* and *other* thesis, not thesis and *anti*thesis, that which is against the thesis. A good name for "other thesis" is *othathesis*.

The two theses are to make an integral (third) thesis having *two* sides due to inclusion *by definition*. The two sides respect feme thinking life and male thinking life *by definition*. The old Greek term *ampho* means having two sides. I call the integral theses of fem and man the *amphothesis*, the *two* theses = a *two*-sided thesis, the *amphothesis* that is sapienity built on facts and truths from which rationality and wisdom are developed by two logic-affirming thinkers. A theory of integration for sapiens is **thesis, othathesis, amphothesis**. The thesis of one *with* the thesis of other one makes a two-sided thesis, an amphothesis that affirms states and keeps the truths Q is Q and 2 = 2 intact.

*Anti*thesis in synthesis is the law of the excluded middle, what is opposite, against the thesis. If we are to call *otha*thesis a law, it is **the law of the included other**, also in *selfual* by definition. *The law of the included other applies to systems of minded beings, profoundly harmonizing and ethical for social thinking animals.* Amphothetic thinking uses the method of dualities in reality by definition where duality exists including *all* those born into the symbolic/speech-using species: Sapiens. *Amphothesis* uses the theses of both fem and man *by definition*, and is thus by definition fair, just, and ethical. No violence need be used to make people *believe* in the lie. No violence need be used to defend its basis, by belief in God. The see-able facts are at ut's disposal to see and use. It is knowledge.

Amphothetic thinking, because it uses the facts of duality, is flexible by the very nature of duality. It includes both state-interest and self-interest, since *selfual citizenship* is based on duality = 2; ut sees life in both perspectives. Mr. Lord #1 is not flexible. So a selfual citizen is the best possible citizen we can aim for, sapiens as related thinkers in the same species, all valued speech users *by definition*. Amphothesis *limits* the two theses done by two finite beings, thus having checks and balances by the very fact of the determinants that impact on the finite two. Sapienity is not like limitless man's hegemony embezzling covert assimilation by making two into a party of one man speaking for the two.

Thesis, othathesis, amphothesis are true to both fem and man as existents. Othathesis is the thesis of the other thinker necessary to achieve rationality. As a law, it is best called "the law of the included other." Including *the necessary other self* is fair, just, and ethical. It is a profound social element needed in the capital of knowledge. It brings *do*ing and *be*ing thinking animals in consonance *with* being social minded animals that ought to be rational and ethical.

With the probabilities in the truths, fem and man predict possibilities. Respecting duality, ut respects dual-based laws in nature walking on two sets of legs for good *balance.* Both *the want and need to be logical and rational* are aims, since symbol and reality must be in consonance with one another *by definition* to be symbols carrying reason and truths.

Lester Pearson and Pierre Trudeau, former Prime Ministers of Canada, put French and English on a level playing field in Canadian law. This helped to make Canada a somewhat gentler and kinder society. They were applying othathesis here, not antithesis. French is not "against" English! Using both expands intelligence.

Where rational attitude *respects the other*, empathy and compassion are more likely to be present. Emotions line up with reason.

Fem having both (1) mind and (2) body can put forth her own thesis as (3) whole thinking being. *Thus the major implication in othathesis is that any symbol, law, or fact affecting or impacting sapiens not affirmed and distinguished—ratified—by fem as fem with man as man is not a symbol for justice, a just law, nor even useable information.* Society consists of fem and man; names and laws ought to be rational to guide moral behavior.

Sapien society is not based on opposing groups, one against opposite as enemies, like hu*man* politics of male and not-male opposing stances, such that few individuals can be members of two at the same time. Sapient society has no one man screaming, "I am the best/highest/holiest/truest," engendering jealousy, envy, hate—and war, many wars, showing *that he himself is not a happy camper in his own man-made system.*

Sapiens using logic-affirming symbols respect the facts of geography; place; available resources; topography; intelligence; talent; pool of rationality; skills; nature, including sexual nature; and reality, including feme reality in correct information that determines and puts limits on their behavior, because they know the *impact on societies*. Differences will always exist in similarity. Truths do not kill the minds in fem and man, nor will truths quash individual and collective differences.

Honesty in cultures and just societies results when differences and similarities are facts arrived at in *amphothesis*. "Opposing" thesis, antithesis, causes factions. German Lutherans, British Anglicans, Roman Catholics, Arab Muslims have opposing-identical *primus inter pares*, enemies, clamoring to be First among F/fathers; *pares* (father) → parish → *peers*, addiction to seminal power, phallic competition among men! Esoteric values in baptism have value only to the flock of believers in Him practicing it *exclusively* to set themselves apart from (and above) all others. Those not baptized in manhood are infidels, enemies, divisive, and not at all unifying. In belief, divisiveness flourishes. Either you believe in God, or Allah, or Emanuel, or Mr. #1—or you do not.

Q is Q is a law that applies to differences and similarities in thinking beings like it does to all other things and issues on planet earth. Consonance assures continuity of correct fact, *a good* as useable knowledge. Integration of mind and body into a reasoning, logic-affirming self is not only possible it is also an ethical aim. Rational laws, symbols, and language have value for developing a sound, flexible mind in a sound and healthy body. Antithesis begets enemies, producing hardcore evidence resistors who lie and use violence.

Standing up for and with the probabilities in evolution are many trial-and-error events, many repeated examinations of "what is" to establish facts and truths seen in the probabilities. Probabilities predict the possibilities for action and wisdom. When Darwin saw the progression of differences in similarities in the multiplicity of animal species, he named it *evolution*. Similarities in relation to differences have implications for finding probabilities, facts, and truths. Darwin, as other evolution scientists showed, was doing creative with scientific thinking, not seminal guesswork as seminarians in seminaries.

Just as we do not call all marsupials kangaroos, we do not call all minded beings men. Seeing the differences-that-distinguish-the-continuity-in-the-similarities sharpens both sight and insight for correct categorization. Evolution in nature shows sapiens that probabilities are inherent with fallibility. But evolution cannot make symbols. We fem and man do categorization using symbols that we make, not an easy task. Selfual language and amphothetic thinking are much more likely to lead to correct categorization.

Language in 2 = 1 man makes man doer (mind) and not-man be-er (body), imposing the selfish and selfless split-life living of one man. Opposing men are enemies and do "the battle of the sexes." Balance is lost in patriarchal language, the speech that is "mankind."

Selfual language, speech including both feme and male selves, is necessary. *Selfual* denotes an integral whole of body and mind in both genders by definition. To develop a balanced self, self-interest with interest in other selves hones the skills of integrating differences and similarities since no self develops in isolation of other selves. It is not possible to make the assertion of two necessary minds in patriarchal English.

Ut as a symbol also denotes both "she and/or he," each as both male and/or fem subject and/or object. Symbols that affirm the existence of two create fairness in speech, and thus are not "neologisms": They are *necessary* to achieve rationality and morality.

We need selfual language to achieve *amphothesis*, to reestablish efficient minds that respect and run on logic. Individual efficient minds see the possibility that collective mind is sufficient. To reestablish efficient minds, facts have to be in thought and knowledge processes expressed in symbols that state what is in reality in correct information. Ut's dignity and serenity as a thinking animal depend on correct information. Tranquility of self, mind, and body follow. This is exhilarating and exciting in its emotional dimension. No one runs around like a chicken with "his" head cut off like "man" does.

Ut is the architect of ut's self when ut keeps sight of other integral selves. Selfual language is integrative; the thesis of self-as-fem and the othathesis of self-as-man make the amphothesis that is sapience, *rationality and wisdom acquired in correct naming. Thesis, othathesis, amphothesis* create an authentic logic-affirming identity of the reasoning, compassionate primate.

As a theory, thesis, antithesis, and synthesis are applicable mostly to non-thinking systems. Thesis, man, antithesis, not-male, synthesis, man, create One Alpha Male in the Sky Causality by The Word, non-existent, esoteric, false, embedded in language used as magic, *a crime against the mind, the source of common evil*. Yet no one is born evil; "he" is made so by the system of error-riddled language that sets up an unfair, unjust, and imbalanced society. Patriarchal Language is made by *higher* criminals zapping in Cause-All Holy Alpha Males to excuse their cosmic seminal crimes against the mind.

In reality, sapiens, like trees, are neither good nor bad. They just are; they exist by accident of evolution. But to be good by ut's own nature, ut must know truths and facts in order to choose from truths. Facts and truths communicate what is/exists in reality in order to *choose* facts and correct knowledge and behave accordingly. Withholding facts, truths, and knowledge, cultured ignorance causes evil beings and unnecessary violence.

Good cannot be bestowed on someone by belief in a religion. But patrists presuppose like they presuppose so many other things that the laws of living systems apply equally *to thinking systems*. Creationists fit the second law of thermodynamics—not applicable to living systems—to the theory of evolution to embezzle that Creationism is as valid as the theory of evolution. But, like you cannot make just any old symbol to name entities, laws are not interapplicable willy-nilly either. Rule-breaking noises teach how to defraud by withholding facts and embezzle error to be deceptive and dishonest, in short, the crime against the mind that is $2 = 1$ common evil. Lies do not lead to moral behavior.

It is rational to say that *the laws of thinking systems are different. The laws applying to minds are different from all other entities, and this difference is to be affirmed and distinguished.* We are not wool makers, nor pearl makers, nor trees, nor machines. Mind really ought to aim at rationality, since neurons and synapses in the brain evolved to do the specific work of relating cause and effect correctly as seen by the senses. The aim creates the basis for a system of many truths in ethics that motivate moral behavior.

In achieving rationality, the relationships between cause and effect, experience, place, time, geography, forebear involvement, insight, knowledge, accidents, circumstances, and consistency play roles singly, together, and cumulatively, since self as integral mind and body is also both subject and object in reality. Thinking life is based on two, pair, duality, *amphorae*, having two sides: There is nothing hard in seeing this.

An organism, says Philip Kitcher (1982), is "a genealogy including a *pair* of organisms and their descendants" (italics mine). *Pair* is *duality*. In all sapiens, all genealogy consists of feme genes and male genes. Hu/man scientists are proportionally accountable for the politico-religious hanky-panky of All-Creating Fathers in colluding with the phallocratic seminal mumbo-jumbo dictated in revelation and creationism.

The tautology Q is Q is meaningful for commitment to 2 = 2 in sapienity. Thinking organisms *are* different from non-thinking ones. The difference does not make them higher or special. Sapiens do not exist in isolation of the ecological system that is all of life. But *all of life* needs 2 = 2 from sapiens to do wise stewardship of all life, including planet earth.

Selfual language names factors in reality as determinants that limit the inter-independence between life forms in existence *probable in fact*, but not said until now. Independence and dependence are like wheels and axle. Wheels work with axle and vice versa. No axle, the wheel becomes a perch for the chickadee.

Inter-independence gives ut the continuity needed to be rational in the face of constant change on both the public and private stages of life. Ut can trust the reliability of ut's feelings and emotions by the soundness and health of ut's speech, Q is Q being one of the keystones in symbol making for all. Just like you don't build a house with toothpicks and ties, you don't build rationality on gender-as-division lies imposed as Holy Truth.

Competency in selfual language, then, is necessary. Selfual language, the language of inclusion by definition, gives the child useable and ethical symbols for development. At the same time, ut gains the skills needed to integrate ut's own dual causation with multiple causations. As ut grows, ut engages in the activity of integrating *other* dual-based selves to develop consonance with others in ut's thinking. Competency in selfual-developed speech, a sonality affirming consonance with reality, leads to sufficiency of mind, a profoundly ethical viewpoint. Ut's competency in inclusive language having a consonality is important to give voice in and to social interaction around shared values that are just and fair to all speech users. Not even the red-haired or blue-eyed races would object to this.

Selfual speech opens the mind to multiple causalities, symbols in consonance with all of life in its multiplicity *by definition*, ecologically sound, acknowledged up front. Authentic as a thinker, ut gains a self-sustaining self-esteem, sufficient to hold a profound respect for the planet we live on—and live off. Ut trusts the reliability of facts and the soundness of ut's speech, since the formula Q is Q applies to all. Ut can trust ut's species in its many societies. Trust is the great motivator of individual and moral behavior.

So if there is anything new in this book, this is it: Real basic *mutual trust* will start to grow again for the first time since 2400 BCE. Seeing the cynicism, apathy, and hypocrisy in man today, there is little if any trust between irrational men of opposite genders. The battle between ad hoc necessary enemies rages on and on as "natural" in humanity. The global arms race testifies! (Testifies, from testicles; patriarchs put a hand on their testicles to show they were telling the truth.)

Where *the right of intelligence is the responsibility to think correctly*, ut must have symbols that state facts to do critical thinking. Ut needs symbols that further good reasoning, *ratiogens*, sources of further good reasoning. This makes thinking easier. Ut has the responsibility to use ratiogenic symbols to do constructive creativity in balance with destructive creativity. This means learning the skills of discernment to call values that lead to moral choices. This means *choosing* to use symbols in consonance with reality for the common good of all. Mind is not a plaything; it is an organ to live conscious life.

Irratiogens cause fatal fissures in the mind like carcinogens cause cancer in cells. These fissures come from predetermined *free*-will lies, making irrationality valid.

Amphothetic knowledge with its premises on the table for all to see is earned in accumulated facts and experiences. Being sapien entails *the responsibility to pass correct knowledge* from self to self regardless of gender, age, color, group, education, intelligence, or social status, implicit in the respect of other self implied in selfual. Amphothetic knowledge makes all fem and man social stewards of mind. *The right to the capital of correct information* comes *with* the *social enterprise of responsibility* to pass it to all the young so that they grow into rational and responsible citizens.

By its very nature, the *capital* that is knowledge is a *social* issue in the species. Kinethics implies the social responsibility to share selfual language—the capital of correct information in symbols—to give every self what is needed to go from individual to collective role without carrying the heavy burden of *Hu*man splits as Truth.

"Education for all," yes, but educate in correct knowledge. How is agreement between correct knowledge as capital property and the social obligation of passing on correct knowledge to be arrived at where Truth is false? How are social coherence and rational continuity infused in the *sense of community* when the false is norm? Too many violations bombard mind in $2 = 1$ ideology, causing a disease of fragmentation and addiction to an abject dependency on irrationality and lies as Truth in manusclerosis.

Addiction to dependency on irrational parasitic life predisposes the potentially rational self to illogical suggestions, especially from L/lords, messiahs, saviors of *men*. Mass appeal, not reasoning, mass rote, not individual knowledge, mass-received revelation, not learning, and mass programs, not valued self-initiative have the masses stuck in anti-rational, anti-nature, and anti-reality language, imposing belief in seminal mantasy-fantasy.

Rofemtic discourse is about the selfual aim in amphothetic thinking. Precise small differences distinguish one entity from another in similarity. Seeing differences in similarity is a skill learned when young, but ut must be taught *correct information to start with*. In duality, the back and forth looking at differences and similarities to see probabilities is to see the possibilities. No probabilities, no sight of possibilities, explaining why we could not see an alternative to $2 = 1$ man for centuries. The probabilities in the partnership of fem with man were not researched, not asserted, not in knowledge, not in truths, not anywhere.

How does an individual learn the skills to balance when One is on a higher plane and the *opposite* on a lower, separate plane? When ut is on the same playing field with all others, ut learns the skills needed to balance ut's self-interests with those of others to achieve a rational, empathic, compassionate self. The respect for difference makes *commitment to rationality* easier and more moral than sinful Hu/*man*ity had ever let us believe. Ut no longer sees the other self as enemy, simplifying the achievement of an honest society.

We need less ritual belief behavior instilled in children by parents, society, and state. We need more genuine and authentic habits of thinking behavior based in good reasoning. We need selfual citizens in society. We need a user-friendly society. We need the knowledge of sufficient mind. Rofemtic discourse with its selfual and amphothetic language names all these *by definition*.

Moreover, rofemtic discourse conceals nothing because it has nothing to conceal. It reveals nothing because it has no "special" to reveal. It does not throw out debilitating beliefs to "the masses" as if they were incapable of understanding, implied in Buber's title *Moral Man and Immoral Society*. Patriarchal speech cannot do constructive creativity; it is at core destructive. Selfual language, on the other hand, affirms two openly, accepting the checks and balances in the limits this implies in the finite characteristics of the two.

It may be argued here that this puts a heavy burden on schools, but it does no such thing; truths are easier to teach. Lies are complex, needing cover-ups, and much harder to teach. Simply read Ernst Cassirer's 1953 *An Essay on Man* to see how complex *man* is. The layers of false-comforting seminal lies in it dazzle you, weakening your mind into a mush needing God. Belief is boxed and mechanical; knowledge is open and purposeful. The task to teach truths rests as much in institutions, the culture, individuals, and societies, everyone. It does not rest only on schools and colleges.

Lord Manu's Law made One the sexual, financial, intellectual, and social predator of fem. It explains to me that by eight years of age my mother and father had talked to me about historical events and their relationships, geography and its influences, politics and its nasty ways, mathematics and its uses, as well as music, farming, to read and write, and that there was a *type of ignorance* much worse than not knowing how to read or write, the ignorance that *resists evidence*. Thinking forebears educate their children to see to think. Sapien forebears see mind as an organ to be developed in every child.

Evidence resistors see the child's mind as some thing(?) to be indoctrinated with their beliefs. They want their child "to transcend" life—to be in God's arms. *Transcend*—how sheep love this concept! Trendy! So we go on century after century exchanging Gods, even inventing more so that we can keep on "transcending."

One Lord is easily replaced with another in "the brotherhood of man." The Shah of Iran (holding the ideology of monarchy) changed the Islamic calendar (holding the ideology of male divinity) into a monarch calendar "establishing" the *first* ancient monarchy of Iran—*by word of law*. In 1971 the Shah celebrated the 2,500th anniversary of continuous monarchy in Iran! He played down Islamic holidays by adding His and His son's birthdays, and more. This did not sit well with Allah believers. Bouts of dominance ensued between Imam L/lords, and in 1979 the Shah was deposed. Islamic theocracy reestablished the pecking order of higher men in command, the veiled on the *loerarchy* far below H/him. Which king was to be the Lord of Lords in Iran? Oh well, the Shah lost the battle.

Sheep do not make steel wool. Yet once a year in the most slemotional of seasons we are reminded that an angel announced to The Virgin—after the fact—that she was "with child." No consent here! Symbolism, it is OK for God to rape when it begets a son who will erase sin from the world! So *Christ*mas, celebrating the birth of a holy son begotten by rape, displaced celebrating the Solstice as a day in nature that would aim at ecological plans. Instead nonsense, a crime/sin that is and is not a crime/sin, is commercialized worldwide. Yes, it's that easy to lose our planet, our selves, and life as life!

But we can deduce from this that rape is the solution to rape, prostitution is the solution to prostitution, violence is the solution to violence—not correct information.

Symbol*ism* is not language. It is a hodgepodge of graphic, stereotyped, seminal seeing for false beliefs, like the swastika. The skirt symbolizes submission to pants as authority and why fem were forbidden to wear pants for centuries. Symbolism is to faith and belief what the symbol is to language and knowledge.

Symbols are reality-based sound units for communication. Symbol*ism* is instant-recognition pictographic messages most often hiding prejudice and bias.

With sapiens as sapiens holding Q is Q, strife as it exists in 2 = 1 is destroyed, not reduced. Military purpose is transformed, not attacked, exploiting classes educated, not annihilated, social and cultural obstacles to achieve rationality deconstructed, not camouflaged in more false pompous ideologies of "a new (2 = 1) man." State power and leadership are redefined in view of the isonomic truths in thinking life with all life forms, reconfiguring institutions of power for *biocratic* purposes. Biocracy puts the *biology of all life forms* at the ruling center of our institutions, knowledge, and cultures to make laws based on the needs of all life forms. A "not-one of us men" is not in rofemtic discourse.

The *love of ritual* repetitiousness necessary to belief is critically examined. Good habits in thinking are encouraged. The habit of doing good and critical thinking means using Q is Q and 2 = 2 to commit to being consistent, fem is fem and sapiens are sapiens. Ritual is unconscious rote speech, mechanical, memorized, trance inducing, and unexamined. The habit of being constant in consistency demands vigilance, conscious behavior. That we *need ritual* is the false belief that we *need ritual* to keep needing rituals in the manmass.

Yes, we need to repeat facts. We do not need repetitiousness of the false. The habits of upholding correct reasoning, correct facts, and correct knowledge lead to wisdom and knowledge that stays reality and nature on their material natural planes. The species is best served by a truthful non-biased account of ut's own material self in space and cosmic time. Ut's responsibility is to acquire solid *habits in good reasoning* by *repeating* the laws of logical relationships seen in reality. Repeating rational items of speech goes into the habit of doing good reasoning over and over again. Redundancy is in most systems. Repetitiousness in 2 = 1 man is overwhelming, false, unnecessary redundancy 10^{10} that blinds conscious behavior and binds it to belief.

It took 4,000 years for Manu's Law to transmute *homo* [sic] *sapiens* into *homo manus*, the manmass. No evolution step, no consensus took place. It was a long, disconnected, haphazard, eclectic program in sexual deception, social imposition, intellectual rape, and economic fraud. In *Homo manus*, Lords are outside and above laws, with lesser men and not-men held prisoners *in manu*. Head-breaking repetitiousness for 4,000 years guarantees the Lie of Man is Truth in methodological solipsism.

Two aspects of the 4,000-year-long transmutation from *homo*, animated being as *sapiens*, to *homo*, male, *in manu*, melds into One con/fusing Truth and Extra-Seminal Power. ESP is a self-fulfilling mechanism in falsifying reality that goes unnoticed because it was developed over forty centuries day by day through a code of lies as "Truth" by withholding vital information. "Truth" is The Word man. Then men like Korzybski would protest (too much) that "The Word wasn't the thing," while upholding the Truth of M/man. This phallic centrality has never been called insanity, but you can say, do, and prove anything in Q is and is not Q that yields 2 = 1 man. The responsibility to respect evidence is nowhere.

To be responsible means to be mature. Maturity is the ability and will to look at and examine critically what you know as an adult to be false. *You choose to know—or to believe.* Belief does not come out of a sky-heaven. Evidence lets ut see the difference between belief and knowledge. To resist evidence is to be immature.

The 2 = 1 ideology of man varies from place to place due to culture, language, geography, resources, societal differences, wealth, and the cleverness and power grabbing of higher men. All went into building symbolism, seminal codification with eclectic elements evident in them. Looking at seminal codes in their cultural characters, one comes to better understand social engineering and economics. The massive prostitution and sex slavery industries growing exponentially show this. Holy virility has this mystical hard drive, so sex slavery, free sex, sex as sin, gender-as-division are all justifiable for $$$.

It is OK to abduct eleven- to sixteen-year-old "virgins" by the hundreds of thousands and take them to brothels in foreign countries to gift each to fifteen to twenty business men a day from every nation on the globe. Mankind is silent on his lucrative big money makers! Little if anything is being done for the *disposable* girls: "Man" is special, favored by God!

One effective way to put a stop to Manu's global influence is for fem to be fem again. The dialectics of Q is Q must be law in society as it is in reality. State and interstate relationships will have to commit to truths more in consonance with reality and more congruent with all of life and nature. Belief in dichotomous man and his chain of splits has to be replaced by *the truth principles in amphothetic knowledge.*

Moral individuals make moral society, whence happiness. Once you see how important symbol making and using is to sapiens, that these are where the basic creative impulses of minded beings start, you will be able to distinguish *the common evil* from the common good. *In the beginning is/was the true-to-reality symbol: Making crude symbols is the first thinking the primitive mind did to experience thinking life.* Lords poisoned it.

The structure of values underlying the cognitive logic on which the content of "the theory of man" is based is false. In it "man" is above all other life, God. Valuation processes and values are false because Q is and is not Q. The common evil—original sin—is implanted into the manmass using lies in symbolism parading as language.

To achieve a critical mass of sapiens standing up as sapiens, it is necessary for as many individuals as possible to come to see that as a species/collective we make ourselves wise by our own symbol making and using. No one else can do it for us. Wisdom and happiness and peace can come no other way but in, with, and through the many truths seen in reality and nature reflected in true-to-reality symbols.

■   ■   ■

What you do with the information in this book is now in your hands. Evidence resistors will hold on to the lie and its belief systems. Open-minded individuals will use the knowledge to build a better understanding of our species, planet earth, and the cosmos. Anatol Rapoport (2000) said that "Money and power were 'conservative commodities': The more one gets of them, the less the other gets. But if A gives B a piece of knowledge, B is enriched while A is not impoverished." My hope is that you will see the responsibility to demand the *right to correct information* to enrich yourself and all others in the process to creating sapienity.

Although the achievements of language are not as evident as the achievements of science and technology, their necessary involvement with science, technology, life, and all that we do is in fact self-evident. But we hardly ever praise "language achievements," more precise naming, and thinking. We were properly scared away from seeking truths when belief in man as Truth took precedence over *knowing* that evolution had brought about fem and man simultaneously as a team of thinkers, that two logic-affirming speakers existed to be critical thinking agents upon which rationality stands. There is no evidence refuting this.

Man as a party of One-for-the-two did away with the foundation of rationality, trust, and stability in the individual, and thereby in society/the collective. Since fem had no power, she had no sphere of influence in civilization, society, history, music, or culture. She was a mere womb, a placeholder between man, and man as Lords bulldozed planet and life. Little development toward justice, respect of others, equitable rights in proprietorship, value setting and knowledge acquisition with equality of opportunity, condition, and value was achieved in $2 = 1$ ideology. We are hardly any further ahead today than in 2400 BCE.

No stability and permanence to live thinking life as it should be lived can evolve if $2 = 1$ seminal lingo is left embracing divisiveness, irrationality, apathy, cynicism, and hypocrisy, as well as magic and superstition on a grand scale. No educational reform can express a true sense of what we are as a symbol-making and symbol-using species if we allow The Word as Truth to bulldoze mind with belief. The worst belief in belief is *that belief has a consequence-free criterion.* This disables the mind to tell the difference between evil and good. President Bush believed gratuitous violence/preemptive strikes to be good for democracy! If your child doesn't want to believe, split his head open with an axe and pour in the indoctrination.

Evolution did not make sapiens name themselves by a gender-as-division method. M/manu's Law started this evil. It spun off on a grand scale: Everyone became enemies. War, be it by conventional arms, nuclear weaponry, germ warfare, biological poisoning, intellectual fraud, or a global lie, always starts with "The Word" first. Used in laws, plans, and policies, lies are the lightning strikes that cause evil. There is always one more way to preach The Lie-Truth in The Word-God where the false abides.

No one today is responsible for the innate flaw-cum-original sin. But to the extent that one does not contribute to the solutions to stopping belief in harmful lies, one is a definitive contributor to the problem, the greatest intellectual fraud of all time. No fraud equals it; none surpasses this crime against mind.

There is only will—volition of mind with energy of body—in self. There is only one life each on planet earth. There is only one species on earth that can be stewards and do stewardship on planet earth. If life is not "life" *by definition*, then evil men can make life-is-death Truth, whence serial warring, global prostitution, and species pornography. If life on our planet, including all life forms, is not in our life plans, then life is doomed, thinking life included, and thus authentic peace, morality, and happiness are not achievable.

Making laws using symbols reflecting reality to guide the process makes you an authentic thinking being. Your efficient mind is sufficient to add to the creation, peace, order, and moral ruling systems, as well as a sane and happy self. Evolution evolved a rule-following species like it did all other species. To be one who follows the rules is to be true-to-ut's-reality as thinking beings. We, fem and man, affirm and distinguish thinking, we are the only ones who can make speech reflecting what reality is. Rational fem and rational man are the foundation of rationality.

It is true that when A gives B an item of knowledge, B is enriched while A is not impoverished—or defrauded, disadvantaged, or disenfranchised. Q is Q, 2 = 2, fem is fem, man is man, and multiple causalities are items of knowledge that affirm this to be true. For your serenity and happiness may the will you possess choose the many truths you see in reality that clarify thinking life to live it fully as thinking life!

BIBLIOGRAPHY

Adams, James L. *The Care and Feeding of Ideas: A Guide to Encouraging Creativity*. Cambridge, MA; Da Capo Press, 1986.

A Dictionary of Believers and Nonbelivers. Translated by Catherine Judelson. Moscow: Progress Publishers, 1989.

Adler, Mortimer J. *Ten Philosophical Mistakes*. New York: Macmillan Press, 1985.

Anderson, Sir Norman, ed. *The World's Religions*. London: Intervarsity Press, 1976.

Anderson, Roger. *The Power and the Word: Language, Power and Change*. London: Paladin Grafton Books, 1988.

Ayer, Alfred Jules. *The Central Questions in Philosophy*. New York: Penguin Books, 1976.

———. *Language, Truth and Logic*. New York: Dover Publications, 1952.

Baker, Gordon P., and Peter M. S. Hacker. *Language, Sense and Nonsense*. Oxford: Basil Blackwell, 1984.

Barnes, John A. *A Pack of Lies: Towards a Sociology of Lying*. Cambridge: Cambridge University Press, 1994.

Barron, Dennis. *Grammar and Gender*. New Haven, CT: Yale University Press, 1986.

Bennett, John G. *Deeper Man*. London: Turnstone Press, 1978.

Bittner, Rüdiger. *What Reason Demands*. Translated by Theodore Talbot. Cambridge: Cambridge University Press, 1989.

Blanshard, Brand. *Reason and Analysis*. LaSalle, IL: Open Court Publishing, 1973.

Bloomfield, Leonard. *Language*. New York: Holt, Rinehart and Winston, 1965.

Bok, Sissela. *Secrets: On the Ethics of Concealment and Revelation*. New York: Vintage Books, 1989.

Bolinger, Dwight. *Language: The Loaded Weapon*. New York: Longman, 1980.

Bowie, Norman E., and Robert L. Simon. *The Individual and Political Order: An Introduction to Social and Political Philosopyhy*. New Jersey: Prentice Hall, 1986.

Britton, Karl. *Philosophy and the Meaning of Life*. Cambridge: Cambridge University Press, 1969.

Bullough, Vern L., and James Brundage, eds. *Sexual Practices and the Medieval Church*. Amherst, NY: Prometheus Books, 1982.

Burtt, Edwin Arthur. *Principles and Problems of Right Thinking*. New York: Harper & Brothers, 1928.

Campbell, Jeremy. *Grammatical Man: Information, Entropy, Language and Life*. New York: Simon & Schuster, 1982.

Campbell, Keith. *Body and Mind*. New York: Macmillan Press, 1970.

Carbone, Peter F. Jr. *Value Theory and Education*. Malabar, FL: Krieger Publishing, 1987.

Carlton, Eric. *Patterns of Belief*, vols. 1 and 2. London: George Allen & Unwin, 1973.

Carney, James D., and Richard K. Scheer. *Fundamentals of Logic*. New York: Macmillan Press, 1964.

Cassirer, Ernst. *An Essay on Man: An Introduction to a Philosophy of Human Culture*. Garden City, NY: Doubleday Anchor Books, 1953.

Cavendish, Richard, ed. *Man, Myth & Magic: The Illustrated Encyclopedia of Mythology, Religion, and the Unknown*. New York: Marshall Cavendish Corporation, 1983.

Chaffee, John. *Thinking Critically*. Boston: Houghton Mifflin, 1988.

Clark, E. C. *Early Roman Law: The Regal Period*. Littleton, CO: F. B. Rothman, 1987.

Conway, David A., and Ronald Munson. *The Elements of Reasoning*. Belmont, CA: Wadsworth, 1990.

Copi, Irving M., and Carl Cohen. *Introduction to Logic*. New York: Macmillan Press, 1990.

Cramp, John Mockett. *A Text-Book on Popery*. London: Houlston and Stoneman, 1851.

Cross, Donna Woolfolk. *Word Abuse: How the Words We Use Use Us*. New York: Coward, McCann & Geoghegan, 1979.

Crossley, David J., and Peter C. Wilson. *How to Argue*. New York: Random House, 1979.

Davies, James W. *Ways of Thinking*. New York: Peter Lang Publishing Group, 1991.

Dawkins, Richard. *The God Delusion*. Boston: Houghton Mifflin, 2006.

de Tocqueville, Alexis. *Democracy in America*. New York: Penguin Books, 1984.

Downes, William. *Language and Society*. London: Fontana Paperbacks, 1984.

Eisiminger, Sterling. *The Consequence of Error and Other Language Essays.* New York: Peter Lang Publishing Group, 1991.

Engel, S. Morris. *With Good Reason: An Introduction to Informal Fallacies.* New York: St. Martin's Press, 1976.

Ernst, Margaret S. *In a Word.* New York: Channel Press, 1960.

———. *Words.* New York: Alfred A. Knopf, 1950.

Farb, Peter. *Man's Rise to Civilization.* New York: Avon Books, 1968.

———. *Word Play.* New York: Alfred A. Knopf, 1974.

Flew, Anthony. *Thinking about Thinking.* London: Fontana Press, 1975.

Frankl, Viktor E. *Man's Search for Meaning: An Introduction to Logotherapy.* Translated by I. Lasch. Boston: Beacon Press, 1962.

Frazer, James G. *The Golden Bough.* London: Chancellor Press, 1994.

Girodet, Jean. *Logos Grand Dictionnaire de la Langue Française.* Paris: Bordas, 1976.

Gouëffic, Louise. *Breaking the Patriarchal Code: The Linguistic Basis of Sexual Bias.* Manchester, CT: Knowledge, Ideas and Trends, 1996.

Harnish, Robert M. *Basic Topics in the Philosophy of Language.* Englewood Cliffs, NJ: Prentice Hall, 1994.

Harris, Roy. *The Language Myth.* London: Duckworth Publishers, 1981.

Hayakawa, Samuel Ichiye. *Symbol, Status, and Personality.* New York: Harcourt Brace Jovanovich, 1963.

———, ed. *The Use and Misuse of Language.* Greenwich, CT: Fawcett Publications, 1962.

Hinderer, Drew E. *Building Arguments.* Belmont, CA: Wadsworth, 1997.

Hitt, Jack, ed. *In a Word.* New York: Bantam Books, 1992.

Hoffer, Eric. *The True Believer: Thoughts on the Nature of Mass Movements.* New York: HarperCollins, 1951.

Howard, Philip. *The State of the Language.* Middlesex: Penguin Books, 1984.

Eliade, Mircea. *Myth and Reality.* Translated by Willard R. Trask. New York: Harper & Row, 1963.

Ireland, David. *The Flesheaters.* Sydney: Angus and Robertson, 1972.

Jordan, William C. *From Servitude to Freedom: Manumission in the Sénonais in the Thirteenth Century.* Philadelphia: University of Pennsylvania Press, 1986.

Jung, Carl J. *Modern Man in Search of a Soul.* New York: Harcourt, Brace & World, 1933.

Kahane, Howard. *Thinking About Basic Beliefs: An Introduction to Philosophy.* Belmont, CA: Wadsworth, 1983.

Katz, Jerrold J. *The Philosophy of Language.* New York: Harper & Row, 1966.

Kitcher, Philip. *Abusing Science: The Case against Creationism.* Boston: MIT Press, 1982.

Koestler, Arthur. *The Ghost in the Machine.* London: Hutchison, 1967.

Kramsky, Jiri. *The Word as a Linguistic Unit.* The Hague: Mouton Publishing, 1969.

Langacker, Ronald W. *Language and Its Structure: Some Fundamental Linguistic Concepts.* New York: Harcourt Brace Jovanovich, 1967.

Levi-Strauss, Claude. *Myth and Meaning: Cracking the Code of Culture.* Toronto: University of Toronto Press, 1995.

Lipset, Seymour Martin. *Political Man: The Social Bases of Politics.* New York: Anchor Books, 1963.

Little, J. Frederick, Leo A. Groarke, and Christopher W. Tindale. *Good Reasoning Matters.* Toronto: McClelland & Stewart, 1989.

Lurker, Manfred. *The Gods and Symbols of Ancient Egypt.* London: Thames and Hudson, 1974.

Magee, Bryan. *The Philosophy of Language* [video recording]. Discussion with John R. Searle. London: British Broadcasting Corporation, 1972.

Mayfield, Marlys. *Thinking for Yourself: Developing Critical Thinking Skills through Writing.* Belmont, CA: Wadsworth, 1987.

McCrone, John. *The Myth of Irrationality: The Science of the Mind from Plato to Star Trek.* London: Macmillan Press, 1993.

McLellan, David. *Ideology.* Minneapolis: University of Minnesota Press, 1986.

Mencken, H. L. *Prejudices: Third Series.* New York: Alfred A. Knopf, 1922.

Michalos, Alex C. *Improving Your Reasoning.* Englewood Cliffs, NJ: Prentice Hall, 1970.

Miller, John William. *The Definition of the Thing.* New York: W. W. Norton, 1980.

Mitchell, James. *Significant Etymology.* Edinburgh: William Blackwood & Sons, 1908.

Munson, Ronald. *The Way of Words: An Informal Logic.* Boston: Houghton Mifflin, 1976.

Nicholas, Barry. *An Introduction to Roman Law.* Oxford: Clarendon Press, 1962.

Niebuhr, Reinhold. *Moral Man and Immoral Society.* New York: Charles Scribner's Sons, 1932.

Nye, Andrea. *Words and Power: A Feminist Reading of the History of Logic.* London: Routledge, 1990.

Onions, C. T., ed. *The Oxford Dictionary of English Etymology*. Oxford: Oxford University Press, 1966.

Pagels, Heinz. *The Dreams of Reason: The Rise of the Sciences of Complexity*. New York: Bantam Books, 1988.

Partridge, Eric. *Origins: A Short Etymological Dictionary of Modern English*, 4th ed. London: Routledge & Kegan Paul, 1966.

Pei, Mario. *The Story of Language*. New York: The New American Library, 1960.

Peters, Francis E. *Greek Philosophical Terms: A Historical Lexicon*. New York: New York University Press, 1967.

Powys, John Cowper. *The Meaning of Culture*. New York: W. W. Norton, 1929.

Putnam, Hilary. *Reason, Truth and History*. Cambridge: Cambridge University Press, 1981.

———. *Representation and Reality*. Cambridge, MA: MIT Press, 1989.

Quine, Willard van Orman. *Word and Object*. Cambridge, MA: MIT Press, 1960.

Rachels, James. *The Elements of Moral Philosophy*, 2nd ed. New York: McGraw-Hill, 1993.

Rand, Ayn. *The Virtue of Selfishness*. New York, Signet Books, 1961.

Rapoport, Anatol. *Certainties and Doubts: A Philosophy of Life*. Montreal: Black Rose Books, 2000.

Reese, William L. *Dictionary of Philosophy and Religion: Eastern and Western Thought*. Sussex, UK: Humanities Press, 1980.

Reynaud, Emmanuel. *Holy Virility*. London: Pluto Press, 1981.

Richter, Horst-Eberhard. *All Mighty: A Study of the God Complex in Western Man*. Translated by Jan van Heurck. Claremont, CA: Hunter House, 1984.

Romero, Francisco. *The Theory of Man*. Translated by William F. Cooper. Berkeley: University of California Press, 1964.

Russell, Bertrand. *A History of Western Philosophy*. London: George Allen & Unwin, 1961.

———. *Human Society in Ethics and Politics*. New York: Simon & Schuster, 1962.

Salmon, Louis B. *Semantics and Common Sense*. New York: Holt, Rinehart and Winston, 1966.

Salmon, Wesley C. *Logic*. Englewood Cliffs, NJ: Prentice Hall, 1973.

Sampson, Geoffrey. *Liberty and Language*. Oxford: Oxford University Press, 1979.

Sapir, Edward. *Language: An Introduction to the Study of Speech*. New York: Harcourt Brace Jovanovich, 1921.

Sennett, Richard. *Authority*. London: Faber and Faber, 1993.

Smith, William, and Samuel Cheetham. *Dictionary of Christian Antiquities.* Toronto: Willing and Williamson, 1880.

Spaemann, Robert. *Basic Moral Concepts.* Translated by Timothy J. Armstrong. New York: Routledge, 1989.

Spender, Dale. *Man-Made Language.* London: Routledge & Kegan Paul, 1980.

St. Aubyn, Giles. *The Art of Argument.* New York: Taplinger Publishing, 1985.

Sterba, James P. *Morality in Practice.* Belmont, CA: Wadsworth, 1988.

Bullock, Alan, and Oliver Stallybrass, eds. *The Fontana Dictionary of Modern Thought.* London: Collins, 1977.

Strawson, Peter Frederick. *The Bounds of Sense: An Essay on Kant's Critique of Pure Reason.* London: Methuen, 1966.

Tagore, Rabindranath. *The Religion of Man.* London: George Allen & Unwin, 1931.

Thomas, P. J. *Introduction to Roman Law.* Boston: Kluwer Law and Taxation Publishers, 1986.

Toulmin, Stephen. *The Place of Reason in Ethics.* Chicago: University of Chicago Press, 1950.

Turner, Nigel. *Christian Words.* Edinburgh: T & T Clark, 1980.

Ullmann, Stephen. *Semantics: An Introduction to the Science of Meaning.* Oxford: Basil Blackwell, 1964.

Urdang, Laurence. *Prefixes and Other Word-Initial Elements of English.* Detroit: Gale Research Co., 1984.

van den Broek, Roelof. *The Myth of the Phoenix according to Classical and Early Christian Traditions.* Translated by I. Seeger. Leiden, Neth.: E. J. Brill, 1972.

Vine, William Edwy. *The Expanded Vine's Expository Dictionary of New Testament Words.* Minneapolis, MN: Bethany House Publishers, 1984.

Walton, Benjamin. *Introduction to Roman Law,* 2nd ed. Edinburgh: William Green & Sons, 1968.

Watson, Alan. *Roman Slave Law.* Baltimore, MD: John Hopkins University Press, 1987.

Watts, Alan W. *Myth and Ritual in Christianity.* New York: Vanguard Press, 1953.

Webster's Word Histories. Springfield, MA: Merriam-Webster, 1989.

Weekly, Ernest. *Words and Names.* Freeport, NY: Books for Libraries Press, 1932.

Weininger, Otto. *Geschlecht und Charakter* (1903). Translated as *Sex and Character* (London: William Heinemann, 1906).

Wiener, Philip P., ed. *The Dictionary of the History of Ideas*. New York: Charles Scribner's Sons, 1968.

Williams, Cecil. *The Foundations of Intelligence*. New York: Comet Press, 1953.

Wilson, Bryan R., ed. *Rationality*. Oxford: Basil Blackwell, 1970.

Wilson, John. *Language and the Pursuit of Truth*. Cambridge: Cambridge University Press, 1956.

———. *Thinking with Concepts*. Cambridge: Cambridge University Press, 1966.

Yule, George. *The Study of Language*. Cambridge: Cambridge University Press, 1985.

Over 100 dictionaries, ancient and modern, in English, French, Latin, Greek, Arab (in translation), Hindu (in translation), German, and more were also consulted in the making of this book.

INDEX

(Symbol necessary for the premise of inclusiveness *by definition* in the theory of integration marked by *)

A

Aboriginal Holocaust, 45

absent symbol(s), 19, 23, 30, 149.
See also knowledge withheld

Adam, 17, 56, 66, 86, 87, 130

Alpha Male(s) in the Sky, belief in 9, 14, 19, 22, 30, 37, 48, 53, 61, 62, 81, 84, 104, 119, 194, 200-201; and causality, 58, 59, 67, 131, 233; and death, 41, 129; and kinship, 189; and neutral hand, 223; obedience to, 89-90; *See also* Holy Books; soul; Word, The

altruism, 6

*amphothesis, 229-230, 231, 232-233

amphothetic thinking/knowledge, 229, 235-236, 241

anonymity, 17, 31

antithesis, 135, 228-229, 231, 232

apathy, 115, 192, 201, 235

apfig, 15-16, 61, 77, 91-92

Aquinas, 143, 193

archimorpheme, 91

archiparadigm, 88, 114

argumentum ad feminam, 103, 135

Aristotle, 143

assimilation, 57, 152, 220, 227-228.
See also dualism; 2 = 1

authentic identity, 6, 175-176, 190-191, 201, 205, 209-210, 216, 217

authority, divine, 81-82, 90-91, 102, 127-128; male, 50, 88, 238-239; seminal, 98, 125

autonomy, dichotomy by gender, 6, 34; moral, 6, 9-10, 22, 36, 58; personal, 6, 9, 10, 33, 36, 51, 92, 215

B

*balance, 146, 148, 150-151, 180

Barnes, John, 169-170

behavior, 212

belief, 14, 63-64, 108-110, 117, 200-201; and knowledge, 15-16, 21, 23, 37, 60, 62, 69, 129; and logic, 64; and reality, 199; and wisdom, 32. *See also* religion; Word, The

Bible, The, 28, 46, 74, 87, 100, 128, 129. *See also by chapter and verse*

*biocracy, 221-222, 224, 239

brains, and evolution, 13, 20, 40, 136, 158, 233; and the mind, 16, 163, 177-178, 188-189; and limits, 164, 166,

Breaking the Patriarchal Code, 78

Buber, Martin, 139, 237

*by definition, 181

C

capitalism, 42-43, 81, 85, 94, 186, 203, 207, 214

Cassirer, Ernst, 237

*causality, 58, 70-71, 134. *See also* cause and effect; multiple causality

evil, 11; and language, 9, 25-28,
42, 93, 98, 101, 144. *See also*
Patriarchal English
patrists, 78, 79, 97-99, 109, 111-112,
113, 114, 131, 233
Pearson, Lester B., 230
phallic-centralism, 113, 240
philosophy, 44, 79, 117, 193
Pitched Manu Syndrome (PMS),
62, 69
*plurality, 146. *See also* multiple
causality
politics, 18, 95, 103, 186, 220-222
Pope, Alexander, 143
pornography, 56, 99, 104, 108,
141, 213
power, money and sex (trinity), 34,
49, 62, 115, 118
prayer, 39, 52, 79, 102, 201. *See
also* belief
pre-determinism, 71, 170-171
premises withheld, 113
*probabilities, 17, 75, 80, 90, 118,
135, 144, 146, 182, 217, 219
progress, 206-207
pronouns, 116, 123, 147, 191
prostitution, 51, 69, 88, 89, 94,
108, 126-127, 132, 141, 173,
188, 240
Providence, 152, 165, 170, 171
*psychephisis, 157, 217, 218
psychology, 28, 64, 67, 92, 178
Ptah, 48, 49, 55, 74

Q
Q is and is not Q, 16, 18, 19, 20, 33,
36, 37, 43, 49, 72, 119, 228
Q is Q, 41, 44, 61, 70, 80, 105, 125,
128, 133, 241; and 2 = 2, 151, 158,
167, 182, 188, 191, 197, 206,
212, 216, 217, 219, 223, 234, 239

R
races, 84, 87
racism, 40, 80, 84, 114, 117, 164, 165
Rapaport, Anatol, 241
ratiocination, 83
*ratiogenic(s), 131, 146, 149, 150,
157, 158, 164, 181
*ratiogens, 235
rational choice, 8
rationalism, 42, 125
rationality, 21, 42, 125, 129-130, 177,
194, 205; foundation of, 5, 13,
30, 61, 72, 134, 170, 182
realism, 10, 49, 103, 115, 134, 137;
and reality, 37, 75, 105, 176
religion, 43, 61, 64, 82-83, 86-91, 93,
107, 109, 127. *See also* belief
re-legion(ing), 60, 68, 71, 72, 82, 103
religion of man, 102-104
repetitiousness, 18, 89, 103, 151, 239
respect, 147, 148
revolving-door belief, 108-110
Reynaud, Emmanuel, 132
rights, and responsibilities, 199-210
"The Rights of Man," 50, 51, 70
*rofemtic, 144-145
rofemtic concepts, 130, 144-145,
146, 148, 152, 196, 237
*Rofemtic Movement, 79, 105, 119,
192-193, 203, 222-223, 224, 226
Romans, 47, 48
Romans 3:8, 112
Rouseau, 143
Rushton, Philip, 35

S
sacred, 20, 37, 53, 61, 65, 74
salvation, 32, 60, 73, 89, 104, 163,
166, 175
sapience, 26, 144, 148, 153, 165,
166, 232

ALSO BY LOUISE GOUËFFIC

Breaking the Patriarchal Code: The Linguistic Basis of Sexual Bias. Manchester, CT: Knowledge, Ideas and Trends, 1996.

Breaking the Patriarchal Code evolved through thirty years of research in language. Louise Gouëffic collected, categorized, and analyzed 20,000 words across the Indo-European tradition addressing our species and its two members (male and fe-male.) These words were gleaned from hundreds of dictionaries worldwide. Louise looked at the etymology, historical background, purpose, meaning, messages, goals, generative use, cross-cultural borrowings, and modern usage of these words and analyzed recurrent themes and recurrent linguistic techniques used in language. ***Breaking the Patriarchal Code*** lists 10,000 words, tabling their linguistic formulas and showing how the techniques used to build words with basic morphemes created concepts and ideas that fit together to make the dominance of one gender appear to be "the way it is."

To purchase this book, please contact the publisher, Knowledge, Ideas and Trends, Inc., at slbkit@aol.com